Guiding Curriculum Decisions for Middle-Grades Science

Barbara Brauner Berns,
Ilene Kantrov, Marian Pasquale,
Doris Santamaria Makang,
Bernie Zubrowski, and
Lynn T. Goldsmith

with assistance from
Michele Browne
and Kristin Metz

Series Editors:
Ilene Kantrov
Lynn T. Goldsmith

HEINEMANN
Portsmouth, NH

Heinemann
A division of Reed Elsevier Inc.
361 Hanover Street
Portsmouth, NH 03801–3912
www.heinemann.com

Offices and agents throughout the world

© 2001 by Education Development Center, Inc.
55 Chapel St., Newton, MA 02458-1060
617-969-7100
www.edc.org

Library of Congress Cataloging-in-Publication Data
ISBN 0-325-00417-X
CIP data is on file with the Library of Congress.

Cover design: Dorothy Geiser

Printed in the United States of America on acid-free paper

05   04   03   02   01   VP   1   2   3   4   5

Contents

Acknowledgments

One of the most rewarding parts of completing a project like this guide is the opportunity to thank the people who have participated in its development. The guide has benefited from the contributions of a substantial number of colleagues, and it is our distinct pleasure to acknowledge them here.

Without the foresight and support of Hayes Mizell, program director at the Edna McConnell Clark Foundation and Leah Meyer Austin, program director at the W.K. Kellogg Foundation, this guide series would never have come about. Hayes and Leah, along with their colleagues from the National Forum to Accelerate Middle-Grades Reform, have championed the efforts to reanimate middle-grades education nationwide. Through their foundations, Hayes and Leah have been providing support to a number of districts and schools throughout the country to promote standards-based instruction. As they worked with their grantees, they learned that many of these districts have faced considerable challenges in identifying and implementing high-quality curriculum materials. Hayes and Leah recognized that educators were in need of more assistance in making curriculum decisions that will promote academic excellence in their districts, schools, and classrooms.

Nancy Ames, our colleague at Education Development Center, Inc. (EDC), who guides the National Forum and shares its members' commitment to middle-grades reform, had the initial vision for this project. Her work provided a solid foundation from which to build, and she supported our efforts throughout.

EDC has been a supportive environment for this work. Nancy and other colleagues helped us to shape the focus of this guide series and to frame its content; still others helped us interview teachers, work out conceptual knots, and prepare the manuscript. Our project staff spent many hours thinking and talking through the overall plan for the guide series: thanks to Christine Brown, Margaret Russell Ciardi, Anne Shure, and Marianne Thompson. Mark Driscoll and Barbara Miller displayed their usual collegial generosity in helping us think through a number of difficult questions and issues. Michele Browne managed a multitude of requests and questions with grace and competence. Carrie Carter, Kerry Ouellet, and Silvia Tracanna established our practitioner database, coded large amounts of data, and kept the project on schedule. Deborah Clark picked up loose ends in the final months and supervised the manuscript production with her signature skill and good humor. Other members of the design and production team included Jennifer Davis-Kay, Dorothy Geiser, Gail Hedges, Catherine Lee, Jennifer Roscoe, and Jane Wilson. Thanks to Kristen Bjork for her design consultations.

It was our good fortune to have assembled an encouraging and thoughtful advisory board whose members helped us to plunge into the task with fortitude and enthusiasm. Members included Ron Adams, Loretta Brady, Everly Broadway, Nancy Clark-Chiarelli, Gerard Consuegra, John D'Auria, Georgette Gonsalves, Kristi Kahl, Lloyda King, Greg Kniseley, Gerald Kulm, Joan Lipsitz, Barbara Reys, Linda Rief, Karen Smith, Albert Talborn, Rob Traver, and Anne Wheelock. We would like to extend a special thanks to Gerard Consuegra, Joan Lipsitz, Rob Traver, and Anne Wheelock for their careful reviews of portions of the manuscript. Anne in particular made a tremendous contribution to shaping the content of the critical questions and practitioner stories.

We would like to extend our thanks to the practitioners who took the time to share their thoughts and experiences with us. Their voices can be heard throughout the guide, and their understanding and eloquence about the challenges of implementing curricula such as those described in this guide provided the core of this project. These include Erin Babin, Debbie Bambino, John Blutfield, Pam Boykin, Elizabeth Chartier, Linda Chororos, Miriam Cooper, Barry Curseaden, Kim Dalton, Scott DeGasperis, Cindy Detwiler, Damon Douglas, Cami Dubie, Dick Duquin, Holly Eaton, Lola Farmer, Lynn Farrin, Denise Finley, Pam Fountain, Jane Gehron, Dean Gilbert, David Gross, Patricia Hagan, Debbie Hobbs, Anne Holbrook, Page Keeley, John Kuzma, Steve Longenecker, Gary Lynes, Ruth Martin, Martin Miller, Vance Mills, Bob Nanney, Nancy Nega, Lisa Nielsen, Linda Peeples, Steve Ralston, Gail Raymond, Larry Reid, Marisol Rosario, Connie Roth, Elizabeth Sanghavi, Jeff Self, Sherie McClam, Jeff Soares, Liz Sorrell, Karen Spaulding, Scott Stowell, Sandy Tauer, Angela Taylor, Roger Twitchell, Brian Vedder, Denise Vizcarra, Larry Weathers, David White, Anne Whitfield, and Jackie Zanotti. Thanks also to those who reviewed selected materials: Roy Chambers, Joellen Killion, Barbara Moore, David Taylor, and Pam Tickle.

Finally, we would like to express appreciation to the developers and selected publishers who reviewed the curriculum profiles for accuracy. And most of all, a big "thank you" to the middle school leaders of EDC's Center for Urban Science Education Reform (CUSER), a collaborative center of 22 school districts across the country, and to our colleagues at the Center: Jeanne Rose Century, Charles Hutchinson, Joe Flynn, Judith Opert Sandler, Jeff Winokur, and Karen Worth.

Guiding Curriculum Decisions for Middle-Grades
Science

INTRODUCTION

Aiming for Academic Excellence in Middle-Grades Curricula

Third period ends with a few, hurried instructions about homework from the teacher as students pack up their pens, pencils, and notebooks. They pour into the halls, moving in small packs to their next classes. Some scurry and others adopt a leisurely stroll, using the time to catch up with friends. The energy bounces off the lockers lining the corridors. Waves of students surge through open classroom doors—they plop their books onto desks and slide into their seats. A soft sigh slips into the emptying hallways as students unpack those pens, pencils, and notebooks and prepare to think and work hard.

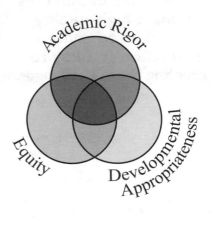

When classroom doors close and lessons begin, we want our children to be intellectually challenged and engaged by their work. And indeed, good things are happening in many middle-grades classrooms throughout the country. Students are learning to think deeply about the subjects they are studying and are enthusiastic about their coursework. Their work requires them to think hard, explain and support their ideas, and apply their understanding to new situations.

How can we extend these conditions to more students in more schools? The answer involves making a number of interconnected changes: establishing district policies that promote and support quality instruction, adopting clearly articulated standards for student learning and performance, using high-quality curricula, improving teacher education, providing ongoing professional development for teachers already in the classroom, and developing community support. This guide will help educators address one of these areas of change—identifying and using high-quality curriculum to promote high standards of student achievement. *Guiding Curriculum Decisions for Middle-Grades Science* is part of a series of curriculum guides for middle-grades mathematics, science,

Good things are happening in many middle-grades classrooms throughout the country. Students are learning to think deeply about the subjects they are studying and are enthusiastic about their coursework. Their work requires them to think hard, explain and support their ideas, and apply their understanding to new situations.

In order to meet these standards, teachers face new academic and pedagogical challenges. They must teach more challenging and extensive subject area content, they must develop different instructional strategies, and they must reach a wider range of students. Having a high-quality curriculum to guide instruction is a key to meeting these challenges.

language arts, and social studies.[1] This guide offers a set of principles for making curriculum decisions and illustrates these principles with practitioners' descriptions of their experiences in implementing standards-based curricula.

This guide series was developed at Education Development Center, Inc. with the support of the Edna McConnell Clark and W.K. Kellogg Foundations. It is based on interviews with more than 100 middle-grades educators who are using standards-based curriculum approaches and materials in their districts, schools, and classrooms. This introductory chapter sets the scene for the scope of the guide series, focusing on science, but drawing examples more broadly from all of the major middle-grades subject areas.

The need for new approaches to curriculum and instruction is clear. Over the past fifteen years educators have been taking a hard look at American students' academic performance. In the realms of mathematics and science, we have learned that American students are outperformed by peers in many other countries.[2] Educators and employers alike express concerns about the literacy skills of America's youth. Within the last decade each major subject area has developed academic standards that raise the bar for student achievement and performance.[3] In order to meet these standards, teachers face new academic and pedagogical challenges. They must teach more challenging and extensive subject area content, they must develop different instructional strategies, and they must reach

---

[1] The anticipated publication date for the social studies guide is 2002.

[2] In an internationally administered proficiency test for science and mathematics, for example, U.S. eighth and tenth graders performed at significantly lower levels than grade-mates from a large number of other countries. For a report of this study, see Third International Mathematics and Science Study, *Attaining Excellence: A TIMSS Resource Kit* (Washington, DC: U.S. Department of Education, 1996).

[3] In 1989 the National Council of Teachers of Mathematics (NCTM) was the first national organization to produce a set of K-12 curriculum standards for a major subject area. Since then, the National Council of Teachers of English (NCTE) and the International Reading Association (IRA) have collaborated on language arts standards; the National Research Council (NRC) and Project 2061 of the American Association for the Advancement of Science (AAAS) have each published science standards (the AAAS uses the term "benchmarks" instead of "standards"), and the National Council for the Social Studies (NCSS) has authored social studies standards. In addition, the National Center on Education and the Economy has published *New Standards™ Student Performance Standards* for language arts, mathematics, science, and applied learning. Information about subject area standards can be found on the websites of all of these organizations.

a wider range of students. Having a high-quality curriculum to guide instruction is a key to meeting these challenges.

Most currently available texts do not help science teachers provide an intellectually rigorous education for all the students in their classes. Frequently, teachers committed to standards-based instruction find themselves at odds with district-mandated curricula and testing programs that provide limited opportunity for students to develop deep understanding of science concepts and to develop inquiry skills. They spend enormous amounts of time searching for resources, planning engaging units that address important concepts, and developing lessons and activities to carry out their goals. This is no easy task. It requires a sophisticated understanding of the subject area and knowledge of the ways that students learn it. Many teachers are only reluctant curriculum developers and are aching for good materials. Others take satisfaction from creating their own curriculum, but still find it a labor-intensive process that reduces their time for classroom planning and for focusing on individual students' academic needs. And, too, the effectiveness of homegrown curricula varies considerably.

However, there are some high-quality published materials for middle-grades educators which can relieve teachers of the burden of inventing their own. Some of these materials have been designed from the outset around the principles of standards-based reform. Their development has

> "Not all teachers are curriculum developers. We find that while they may create fun activities, their lessons don't necessarily lead to solid student learning. It's really difficult because many teachers think that to be a good teacher you have to be creative and develop your own materials. There's a prejudice that you're not a creative, innovative teacher if you rely on a piece of commercial material. I have to dispel that idea. You can still be creative and innovative, but published materials give you a structure, a sequence, and they guide you in the right direction. But there is a misconception among some teachers that just developing their own materials automatically means their lessons are better, or that the kids will be more engaged."
>
> — State-level curriculum specialist

included review by content area experts and a significant amount of pilot and field testing in a range of schools to ensure that they are effective in classroom settings. Such carefully constructed and tested materials offer teachers an effective alternative to constructing an entire curriculum from scratch.

What do we mean by "curriculum"?

In a broad sense, curriculum refers to the ideas, skills, and dispositions that educators and content specialists identify as the important ones for students to learn. Many states and districts have developed curriculum frameworks that articulate these learning goals. (Districts may further refine this articulation by indicating the concepts and skills to be learned at each grade level.) Curriculum materials—the written lessons, activities, exercises, and supporting materials—provide the means through which teachers engage students in learning, articulating the important content to teach and offering teachers a structure and organization for instruction. Districts build their instructional programs by selecting curriculum materials that will help them meet their curricular goals.

Adapted from Lynn T. Goldsmith, June Mark, and Ilene Kantrov, *Choosing a Standards-Based Mathematics Curriculum* (Portsmouth, NH: Heinemann, 2000), 2. Copyright © 1998 by Education Development Center, Inc., K-12 Mathematics Curriculum Center. Published by Heinemann, a division of Reed Elsevier, Inc., Portsmouth, NH.

Because quality curriculum materials are now available, teachers can invest their time in adapting fundamentally sound materials to the particulars of their own students and situations rather than trying to invent a science program out of whole cloth. The challenge, then, is to help educators choose wisely among the available materials.

> "Every year I say I am tired of creating my own curriculum. I can't do a great job. It is very hard to interlace all the lessons. For two years, I had the opportunity to teach one of the reform mathematics curricula, with four weeks of professional development for that. I couldn't invent a better curriculum. So when the science coordinator in my district asked me to pilot a new standards-based science curriculum, I was happy to volunteer."
>
> — Middle-grades science teacher

Publishing curriculum materials is a big business, and with the national spotlight on standards, many programs describe themselves as "standards-based." Some of these have been newly developed, designed from the very beginning to promote the kinds of deep and flexible understanding that standards support. Some others, though published before the release of the national standards, were also designed to promote such deep understanding. Others, however, have undergone a kind of curricular cosmetic surgery, repackaging established approaches to familiar content with some additional activities and problems, for example, open-response exercises or journal writing assignments. Reform-minded teachers, school principals, and district administrators can wade through a vast number of choices—some very good and others rather poor—trying to find programs and materials that will help their students develop the skills, knowledge, and understanding they need to reason and communicate about the subjects they are studying. Educators seeking curricula that will move students to high standards of learning and performance need help determining their criteria for evaluating materials, winnowing the options, and identifying the important implementation issues.

Within the past few years several evaluations of middle-grades science materials have been published.[4] These reports are valuable resources, but there are several reasons why they cannot stand alone as guides for curriculum decisions. For one, the evaluations have used different strategies for identifying materials to evaluate and different criteria for their actual evaluations. Taken together, they offer a good sense of the kinds of materials promoting academic excellence that are currently available, but no one evaluation offers a definitive list from which to choose.

For another, curriculum decisions must include a consideration of the match between prospective materials and the particular circumstances of a district, school, or classroom. Such a very specific analysis is, of course, beyond the scope of the general evaluation these reports provide. Moreover, the reports' recommendations about specific materials will become outdated as new programs are developed and old ones modified. Potentially more useful over the long run are the evaluation criteria themselves, which educators can use on their own to review materials they are considering. As you might expect, however, the most rigorous criteria are also extensive and detailed, making their use quite labor-intensive.

There are also some guides that lay out the general process of curriculum design and selection.[5] The kind of resource that

> **Curriculum decisions must include a consideration of the match between prospective materials and the particular circumstances of a district, school, or classroom.**

---

[4] Science curricula have been reviewed in reports by the National Science Resources Center and Project 2061. See Chapter 4 for information about these reports.

[5] See, for example, National Academy Press, *Designing Mathematics or Science Curriculum Programs* (Washington, DC: National Academy Press, 1999); National Research Council, *Selecting Instructional Materials* (Washington, DC: National Research Council, 1999); and Lynn T. Goldsmith, June Mark, and Ilene Kantrov, *Choosing a Standards-Based Mathematics Curriculum* (Portsmouth, NH: Heinemann, 2000). Although this last guide is about choosing mathematics curricula, many of the points it makes are applicable to choosing science materials as well.

currently seems to be missing is a practical guide that combines a view of the decision-making process and descriptions of quality standards-based curricula, and that frames these within the experiences of practitioners who have been at the forefront of classroom reform. It is this niche that the *Guiding Curriculum Decisions* series seeks to fill.

This guide includes:

• Critical questions that embody a set of principles to guide curriculum decision making.

• Vignettes about curriculum selection and implementation that use practitioners' own voices to illustrate how the principles are addressed in practice.

• An overview of the curriculum decision-making process.

• Profiles of selected, exemplary curriculum programs.

• An annotated list of other resources that may be useful to curriculum decision making.

The principles we propose to guide decision making are general ones that pertain to any subject area. They articulate three essential components of any academically excellent curriculum. These three components provide the foundation on which the guides are based. The next section introduces these components, and is followed by some additional information about this guide: a brief tour of the remaining chapters of the guide, some suggestions of different ways to use the guide, a description of our process for identifying and interviewing practitioners about their experiences with standards-based curricula, and our methods for identifying materials to profile.

Principles to Guide Curriculum Decisions: Three Components of Academically Excellent Curricula

Before you can judge a curriculum's potential for promoting academic excellence, you need to know what to base your judgements *on*. The framework we describe below specifies three key components of academically excellent curricula—academic rigor, equity, and developmental appropriateness. These components, which are illustrated by the diagram of interlocking circles pictured throughout this introduction, were first proposed by members of the National Forum to Accelerate Middle-Grades School Reform, a coalition of funders, educators, researchers, state and local leaders, and representatives of national associations that promotes a vision of effective schools for young adolescents.[6] This section describes each of the components and discusses how each pertains to middle-grades students.

A view of middle-grades students

"Teaching middle school is like being inside a kaleidoscope—the view of the kids is always changing, and it's always interesting. I've heard middle-grades kids described in a lot of ways—mostly contradictory. For example, they're really learning how to take responsibility for themselves; they're really wild. They're vigilantly watching everyone and everything around them so they can figure out who they are; they're completely oblivious to the rest of the world. They're kind and thoughtful; they're rude and obnoxious. You can get someone in this school to agree to every one of these descriptions, and most of us would say that, at one time or another, they're *all* true.

"I think about middle-grades students like kernels of popcorn. They pretty much all enter sixth grade as young kids, and during the three years we have them, they start popping at different rates, transforming into these new adolescent creatures. The most obvious part of the transformation is the physical one. There are always a few kids who enter the sixth grade looking 16 instead of 11 or 12 (or who are older to begin with because they've repeated grades somewhere along the way), but mostly the sixth graders still have the bodies of children. And then, they start popping. By the end of the first year, there are a handful of boys who are shooting up and have feet the size of canal boats, and a bunch of girls who are beginning to look like young women. When everyone comes back to school the next fall, there are more kids who are making the change, and during seventh grade, even more. It's fun to watch friends catch up with each other—one month, two boys will walk down the hall looking like Mutt and Jeff, and two or three months later, they're standing shoulder to shoulder. By the time they leave for the high school, better than half of the girls are taller than I am—and let's not even talk about the boys!

"These kids are such a funny mix of becoming more grown up emotionally and intellectually and still remaining quite young. I really enjoy their class discussions, because you can see the kids

---

[6] Joan Lipsitz, Hayes Mizell, Anthony Jackson, and Leah Meyer Austin, "Speaking With One Voice," *Phi Delta Kappan*, 78, no. 7 (1997): 553.

revving up their mental engines. They're thinking deeply and figuring out some really sophisticated stuff. Kids will argue for their ideas and make pretty convincing cases, too. Even though they're beginning to become really passionate about some of their ideas and beliefs, they're also learning to listen to other people. Lots of times they can understand why someone else might see things differently. Sometimes they can even convince others to change their minds.

"But this growing intellectual power is only part of the story. Kids can be having this really intense and interesting discussion in class, say about how to control variables in an experimental design. Then, as soon as class ends the girls may shift seamlessly into a debate about the 'hottest' TV star on their way out the door and the boys may start to talk up the latest basketball game or exchange tips for avoiding skateboard wipe-outs."

— Middle-grades educator

Academic rigor: Meeting high standards

The current efforts to set standards for student performance at national, state, and district levels are, in essence, efforts to define academic rigor. At the heart of the standards movement is the question, "What is the essential knowledge of the discipline?" Or, as one Massachusetts teacher has put it, the fundamental question is: "What do I want my students to know ten years after they've been in my class?" For reform-minded educators the answer to these questions includes understanding the major concepts of a subject area (the "big ideas"), acquiring characteristic ways of thinking within the discipline ("habits of mind"), and learning its particular methods of investigation and argumentation. The answer also includes mastering skills, facts, and useful procedures, but it reframes these as part of a larger intellectual enterprise rather than as the primary goal of curriculum and instruction.

Standards are more than a list of expectations for student accomplishment—they're not simply a scope and sequence for the topics to be covered over the course of a year, a grade level, or an entire K–12 career. Standards are guideposts to help keep students on track for mastering the fundamental ideas of the subject area, reasoning according to the methods and conventions of the discipline, and presenting (and, if necessary, defending) their thinking to others.

This view of standards is pushing curriculum and instruction in new directions. Drawing on models of apprenticeship-style

Academic Rigor

Standards are guideposts to help keep students on track for mastering the fundamental ideas of the subject area, reasoning according to the methods and conventions of the discipline, and presenting (and, if necessary, defending) their thinking to others.

learning and on the theory that students construct their knowledge and understanding by actively engaging with the central ideas of a discipline, the current educational reform movement focuses on creating opportunities for students to build and use their understanding in rich and complex learning contexts.

An academically rigorous curriculum articulates a clear set of goals for learning. It gives teachers and students a reasonable picture of the nature of the discipline and connects them with the same kinds of work that engage professional practitioners. For example, students make and test mathematical conjectures, design science experiments to test hypotheses, or research and write persuasive essays. A rigorous curriculum helps students exercise general reasoning processes, develop ways of thinking that are particular to the subject area, and acquire an understanding of the methods for establishing and evaluating knowledge in the discipline. For example, the science curriculum should help students begin to evaluate the characteristics of a good scientific investigation, while language arts classes should help students understand the criteria by which we judge a well-reasoned essay.

In addition, a rigorous curriculum offers students (and teachers) a coherent view of the subject area by making connections among important ideas within the discipline. These connections have an effect similar to that of viewing an Impressionist painting from across a room. From up close, the painting looks like little more than individual patches of color floating on the surface of the canvas. From a distance, these colors coalesce into the rendering of a three-dimensional scene. A rigorous curriculum offers connections that help students recognize and appreciate the recurring themes, ideas, and methodologies of the discipline instead of only small, isolated pieces of the picture. In addition, it emphasizes connections between classroom study and real-world applications, helping students to recognize the practical utility of their developing knowledge. Finally, a rigorous curriculum uses a variety of strategies for assessing students' understanding and ability to apply their knowledge to new problems or in different contexts.

In the particular case of the middle grades, it is important that curricula not underestimate students' intellectual capabilities. Early adolescence is a time of significant growth in reasoning capacity, and students' coursework should reflect their increasing ability to think hypothetically and systematically. Jean Piaget, the

The current educational reform movement focuses on creating opportunities for students to build and use their understanding in rich and complex learning contexts.

An academically rigorous curriculum for the middle grades acknowledges students' growing cognitive capacities and provides them with intellectual challenges to help them shape and sharpen their growing interests.

grand master of cognitive developmental psychology, characterized the young adolescent as navigating the final major stage of intellectual growth.[7] Young adolescents become increasingly adept at considering a variety of perspectives, examining situations from different angles, assessing contingencies, and acknowledging possible outcomes. They can think about what might happen (or what might have happened if conditions had been different). Their reasoning becomes more complex and systematic as they develop the capacity to coordinate their thinking about several ideas at once. A classic example is the young adolescent's developing ability to understand that a balance beam's balance point is affected by the coordination of several factors: the amount of weight on each arm, the placement of the weights, and the location of the fulcrum.

The typical middle-grades curriculum is often criticized as a rehash of previous material, a time for review to ensure that students are prepared for their work in high school. Students are often seen as marking time instead of encountering new ideas and challenging work. An academically rigorous curriculum for the middle grades acknowledges students' growing cognitive capacities and provides them with intellectual challenges to help them shape and sharpen their growing interests. It helps students develop their reasoning abilities and their capabilities for inquiry. It also helps them learn to monitor and critique their work by tapping their growing "metacognitive" ability—the capacity to guide their learning by reflecting critically on their own thinking.

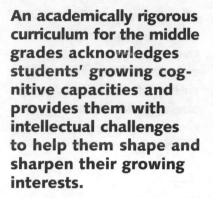

"In reviewing curricula, we found some books had hardly anything new from year to year. Those books presented the same activities, the same concepts, year after year. There was just no depth. If you looked at only one year in isolation you might say, 'Oh, this is really good,' but then when you looked across the three years of the program, you found that it was the same stuff. Kids would go through those books each year and they wouldn't learn anything new. We need a curriculum that will make sure we're not teaching the same material over and over again."

— District curriculum supervisor

Many schools have looked to using interdisciplinary approaches as a way to create more overall curricular coherence and enriching experiences for students. The team structures common in

---

[7] For an introduction to Piaget's theories, see Herbert Ginsburg and Sylvia Opper, *Piaget's Theory of Intellectual Development* (Englewood Cliffs, NJ: Prentice-Hall, 1969), or Jean Piaget, "Piaget's Theory," in *Carmichael's Handbook of Child Development*, ed. P. H. Mussen (New York: Wiley, 1970), 702–732.

middle schools can facilitate this effort by providing opportunities for teachers to work more closely together to establish and coordinate lesson plans. In some schools, the same teacher may even be responsible for instruction in more than one subject area. In addition to emphasizing connections among different disciplines, interdisciplinary studies have the potential to explore subject area content in much richer and more realistic contexts. After all, the activities and studies that comprise adult work rarely require the skills and ideas of only a single discipline.

It is important, however, to beware of a potential pitfall to interdisciplinary studies. In practice, it is less common to create a truly interdisciplinary curriculum than it is to integrate some of the themes, skills, and tools of one discipline into the study of another. For example, it is becoming increasingly common to ask students in science class to write in journals about their experiments or to articulate and defend their views about science-related social issues. This is a valuable addition to science classes, as it provides opportunities for students to articulate their thinking and use communication skills. However, teachers rarely respond to this written work as they would to writing assignments in language arts class. It would be unusual for teachers to require several drafts of writing done in science class in order to help students clarify their ideas, shape their reasoning, and produce effective and grammatically correct prose. Writing assignments may integrate language arts skills into science class, but they generally are not treated with equal weight. Similarly, having students read a novel about the Revolutionary War in language arts class while they study the colonial period in social studies does not, in itself, constitute an interdisciplinary approach to language arts and social studies. Making such links may offer students the chance to practice skills and reinforce knowledge gained in another subject area, which is well worth doing. But a truly interdisciplinary curriculum addresses the full set of academic standards for each subject area involved and requires more time than is allotted for study of a single subject.

Equity: Holding *all* students to high standards

Our public education system is built on the commitment to prepare all of the country's children for productive lives as adult members of our society. Unfortunately, the realization of this commitment has been imperfect, and it is often those students at

> **A truly interdisciplinary curriculum addresses the full set of academic standards for each subject area involved and requires more time than is allotted for study of a single subject.**

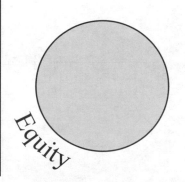

Equity

An equitable curriculum promotes high levels of achievement among a wide range of students by having more than one way to convey ideas and help students master skills.

most risk for being marginalized—those with the fewest resources and poorest prospects—who receive the least adequate education.[8] By articulating high standards for all students, the current education reform movement raises expectations for student performance, with particular attention to students who have traditionally not excelled in school. Hand in hand with these higher expectations comes the assumption that all students can learn important concepts and skills when instruction builds from their current understanding, focuses on making learning meaningful, and engages students' intellectual strengths to drive the learning process.

Educators who embrace this assumption commit themselves to finding a wide range of instructional approaches and classroom activities in order to meet the specific learning needs of individual students. In the past, the most common approach for working with students at risk of falling behind has been to "re-teach," going over material students have previously failed to master by using similar (if not identical) explanations and exercises in the hopes that more exposure will eventually lead to greater understanding. This "more of the same" approach is the educational equivalent of trying to communicate with someone who doesn't speak a word of English by repeating yourself, taking extra care to enunciate clearly and to speak more slowly and more loudly. If the listener has no way to make sense of your speech in the first place, you won't accomplish much by saying it again. You might, however, make some progress if you try something different, like supplementary gestures or even pantomime.

An equitable curriculum promotes high levels of achievement among a wide range of students by having more than one way to convey ideas and help students master skills. It includes approaches and activities that accommodate a variety of learning styles and provides different kinds of opportunities for students to gain understanding of the subject area content and demonstrate their mastery. For example, in a classroom study of hurricanes, students approach the topic from a variety of perspectives. They view videotape footage of television news coverage of Hurricane Andrew, read weather maps, track hurricanes, learn how to use weather instruments, and do hands-on investigations of surface

---

[8] Some also make the case that our educational system fails to meet the needs of very academically oriented students, who would benefit from more accelerated and in-depth learning.

heating and its effect on the air. Students also prepare a newspaper about hurricanes, with each student taking on the role of a different "expert" needed to produce the stories for the paper: hurricane specialist, meteorologist, natural hazards planner, and environmental scientist.

An equitable curriculum offers content that is rich and deep enough that students with different levels of understanding can all extend their learning. Both the kinds of topics addressed and the kinds of work students are asked to do must be sufficiently broad to allow everyone room to learn. In science, for example, investigations can offer less advanced students the opportunity to make observations, organize data, and seek explanations, while more sophisticated students can extend the activity by posing additional questions, designing follow-up inquiries, and carrying out further research. An equitable curriculum creates opportunities for all students, not just the most successful, to do work that challenges them to take charge of their work, reason, organize their thoughts, and communicate them to others. As educator and author Anne Wheelock has observed, "All students can benefit from the thinking skills and enrichment activities often offered only to those labeled 'gifted' and 'talented.'"[9]

Student diversity takes a number of forms: different approaches to learning; gender-related differences; a variety of home cultures, languages, and life experiences; different forms of physical challenge. Curricula should be sensitive to such differences. The contexts (and, where appropriate, content) should represent a variety of perspectives and experiences. The work and lives of those "dead, white, European males" are only part of the picture. An equitable curriculum makes sure that other parts of the picture are developed as well.

How do issues of equity apply to middle-grades curricula in particular? Curricula for young adolescents need to be particularly sensitive to providing all students with opportunities to exercise their newly developing logical and critical thinking skills. Because early adolescence is a time of intellectual growth spurts as well as physical ones, middle-grades students are developing their new cognitive resources and capacities at different rates and times. A typical middle-grades classroom, therefore, is likely to contain students with an especially wide range of cognitive

---

[9] Anne Wheelock, *Crossing the Tracks* (New York: The New Press, 1992), 13.

An equitable curriculum creates opportunities for all students, not just the most successful, to do work that challenges them to take charge of their work, reason, organize their thoughts, and communicate them to others.

Developmental
Appropriateness

In the middle grades, a developmentally appropriate curriculum takes into account the young adolescent's growing cognitive capacities, helping students move from their informal and intuitive ways of understanding toward more formal and systematic approaches to the subjects they are studying.

resources and capabilities. This intensifies the challenge of finding curriculum materials that can promote learning for students who bring a range of skills, prior knowledge, and reasoning abilities into the classroom.

Developmental appropriateness: Attending to characteristics of young adolescents

Effective curricula are geared to the students they are designed to reach. Their subject area content is developed at a level of complexity that builds on students' current knowledge and encourages them to push toward deeper and more extensive understanding. If the ideas developed in the curriculum are too far removed from students' experience or current ways of understanding, they will be too difficult to grasp; if the ideas are too simplistic, students will be bored by work they already understand.

Developmentally appropriate curricula are based on knowledge of how students' thinking develops. This ensures that the curricula deal with central ideas and skills in ways that address students' typical questions, confusions, and evolving understandings. Curriculum developers use their own experiences with students, educational and psychological research regarding children's acquisition of subject area concepts and skills, and pilot-test results to ensure that their materials are effective learning tools for students in the target grades.

Curricula must not only engage students at an appropriate intellectual level; they must engage students' interest and attention as well. Unless students are motivated to connect to the ideas in the curriculum, they will just mark time with studies that they don't "own." Developmentally appropriate curricula must therefore set students' academic work in contexts that are suited to their age and interests.

In the middle grades, a developmentally appropriate curriculum takes into account the young adolescent's growing cognitive capacities, helping students move from their informal and intuitive ways of understanding toward more formal and systematic approaches to the subjects they are studying. It is also particularly important that curricula motivate and engage middle-grades students, since young adolescents begin to question the purpose and value of adult-initiated assignments. As many students move to the middle grades, they leave their tractability behind as a souvenir for their elementary school teachers. Many students become less willing to work hard simply because a teacher requests it, asking, "What's the use of learning about this?" Students are more likely to put effort into their schoolwork when they perceive the contexts for lessons and activities to be interesting, important, and relevant to their lives. A developmentally appropriate middle-grades curriculum capitalizes on students' growing interest in their own communities, other cultures, and other eras to motivate their studies.

On the social front, the young adolescent's more flexible and far-reaching ways of thinking lead to a seeming paradox: an increasing attention to others which is paired with a growing self-consciousness. Students in the middle grades begin to think more deeply about the consequences of people's thoughts and actions, and are willing to consider complex and important questions like, "What makes a good friend?" "What does it mean to be a slave, or a slaveholder?" "What do the statistics on driving age and accident rates tell us?" "What is the effect of human activity on the environment?" Middle-grades students also think a lot about their own character and role in the world. Their questions about identity aren't idle ones. With bodies that often look and feel alien, and with newly emerging observational and analytic skills, young adolescents are often genuinely in a state of flux. As middle-grades students grapple with questions about themselves and their world, they turn to their compatriots in struggle—their peers—for self-definition and validation.

Developmentally appropriate curricula for the middle grades capitalize on this attention to self and peers by offering students opportunities to develop social skills and to use their classmates as resources for learning. Because middle-grades students are particularly oriented toward their peer group, providing them opportunities to work together offers a way to harness their keen interest in one another toward productive educational ends. Students can develop their collaborative skills as well as engage their capacity to compare and critique ideas from different perspectives.

A caution. A common misinterpretation of standards-based reform is that it is first and foremost about offering students motivating and engaging activities. But an effort directed only at making lessons appealing and engaging may lead to trivial intellectual

Developmentally appropriate curricula for the middle grades capitalize on this attention to self and peers by offering students opportunities to develop social skills and to use their classmates as resources for learning.

work—in an effort to hook students on learning, students may be let off the hook of mastering content.

Choosing fun classroom activities, using concrete, "hands-on" lessons, and having students work in cooperative groups do not by themselves guarantee student learning. Without clear academic goals and an understanding of how to reach them, efforts to provide engaging and interesting activities are simply form without substance. Yet, because subject area standards all stress the importance of student involvement, it's not unusual for educators to assume that active and engaged students provide adequate evidence that substantial learning is taking place.

There is no question that it is better for students to find their work engaging and interesting than to be bored and unconvinced of the value of their efforts. However, activities may prove engaging without stretching students' understanding. When this is the case, neither the criterion for academic rigor nor that for developmental appropriateness is being met. Quality education isn't simply about having students busy and happy in the classroom. It's about having them engaged in work that has intellectual teeth.

Integrating the three components

Only when all three components described above are present can a curriculum offer the intellectual depth and pedagogical perspectives that create powerful learning opportunities for a wide range of students. Academic excellence lies at the intersection of academic rigor, equity, and developmental appropriateness.

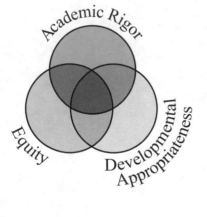

Because the three components work in concert to support learning, when one or another is missing or weak, the curriculum will not promote academic excellence. Without academic rigor, the curriculum will have no edge as a tool for intellectual growth and students will be denied important resources for building knowledge and understanding. However, if an academically rigorous curriculum is inequitable (by being successful at promoting learning for only a narrow segment of the student population), its effectiveness is also compromised. It runs the risk of shortchanging students who have interesting minds and the potential to make significant contributions, but whose modes of learning or whose academic or social experiences are inconsistent with the limited approaches taken by the curriculum. And even an admirably rigorous curriculum will fail to promote learning if it does not address students' typical patterns of developing concepts and skills, or if it fails to capture students' interest or attention. In curriculum, as in other aspects of life, a balance among important components is the key.

We want this guide to speak to educators . . . from the place where, ultimately, the work of the curriculum is carried out—the classroom.

About This Guide

This guide, like the others in the series, uses the framework described above to examine standards-based curricula and their implementation. It also relies on the insights of a number of teachers and advisors, who shared with us their thoughts and observations about using standards-based approaches to curriculum. In addition to providing information about the implementation of particular materials, they talked about the "big picture"— how curriculum related to their standards for student performance, the instructional approaches they saw as most effective for student learning in diverse populations, and their commitment to professional development. Below is a summary of the contents of *Guiding Curriculum Decisions for Middle-Grades Science.*

A brief tour of this guide

Guiding Curriculum Decisions for Middle-Grades Science looks at curriculum from several different perspectives. The introduction has offered a set of principles—the three components of academically excellent curricula—as an overarching guide to curriculum decision making. Subsequent chapters use these principles as a framework for considering curriculum decision making and implementation.

Chapter 1. In this chapter, we look at practitioners' experiences with exemplary curriculum materials to help us draw explicit connections between these principles and the ways teachers actually use exemplary materials to promote students' learning. We want this guide to speak to educators (teachers, curriculum specialists, staff developers, principals, and central office administrators) from the place where, ultimately, the work of the curriculum is carried out—the classroom. By grounding the guide in practitioners' own descriptions of their experiences, we aim to give readers a fuller and more vibrant picture of what makes an excellent curriculum excellent.

The chapter is organized around "critical questions" to ask when making curriculum decisions. These questions are tied to the three critical components of academically excellent curricula we have described above: academic rigor, equity, and developmental appropriateness. Each of the critical questions is then illustrated by vignettes with practitioners' observations of ways they (or their districts) have addressed the question.

Chapter 2. This chapter offers a practical guide to the curriculum selection process, sketching important steps to take and issues to consider. It may outline a process that is more complex and time-consuming than you have used in the past; remember that the kinds of curriculum materials that will help promote academic excellence are themselves more complex and require more study. The "flip test" that worked when materials were all more or less the same—flip through a few pages or a chapter, check for layout, readability, and coverage of topics in the district's scope and sequence—is no longer sufficient. Because concepts and skills are developed in the context of carefully sequenced activities and investigations, the materials generally require more thorough study in order to identify the ways content is developed in lessons and units. Since the scope of different materials varies significantly as well, it is important to review them closely to make sure not only that the content is rigorous, equitable, and developmentally appropriate, but that it meets state and district standards.

Chapter 3. Chapter 3 presents profiles of eleven examples of science curriculum materials worthy of consideration by schools that want to help middle-grades students meet national science standards. These profiles do not represent a definitive list of high-quality materials, but rather examples of the kinds of materials that are designed to promote the science concepts, skills, and processes that are emphasized in the national science standards. The profiles provide an overview of each curriculum; identify its content focus; describe its format; suggest how it addresses the criteria of academic rigor, equity, and developmental appropriateness; note the available teaching resources and support; and include comments and suggestions from teachers who have used the materials. The profiles of these curriculum materials are designed to give you a sense of the distinctive characteristics of the materials. They may whet your appetite for a closer look at the curriculum, but should never substitute for a more careful review of the materials themselves. They may also encourage you to look at materials similar to those profiled—ones that take a similar approach but address different topics or standards.

Chapter 4. This final chapter provides an annotated list of additional resources to assist you in making curriculum decisions. These resources include professional organizations, sources of information about designing or implementing curricula, professional development programs, and additional curriculum materials, including forthcoming publications.

Some suggestions for using the guide

For some who are looking for guidance in making decisions about new curriculum the only real question they may have is, "What should we buy?" and the only part of this guide that may seem relevant is the chapter that includes the curriculum profiles. While we certainly cannot argue about the importance of this question, we do not see it as the only one to ask, and we encourage you to use this guide (and the others in the series) for more than a quick pointer to the publishers you will contact for sales presentations.

In fact, we think that the temptation to look at the profiles and nothing more is kind of like eating dessert before your main course—it may satisfy your immediate craving, but it's not very nutritious by itself. The profiles are intended to give you a sense of how different exemplary programs approach important issues, but this information alone isn't enough to help you make good curricular decisions for your particular circumstances. The other parts of the guide are constructed to help you put the profiles in some broader contexts: the context of general characteristics of academically excellent materials and the context of other practitioners' experiences, which you can then compare to the particulars of your own district, school, and/or classroom.

We strongly suggest that you read Chapter 1 before you go on to the rest of the guide. This chapter grounds the conceptual framework outlined above within the actual experiences of teachers. More than any other part of this guide, and more than most other resources we have seen, this chapter offers the voices of fellow educators reflecting on the challenges and rewards of using standards-based curriculum materials.

You may want to read the guide front to back, but you may also choose to use it more as a resource book, choosing chapters to read as the need arises. However you use it, we hope that one idea shines through: that the movement toward standards for learning and performance that focus on conceptual as well as skill-based achievement has required a serious reconsideration of what makes an academically excellent curriculum. And this reconsideration, in turn, has lead to the need to conceptualize both the decision-making process for curriculum selection and plans for implementation in different terms.

Interviews with science educators

In preparing this guide, we spoke to a number of science educators throughout the country about their curricula. Because there is a large array of science materials, which vary in terms of the instructional time they require, we found that many teachers used a variety of materials over the course of the year. We were interested in learning from them about district-level curriculum choices and decisions, their thoughts about different curriculum materials, some of the challenges they had encountered in implementing standards-based curricula, and ways they had resolved those challenges.

All told, we interviewed 37 full-time sience teachers and 20 former full-time teachers now working as teacher leaders, curriculum coordinators, coaches, or resource teachers. They work in different community settings (urban, suburban, and rural) and in different geographical regions of the country. Their districts range in size from large urban systems serving tens of thousands of students to a district with a total of fewer than 1000.

We identified educators to interview in several ways. Colleagues and members of the advisory board for this guide recommended practitioners they knew and respected. Sometimes these practitioners, in turn, recommended that we speak with colleagues of theirs. Curriculum developers and selected publishers also recommended teachers who were familiar with standards-based instruction and articulate about meeting the challenges of implementing a standards-based curriculum. We also contacted several of the curriculum supervisors and coordinators whose districts are associated with our granting agencies, the Edna McConnell Clark and W.K. Kellogg Foundations, and with the National Science Foundation-funded Center for Urban Science Education Reform based at Education Development Center, Inc. These practitioners were not necessarily using standards-based curricula, but were quite helpful in assisting us to develop a fuller picture of the kinds of challenges that teachers face as they work to meet standards in their classrooms.

The interviews themselves consisted of conversations of approximately an hour in length, which followed a flexible interview protocol. The interviews included discussion of curriculum selection decisions, overall experiences with standards-based curriculum materials, experiences with particular lessons, ways the curriculum materials affected students who were succeeding or struggling in class, and specific challenges of the materials for teaching and learning. We have used these interviews in creating the vignettes in Chapter 1 and in developing the curriculum profiles that comprise Chapter 3.

Identifying examples of standards-based curricula

The exemplary middle-grades science materials identified in this guide represent two different types of materials currently used by reform-minded school districts across the country. These are (1) yearlong and multiyear materials that constitute comprehensive, core instructional programs, and (2) modular materials that can be used over shorter periods, either as supplements to a core curriculum or as part of a tapestry of modular units that are woven together to create a comprehensive program. Modular units often use social issues or everyday phenomena as the door into the study of the science. Among the materials identified in this guide are examples of social issues-focused curricula and curricula that involve extended inquiry. This guide does not focus on activity books, CD-ROMs, or individual curriculum units that stand alone rather than serve as part of a series or larger science program. Some of these other kinds of materials are, however, described briefly in the annotated list of resources included in Chapter 4.

We began our identification of exemplary middle-grades science curriculum materials by reviewing materials that had been developed with support from the National Science Foundation, designed in accordance with the national science standards, and field tested in a variety of different classroom contexts. In addition, we contacted leading science educators and asked for suggestions of additional curriculum materials that address the criteria of academic rigor, equity, and developmental appropriateness. We further consulted resource lists developed by science education organizations and professional associations. Once we had identified a list of candidate materials, our staff of science educators reviewed them and also looked to practitioners for corroboration of their merits. As we interviewed science educators who were using the materials initially identified, we also asked them to recommend additional materials. Finally, we gathered as much information as possible about other ongoing curriculum evaluation efforts to ensure that we did not appreciably duplicate their efforts. For example, because Project 2061 of AAAS was conducting an extensive review of the most commonly used comprehensive textbook-based curricula, we decided to focus primarily on modular programs and inquiry-based materials.

A final word

As we have worked on this guide, we have spoken with many teachers who have come to believe that standards-based curriculum materials have helped them to teach better because they have helped focus on providing rigorous, equitable, and developmentally appropriate instruction for students. For many, learning to use these materials effectively has been a challenge, but ultimately a rewarding one. As one seventh- and eighth- grade teacher noted,

> "After the pilot testing of the curriculum there was some controversy in the district about whether it was going to be approved for adoption or not. But all the middle school teachers just looked at each other and someone said, 'The school board can do what they want. I'll never teach like I did before.' So this curriculum really had a big impact on how we taught and how we saw students learning. I think it has been very powerful."

We hope that you, too, will find that standards-based science materials can be a powerful force in your district, school, or classroom. And we hope that this guide will help you to make thoughtful decisions about choosing and using science curriculum materials in the future.

CHAPTER 1

Critical Questions in Curriculum Decision Making

The three key components of academically excellent curricula described in the introduction provide a framework for educators faced with making curriculum decisions. However, it is one thing to talk in the abstract about the important components of an academically excellent curriculum and another to have an image of what such a creature looks like and how teachers make it work in the classroom with 150 students each day. This chapter focuses on what curricula that are academically rigorous, equitable, and developmentally appropriate look like in action. Drawing on interviews with teachers and school leaders around the U.S. who have experience using exemplary science curriculum materials, this chapter takes you inside classrooms and schools to see how educators use these materials to promote student learning.

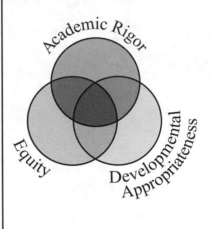

Critical Questions

This chapter poses a set of six "critical questions" to ask about middle-grades curriculum. A series of vignettes—stories told in the voices of practitioners—illustrates how the answers to each question emerge from the intersection of excellent curriculum, effective teaching, and the support of school and district leadership.

The first four critical questions, and the corresponding sections of this chapter, focus on the components of the curricula themselves—academic rigor, equity, and developmental appropriateness. (Rigor accounts for two of the questions, one focusing on how curriculum supports standards for teaching and learning and the other on how the curriculum achieves coherence.) A brief introduction to each section explains the particular aspect of curricular excellence that the question highlights.

It is one thing to talk in the abstract about the important components of an academically excellent curriculum and another to have an image of what such a creature looks like and how teachers make it work in the classroom with 150 students each day.

The remaining questions focus on factors influencing curriculum implementation, including the kinds of professional development for teachers that are necessary to ensure effective implementation and the particular challenges faced by teachers using exemplary curriculum materials in the classroom. The introduction to the section on professional development describes why this is so important for teachers using standards-based curriculum materials, and characterizes strategies for effective professional development. The introduction to the section on implementation challenges provides an overview of the kinds of challenges teachers encounter when using standards-based materials in the classroom and the kinds of strategies they employ to address these challenges.

Vignettes

Each critical question is illustrated by several vignettes that focus on the curriculum component or implementation issue addressed by that question. Because the qualities of excellent curricula are intertwined, there is some overlap between the vignettes within each section and across different sections. For example, an exemplary curriculum that is academically rigorous will necessarily take advantage of students' growing cognitive capacities in the middle-grades years—a key aspect of developmental appropriateness.

Vignettes also vary in length, usually depending on the complexity of the curriculum features and implementation challenges they illustrate.

The names and locations of the teachers, school leaders, and districts in the vignettes are fictional. However, the kinds of districts (for example, urban, rural, suburban, small, large, relatively resource-rich or -poor) and the areas of the country mentioned do correspond to the types of districts and geographical areas represented by the practitioners interviewed. The practitioners' words have also been edited, and in some cases a particular vignette represents a composite of several people's experiences and perspectives. However, the vignettes do reflect the views represented in the interviews on which they were based.

Because this chapter focuses on the features that exemplary curricula share, the vignettes do not name particular curriculum materials. Naming the materials would shift the focus from the shared features of high-quality curriculum materials to the strengths of particular ones. In addition, the choice of which curriculum to highlight in a particular vignette is relatively arbitrary. Naming a particular curriculum in a vignette about equity might suggest that that curriculum was more likely to promote high achievement for a wide range of students than other curricula. Yet it might have been selected to illustrate this feature simply because the interview data provided a particularly good description of how it exemplifies this feature. Because we do not want readers to mistake an example for an endorsement, we have chosen to forego identification of specific materials in this chapter.

Many of the vignettes do describe curriculum materials in terms of the approaches they take: inquiry-based, extended investigations, social issues-oriented, technology-focused. These approaches correspond to the types of particular curriculum materials that are profiled in Chapter 3. To learn about how a particular curriculum addresses the critical questions, you can consult the individual profiles.

The *National Science Education Standards*[1] and *Benchmarks for Science Literacy*[2] present an ambitious vision for science education. These standards and benchmarks challenge middle-grades science teachers to engage students in the process of scientific inquiry and build their understanding of important concepts within and across a range of scientific disciplines: physical, life, and earth sciences.

The hallmark of these curricula is the development of student learning in a disciplined manner that reflects the ways in which scientists work and learn in the real world. Students learn to formulate questions, design and conduct experiments, collect and analyze data, reach conclusions, and cite evidence to support those conclusions. Students delve into concepts (for example, mass and density, force, transfer of energy; structure and function in cells, organisms, and ecosystems; climate, planetary motion) so that they can understand and apply them in novel situations. Students demonstrate their understanding of scientific concepts by using them to explain observations and make predictions, and

ACADEMIC RIGOR

How will the middle-grades science curriculum support the standards for teaching and learning?

---

[1] National Research Council, *National Science Education Standards* (Washington, DC: National Academy Press, 1996).

[2] Project 2061, American Association for the Advancement of Science, *Benchmarks for Science Literacy* (New York: Oxford University Press, 1993).

by representing their ideas in different ways (for example, in writing and with diagrams, graphs, and charts). Students are able to use scientific tools and technologies, including laboratory equipment and computer technology, to conduct experiments and analyze results.

What makes curricula developed to meet these standards effective tools for teaching and learning? Curricula that support academically rigorous science standards seek to deepen students' understanding of key science concepts, challenge students' current conceptions, and structure student learning in a logical and systematic way. In general, these curricula offer:

- Investigations that enable students to engage in scientific inquiry and build their understanding of important concepts.
- Carefully structured sequences of activities that provide students with the necessary support to understand and learn to apply scientific concepts.
- A focus on the intuitive conceptions of important scientific ideas that students bring to the classroom and many opportunities for teachers to elicit and develop students' ideas.
- Integrated learning of scientific skills, concepts, and processes.
- Assessments that require students to demonstrate their ability to understand and apply important concepts, use scientific tools, and communicate results in appropriate ways.
- Assessment scoring guides that make clear to students what they need to learn and be able to do.

Because rigorous science learning depends on student access to all these features, teachers advise that new materials are best used as a package. Although teachers adapt and "tweak" the written materials to fit their own particular students, classrooms, and communities, students derive the greatest benefit when teachers use materials as a single, coherent program, not in bits and pieces. The following vignettes illustrate the important features of academically rigorous curriculum materials.

Deepening students' conceptual understanding

Rigorous curriculum is designed to help students learn science concepts in depth through activities that become increasingly complex. For example, one unit of an inquiry-based curriculum challenges students to design and build windmills. In the initial activity of this extended investigation, students have to construct a windmill from some simple materials (including index cards for arms and a yogurt container for a hub). They have to get the windmill to work, observe its functioning, isolate important variables, make sense of what is happening (that is, why does the windmill work?), and explain it to others. Later in the investigation, students are challenged to get their windmills to lift a cup of nails. In the context of meeting this challenge, students learn about physical science concepts related to simple machines, rotational momentum, transformation of energy, work, and power. By engaging in increasingly systematic inquiry, students develop an understanding of these concepts so that they can apply them in novel situations.

Suzanne Bourque, who teaches seventh- and eighth-grade science in a large urban district in the Midwest, talks about how she starts the unit. "At the beginning of the unit, students use their own intuition and creativity to make a model, which may barely function." An observer in Suzanne's seventh-grade classroom would see groups of students trying to determine the best place to position a fan to get their newly constructed model windmills to lift the nails. Some groups hold the fan to the side of the windmill. Others hold the fan directly in front of it. A group that holds the fan on the side notices that their windmill doesn't lift as many nails as the windmill of a group holding the fan in front. At this early point in the unit, the students aren't yet sure what is most important: the size of the blades, the position of the blades, or the position of the fan. So they keep on experimenting to determine what makes the difference.

"In the process of attempting to improve the windmill's performance, they identify important variables. One student says, 'I think we need four arms.' Another student thinks the windmill needs more than four arms. They figure out that they have to consider the angle of the blades. Each group collects data, then they compare the data, and then they have to analyze it. Sometimes they hypothesize what will happen before they collect data, but then they see the importance of the data in order to reach a conclusion.

"These experiments help kids to build a knowledge base which enables them to improve the performance of the windmill. It also is a concrete context for introducing concepts such as energy transformation, work, and power. Technology topics like this offer great opportunities to help kids develop an understanding of physical science concepts. But this approach, which integrates

By engaging in increasingly systematic inquiry, students develop an understanding of these concepts so that they can apply them in novel situations.

"The deeper into the investigations they go, the more skills and content they learn. In addition to learning the concepts, they learn process skills such as collecting and recording data, and designing experiments that isolate variables."

science and technology, requires an extended period for students to develop a really firm understanding of the concepts.

"The unit on windmills in seventh grade is a good example of how learning with these inquiry units really is serious work. And it's hard. Sometimes when the students get to the tough part, they want to give up. But then we begin to see a growth in their skills. The deeper into the investigations they go, the more skills and content they learn. In addition to learning the concepts, they learn process skills such as collecting and recording data, and designing experiments that isolate variables. The hardest part is learning to be systematic. Not many kids at this age are naturally systematic in their investigations, and it's especially hard for them to isolate variables. But they can learn to do this if they keep working on the investigation over time." Through the sequence of activities in this unit, students learn that they need to plan ahead and address one variable—number of blades, angle of blades, direction of power source—at a time.

Suzanne has struggled to select curriculum materials that respect her students' natural curiosity, recognize the experiences they bring into the classroom, and help them develop a deep understanding of critical concepts. Her district has learning standards that are based on state standards, and designates topics at each grade level. The curriculum must align with the district's standards, grade-level topics, and also a new statewide assessment. Suzanne says, "The reason I like these kinds of materials so much is they really get at important concepts, the big ideas of science, and they're a good match with our learning standards. They focus on just a few fundamental ideas, but really develop a conceptual understanding in depth, rather than just superficially touching on these topics. They start out with very basic, simple ideas and through carefully scaffolded activities the sophistication level builds."

Suzanne explains her confidence that her students will do well on the new state assessment. "If the curriculum can help kids tackle problems and make connections, which it does, they're going to do well on the state test. The test really does have the big ideas, and that's what they're getting from this curriculum. Sometimes after they've completed an extended investigation and learned specific concepts, I give them related problems from a textbook. Even though they haven't yet learned the specific formulas, they're still able to solve the problems. In fact, they seem to be able to do these very well." Students' success in applying their scientific knowledge in an unfamiliar context is evidence to Suzanne of their depth of understanding.

Suzanne acknowledges, however, that, by offering such in-depth learning experiences, she is making some tradeoffs between depth of understanding and breadth of coverage. "In the extended investigations we do, I think a lot about student understanding versus content coverage. Kids have the chance, with these investigations, to apply the concepts they learn. But to do this really well, we will, in fact, be covering less content. Their understanding will be deeper, though, because we won't be jumping around so much. We'll use the content they have learned and connect it to other pieces of content they have learned. I think they're going much deeper. I see that when they bring up something they've learned in one unit—about momentum, for instance, from the windmill unit—in another context. I can see it in their increasing capacity to explain convincingly—to me or to others in their group—their evidence for a particular conclusion. And I see it in the kinds of questions they ask. They're not just looking for 'the answer' from me, but they want to know why."

While noting the focused and in-depth nature of the materials, Suzanne also points out that each unit makes connections to other important scientific ideas. Rather than promoting superficial "coverage" of many topics, the materials enable students to make conceptual connections. She says, "You're not focusing only on one thing. There are other ideas that connect, that come out, through focusing on this big idea."

Suzanne adds, "I think you need to go for in-depth understanding and it is often at the expense of coverage. It does take longer to teach this way. But if you're seeing an increase in your students' understanding, then you really need to trust your decision."

Moving students too quickly through the curriculum can undermine the overall thrust toward deeper understanding. Standards-based curricula assume that students need time to experiment. They assume that faster is not necessarily smarter, that the first solution to a problem is not necessarily the best solution. Though she admits feeling frustrated at times at not being able to move more quickly, Suzanne cautions teachers against hurrying students through the materials. "Don't rush the kids. I know

"They're not just looking for 'the answer' from me, but they want to know why."

"Don't rush the kids. I know that's a hard one, but each part of the unit has a purpose in the whole picture."

that's a hard one, but each part of the unit has a purpose in the whole picture. Say the kids have a class period to build something. Towards the end of the class, they're starting to get something done. Well, you might feel frustrated about that and think, 'Oh, we should have finished.' So it's a tough call. 'Am I going to give them time again next class to continue with this?' It depends on your evaluation of how far they've come in their understanding. If I'm not sure, I might take time during the next class to do some assessment—look at what they've written up about what they've learned so far—to see where they are in terms of the concepts. These are all hard decisions, but you definitely want to keep pushing for the understanding, not rushing to get through the materials."

Challenging students' intuitive conceptions

Lois McCullough is a professional development coach who works with science teachers in small cities and rural areas of New England. Lois has particular praise for materials that are designed to help teachers identify and build on students' existing conceptions in order to develop a sound understanding of difficult concepts such as matter and energy. She tells about a classroom where students are learning about evaporation. "Even though they often use the term 'evaporation,' they can't explain where water or some other liquid has 'gone.' For them, the water has just disappeared. To help them understand what really happens, students start out by reading a story that involves two cups of liquid left out in the heat.

"Students have to figure out what happened to the liquid. First, they have to draw the two cups in their journals and show how much they think would be left in each cup. Then they have to explain why they have drawn the cups in particular ways: the shape and size of each cup and how much is missing from each. From this activity, they move on to develop a list of factors that affect the rate of evaporation. They divide into groups that design, set up, and carry out an experiment to test their ideas. Then they analyze and interpret the data and draw a conclusion."

Lois describes what she especially values in the curriculum: "One of the things this curriculum does is identify what students' 'misconceptions' are, that is, the alternative conceptions that they bring to their learning. It makes you aware of those common misconceptions up front before you teach the unit. In the evaporation unit, it's the idea that the liquid has 'just disappeared.' The units are carefully designed to address these ideas that research has shown us kids bring into their learning."

Standards-based curriculum materials push students to examine the ways they think about phenomena by having them construct hypotheses, evaluate their ideas in light of the evidence and data, and invite others to critique their ideas. Lois explains, "The way it works with the curriculum is that a problem is presented and you get kids engaged in thinking about the problem, and then kids have opportunities to explore all different aspects of that particular problem. Kids work in groups, brainstorming solutions. If you look at all the cross-cutting process standards that are part of our state learning results, these materials are very strong in terms of group work and eliciting student ideas. Students are constantly being asked to explain their reasoning. So you can see how their ideas are developing, and where they still need more work.

"Take the whole notion of molecules and the kinetic theory of matter. That's such a difficult concept to teach. So there are units that focus on evaporation and condensation, and on freezing and melting, all using the idea of molecules. There's another unit that really develops an understanding of photosynthesis and the connection with respiration and structure and function in plants, and the whole idea of food and food energy. These materials target some really important big ideas, and kids stay really focused on a particular idea that plays out over time."

Lois also notes that the assessments accompanying these materials ask students to explain their thinking, rather than asking just for answers or conclusions. For example, students might correctly answer that sunlight, carbon dioxide, and water are all necessary for photosynthesis, but their explanations of the process might suggest that they are still uncertain about whether plants make their own food. Teachers can use that information to guide their teaching as students work through the rest of the unit.

Structuring learning experiences

Sam Ruocco, who teaches seventh-grade science in a suburban district in the Northwest, describes how another inquiry-based curriculum also systematically develops students' skills, knowledge, and understanding of important scientific concepts. The unit Sam describes focuses on properties of matter, introducing concepts of mass, weight, volume, and density. He says, "Students do a series of experiments to investigate floating and sinking. At

Standards-based curriculum materials push students to examine the ways they think about phenomena by having them construct hypotheses, evaluate their ideas in light of the evidence and data, and invite others to critique their ideas.

"We're developing those lab skills at the same time as we're developing concepts."

one point, they have two cartons of different sizes. They add the same mass to each, and put them in water. The cartons don't sink to the same level, even though they have the same mass, and the one the students expect to sink deeper doesn't. That's an anomaly to the students, and it piques their interest. So they learn that they have to consider volume as well. Now, we've calculated volume and measured volume. And we put it all together and come up with density as the reason for floating and sinking.

"Right now they're measuring the densities of different objects. They're doing it as a lab, they aren't just reading about it. They're actually measuring the mass and the volume of these objects and categorizing them as floaters, sinkers, and subsurface floaters. They graph their results, and then they're able to explain the anomaly that they saw earlier. Next they'll go on to a much more sophisticated lab, in which they'll correlate the mass displaced with the mass of the floating object. They'll see that even though you have liquids of different densities, the object still displaces its own mass. That will allow us to explain buoyancy."

Sam points to the way the unit integrates learning of skills with understanding of concepts. "We start out with a very simple lab skill, like learning to count, learning to use a metric ruler. They learn graphing skills, and interpolating and extrapolating on a graph. Later on, when we're working on the concept of mass, they use a balance and learn to measure mass. Then they learn to measure density and volume. So we're developing those lab skills at the same time as we're developing concepts."

Sam explains how the inquiry approach of the curriculum encourages students to think carefully about the phenomena they are investigating and provide evidence for their conclusions. "At the end of the unit, in the culminating project, the kids build a submarine. It has to float, sink, and then float again. In other words, they have to be able to change the density of that object." But students don't just build the submarine, Sam points out. "They have to be able to explain why their submarine works. That's the key in these units, to get the kids to do the thinking. Inquiry is a whole philosophy of teaching. It means that the student is involved from the start to the finish. There's good hands-on stuff out there, but it's not necessarily inquiry. Because with inquiry goes an entire philosophy and strategy about questioning students. It's not just, 'Guess what the teacher wanted me to say.'

Here's an example: instead of saying, 'How many BBs did it take to sink this straw?', you'll say, 'What do you notice about this data?' When a student answers that mass is equal to the displaced volume, you don't just say, 'Oh, that's great.' Instead you ask, 'What is your evidence for that? How do you know that? Is there anyone who disagrees?'"

Curriculum units like this also promote both development of skills and learning for understanding by asking students to do a significant amount of writing. For middle-grades teachers who work on teams with teachers of other academic subjects, this offers the opportunity for interdisciplinary collaboration. Sam describes a unit on ecology in which students design and carry out their own investigation and then report upon it in a scientific format. The writing assignment is designed and carried out jointly with the English teacher on the team, so that, as Sam says, "the English teacher teaches them technical writing while they're doing their soil reports. The vehicle for the teaching of the technical writing is the soil report. So they hone their technical writing skills, and it counts as both an English and a science grade." Sam adds, "One of the things I see that kids don't like to do is to write. But they're finding that in every single discipline, mathematics and science included, they have to write. That's one thing that kids sometimes find difficult, so the teacher needs to establish the criteria and give kids lots and lots and lots of practice at it."

The ways in which these materials address the science learning standards is also made explicit in the assessments they provide. For example, the curriculum Sam uses includes an evaluation guide which helps him identify a list of skills, processes, and content areas that kids should know by the end of seventh grade. Sam has also adapted a scoring guide—which was developed by other teachers using the curriculum—for lab assignments in his class. He says, "The kids each have a copy of the scoring guide, and each time I grade a lab now, I pull out a grid that has the criteria on it. It focuses on the lab write-up, the work in cooperative groups, collecting and analyzing data, summary and conclusion, and communication. And it has ratings of one, two, three, and four for each of the criteria. This not only becomes a way to score the kids' work, but students can look back at the guide and say, 'Well, I got a two on writing,' and look at the comments on the writing to figure out where they could improve. It lets me hold them to a certain standard that they can see and refer to

Curriculum units like this also promote both development of skills and learning for understanding by asking students to do a significant amount of writing. For middle-grades teachers who work on teams with teachers of other academic subjects, this offers the opportunity for interdisciplinary collaboration.

each time. For their science investigation, I took the scoring guide that is going to be used for the kids in the tenth grade, when they do our state certificate of mastery. I tweaked it a little bit, and I'm now using that same scoring guide for them. So they'll be seeing this scoring guide for the next four years, and be working to that."

ACADEMIC RIGOR

How will we create a coherent science program that has a deliberate and integrated design?

With an abundance of middle-grades science curriculum materials from which to choose, educators not only face the challenge of selecting rigorous, developmentally appropriate, standards-based materials, but they must then create a coherent curriculum from among those materials. As they take on this challenge, educators face a choice. They can select a yearlong or multiyear program from among the few designed for this purpose. Alternatively, they can choose from a wider array of materials that offer four- to eight-week units or modules, weaving these together into a varied but comprehensive and high-quality program of their own.

Whichever approach they choose, educators have to ensure that the parts that make up the year's curriculum create a coherent whole in which key teaching strategies and expectations for learning reinforce one another from unit to unit. A coherent curriculum:

- Integrates science content and process skills.
- Builds students' understanding of concepts over time.
- Makes connections across different scientific disciplines (earth, life, and physical sciences).
- Links science learning to the real world.

In addition, because young adolescents are "in the middle"—ready to be stretched intellectually, but still developing the habits of mind necessary for more complex work—middle-grades curriculum must do one more thing. It must build on what students have learned in the elementary grades and also set the stage for learning science in the high school grades.

The following vignettes describe the experiences of two reform-minded districts that have taken different approaches to curriculum design. Each approach depends on teachers and district leaders who first identify high-quality curriculum materials that reflect the expectations for middle-grades science learning defined in local standards, and who then ensure that every aspect of the program develops students' understanding of the concepts identified in those standards. In one district, teachers are carefully piecing such a curriculum together. In the other, teachers have selected a comprehensive program, supplemented with additional lessons and a textbook. A number of factors, including availability of district resources and time for planning, can influence the choice of approach to achieving coherence. Whatever the approach, the outcome should be a curriculum in which objectives for student learning support one another as the year progresses.

Carefully choosing the parts to make a coherent whole

The Newcastle School District, a large urban district in the Northeast, received a five-year National Science Foundation (NSF) grant to improve the middle schools' science program. Using NSF-sponsored resources to support study and planning, the district thoughtfully crafted a coherent curriculum from a variety of published science materials that align with its state science standards and the district curriculum framework.

In the beginning, district science specialist Sophia Engels worked with her colleagues to establish two major initiatives. First, she created a district curriculum framework committee whose job was to work over three years to develop student performance goals for science content and processes, gather comments from the local scientific community, and, finally, refine those goals. Second, Sophia led the committee in a process of identifying and selecting specific materials that would support students and teachers in achieving those goals in grades 6, 7, and 8. She tied this identification and selection process to summer and academic-year professional development programs where teachers tried out new instructional strategies, materials, and assessments, so they could implement the new materials effectively.

Given the district curriculum framework, the science staff proposed an integrated program, which includes concepts from earth, life, and physical sciences at each grade level. The units selected use instructional strategies—including inquiry; cooperative groups; real-world applications; and rigorous reading, writing, and mathematics—that are mandated by the state standards.

The opportunity for teachers to pilot new materials and then meet together to evaluate them before they become an official part of the curriculum is key to the success of the curriculum design process. Sophia says, "This makes a big difference. I know that in the past I have picked materials that looked good, but when I used them, they were awful. This process ensures that won't happen."

The opportunity for teachers to pilot new materials and then meet together to evaluate them before they become an official part of the curriculum is key to the success of the curriculum design process.

Different units used in physical and life science classes in seventh grade and earth science classes in eighth grade all integrate three different approaches to science study—inquiry, textbook use, and a focus on social issues.

One of the middle-grades science teachers, Antonia Barada, who has piloted many science curriculum units, elaborates on the benefits of the approach Newcastle adopted. She says, "I feel pretty strongly that using a variety of curriculum materials is important. I have not yet seen any one thing that does it all. Kids need a lot of different experiences. They need to be able to design investigations, ask questions, and pursue those questions. They also need some more structured experiences, and also some time to deepen their knowledge by reading texts and other resources. And they need to know how the content relates to real life and to societal issues. We didn't find one published curriculum that does all of that really well. But we were able to find materials that, if pulled together, can work together well."

Teachers in the district have put significant effort into thinking about how individual materials work together to make a coherent curriculum. Antonia explains that there are curriculum themes selected for each year which are key to organizing the curriculum, and that each year's curriculum is designed to build on concepts introduced in earlier years. "There is a grade 6, 7, 8 curriculum with life science, earth science, and physical science at each of those levels. And one year builds upon the next. So, for example, in life science, the focus in seventh grade is diversity and variation, and then in eighth grade the focus is genetics. Each year the previous year's content is built upon and extended."

Antonia describes how different units used in physical and life science classes in seventh grade and earth science classes in eighth grade all integrate three different approaches to science study— inquiry, textbook use, and a focus on social issues. She says, "For the physical science third of the year in seventh grade, the focus is really on chemistry. First, we use an inquiry unit on ice cream making and cake baking. It's guided inquiry, but it's far less guided than many programs. It's pretty intense. Kids are experimenting. They're collecting data. They're really trying to come up with some concepts about the way the world works, based on the experiments. We then use a textbook coupled with a unit on plastics that has a social issues orientation and engages students in problem solving. Then for life science we have a unit on biodiversity. We also use a textbook during the seventh-grade life science third of the year.

"Eighth grade starts out the year with earth science, focusing on a unit about hurricanes. The philosophy of this curriculum unit is to use real-life events to spark the interest of the kids so they will want to learn the science behind the events. We use it as an umbrella for that third of the year. We can hook together all the concepts that are important for kids to know about in the hurricane unit—air pressure, precipitation, wind, and water vapor. The hurricane study pulls it all together and connects the concepts for the kids. We also use a section of the textbook on weather. Then we slide into another social issues unit, which is actually a simulation that addresses how human activities have affected the environment. So all the components of the curriculum combine to build kids' understanding of these concepts.

"The culmination of this part of the year is a project in the hurricane unit where students produce a newspaper. Each kid becomes a specialist—one is a meteorologist, one a natural hazards planner, one an editor. They have to do research on their own; some of it they have to get on the Internet. And each kid writes four or five articles." This newspaper is distributed throughout the school and sent home to families.

Antonia observes that the time the district took to work with teachers to plan and pilot the curriculum paid off. Teachers have been able to make the conceptual links between the different components of the curriculum, and in turn have been able to help students better understand key science concepts. She says, "I saw that my eighth-grade students this year were starting to connect what they had learned last year about heat and heat movement to the weather that they were learning about this year when we studied hurricanes and low-pressure systems, and high-pressure systems. It motivated them to look deeper and question what was going on."

Supplementing a core curriculum

Not all districts have the resources that Newcastle has had to engage in such an extended curriculum design and selection process and to try out so many materials. However, even districts that have traditionally depended on textbooks to guide teaching and learning have found that the depth and breadth called for by new district and state standards mean they must seek out non-textbook materials for use in their middle-grades classrooms. The Marston School District, a suburban district in the Midwest,

The inquiry-based curriculum makes connections across science disciplines, enabling students to study the same phenomenon through more than one lens.

recently adopted a standards-based yearlong modular curriculum for the seventh grade that takes an inquiry approach to science. The district made this choice with the understanding that teachers would need professional development if they were to implement the new curriculum effectively. Teachers would also need to supplement this core curriculum to assure that students fully meet state standards and local high school requirements.

The heart of the teaching and learning in Bob Tiller's seventh-grade Marston Middle School classroom is the yearlong inquiry-based curriculum. Bob supplements the curriculum with a textbook that the district purchased several years ago and some lessons he and other teachers have developed to address particular requirements of the state standards.

Bob describes how the inquiry-based curriculum makes connections across science disciplines, enabling students to study the same phenomenon through more than one lens—for example, both physical science and ecology. The curriculum, which is packaged as a series of units grouped into sections, "has three sections in it. There's a physical science section, there's an ecology section, and then there's a third section that integrates what students learned in the other two. All the components focus on ensuring that students develop a working understanding of energy and its transformation. Instead of studying all physical science for a quarter or a half-year and then switching to ecology, we initially study properties of light. We look at the physical components of it, we look through spectroscopes, we do a number of physical investigations on the properties of light.

"Then we switch into ecology, and one of the questions we ask is, 'How do these light properties affect living things?' We extract the chlorophyll from a leaf and look at it through a spectroscope, which returns students to all the things they learned about light, transmission, absorption, and reflection. Then we make graphs and investigate that information, and as we study ecology a little bit more, we find out that the plant has energy. The class just finished a lab on measuring calories in peanuts. We burn the nut, collect the heat in water. Now we're making a connection between the sunlight, the plant, and heat energy. So then later we're going to go back into physical science, do some chemical properties, then we'll go back into ecology and look at how plants respire. Some of the stuff can be very sophisticated, but the kids actually ask questions that the next unit deals with. That's how logically this has been laid out."

Because of the way the curriculum gradually builds connections between concepts in different scientific disciplines, Bob emphasizes the importance of using it as a whole. He says, "You can't pull this curriculum apart and use a piece here and another piece there. It's been constructed so carefully, so it all fits together. And you really need to follow it through to take advantage of that design."

Bob identifies another feature of the curriculum that links ideas together across the disciplines: "The third section of the curriculum has a number of activities that combine the physical and the ecological units. The same key concepts keep spinning through the curriculum. If they don't get the concept of the different forms of energy in ecology, they'll pick it up in physical science. Because these kids are at different levels of abstract thinking, they're not all going to understand it at the same time, and that's designed into the program. So if you teach the material the way it can be done, you will see lights go on in students' heads. And that's really the exciting part of the whole process."

Bob explains that the curriculum also helps students to develop particular habits of mind—ways of approaching science learning through problem solving. "Each lesson is open ended. It's all hands-on. It's all inquiry, and there's a lot to it. Basically every unit that I do starts off with a problem, an anomaly or something that the kids can't understand, and they have to solve the problem using a series of labs. There's a lot of processing, discussing of the data. The students have to take responsibility for the things that they need to know. Every unit also has a final project where they have to use the knowledge that they gain during the earlier labs to carry out the final project."

Bob notes that, overall, the curriculum meets the national standards on which it is based, allowing him to couple the units to the corresponding state standards. He notes the challenge of trading off a certain amount of content coverage in order to engage students in scientific processes and build their understanding of concepts. But he disputes the concern of some teachers that the curriculum sacrifices too much content in favor of process. He says, "There's a lot more processing in this curriculum than there is factual learning, so you have to give up a little bit of what you

"You can't pull this curriculum apart and use a piece here and another piece there. It's been constructed so carefully, so it all fits together. And you really need to follow it through to take advantage of that design."

Teachers have worked together to identify gaps in the core curriculum, and they share resources and strategies for supplementing it.

normally cover in order to gain ground on the process part, and that's the toughest thing for teachers to do. They think, 'Oh, it's all process.' But it isn't all process, and learning the facts happens as part of engaging in the process."

Bob and other science teachers in the district do supplement the published curriculum in order to fully address the state standards and the requirements of the local high school. Teachers have worked together to identify gaps in the core curriculum, and they share resources and strategies for supplementing it. He reports, "Some of what I do now is not just this curriculum. Because of our standards, for example, we have to teach Newton's Laws. But I've developed my own way of doing that, based on the standards and using the same inquiry approach as the curriculum program we use." Bob has shared his lessons on Newton's Laws by offering workshops to colleagues. He adds, "Also, we don't think the core program has enough reading. Students still have to go through the mental discipline of reading information, and I have an obligation to have them experience that. But I don't want that to be the end-all either. So we use the readings in the textbook as a supplement. I also sometimes supplement with assessments from the textbook—a vocabulary list, a matching assignment, or labeling."

Bob also cautions that not all of the connections he enables students to make in his classroom are explicit in the curriculum materials. However, his professional development experiences have taught him how to focus on the conceptual links: for example, to help students understand how the physical properties of light they have studied relate to the function of light in photosynthesis. Bob believes that the key is to "make the science meaningful. If we can make it meaningful, applicable to their world and things around them, they really learn a lot of science."

EQUITY

How will the curriculum both challenge and support students with diverse social and academic experiences to learn science successfully?

The expectation that all students will meet or exceed standards propels reform efforts in many school districts. Realizing this expectation requires schools to provide students who are vulnerable to falling behind with the kinds of instruction and learning experiences that are often reserved for only the most academically proficient students. In science, this means ensuring that every student has opportunities to use skills that mirror those of working scientists, for example, engaging in problem solving, participating in substantive conversation about scientific concepts, and collecting and analyzing data. Curricula that provide these key opportunities to learn help students see connections between what they learn in school and what they observe in the world beyond school. Skilled teachers can use such curricula to enable students to understand science concepts, use science processes, and apply their knowledge and skills in novel situations.

Teachers who have used standards-based curriculum materials find in them the tools they need to improve science achievement for a wide range of students. The following vignettes illustrate how teachers can use standards-based materials so that students receive both the challenge and support necessary for significant learning. In the first vignette, a teacher explains how she must stretch the curriculum to enhance skills development and account for the particular experiences and knowledge of her students. In the second vignette, another teacher describes the adjustments students must make to the curriculum's demands. These are adjustments that even those students who are accustomed to success with a traditional science curriculum must make if they are to engage in a deeper way with a hands-on, inquiry-based curriculum.

All students become scientists

In a large urban district in the Northeast, Lorena Torres teaches science to sixth and seventh graders in bilingual classes. Some of her students have good conversational English skills but still need support in reading and writing; others are newcomers to the country and speak almost no English. In addition to their range of conversational skills, students' reading levels in English vary from second to sixth grade. Their mathematics achievement scores reflect similar skill levels, and Lorena finds great individuality in their accomplishments. Thus, students who score well in mathematics do not necessarily achieve high reading comprehension scores and vice versa. Lorena's class also includes several students on education plans because of special needs, and several students designated "gifted and talented," but who currently have limited English language skills.

Given the diversity of her classes, Lorena knows she needs curriculum materials that will reach all her students in a way that both challenges and supports each of them. At a district staff development workshop, she learned about a set of modular units that combined an exploration of social issues with learning in science

When students realized that particular concepts and skills were essential to the experiment, they did not dismiss them as irrelevant to their interests or beyond their abilities.

and were designed to motivate young adolescent students. Other teachers in the district were using these modules in their heterogeneous classrooms, and Lorena wanted the bilingual students in her classes to have learning experiences that were of equally high quality. She believed she could figure out a way to make these modules the core of her students' science curriculum.

From Lorena's perspective, the most appealing aspect of the modules is the guided inquiry experiences designed to make science concepts like permeability accessible to a wide range of students. Lorena has learned through experience that engaging students requires her to step back and allow them to experiment with the assignment and the materials. She says, "Last year when I taught a groundwater contamination unit, I conducted several test procedures while the students watched. But this year I had the students testing each of the earth materials themselves. This year everyone was thoroughly engaged in the activity, and they were observing closely what was going on and why. They were much more involved. They came up with a lot of questions. And I could see that they understood because after they had conducted all the experiments, collected and analyzed their data, they could explain to me why certain earth materials were more permeable than others."

Lorena also knew that her students would need some direct instruction in relevant mathematics skills to supplement the modules and ensure that they would be able to carry out the activities. But Lorena also wanted her students to practice those skills in a way that connected them to the work they were doing. In fact, Lorena found that when students realized that particular concepts and skills were essential to the experiment, they did not dismiss them as irrelevant to their interests or beyond their abilities.

Lorena explains, "Some of my students are weak in math and in reading, as well as in writing. In order to do the groundwater contamination unit, they have to have an understanding of some particular math concepts. So I devised a couple of lessons on percentages and on fractions, using hands-on activities because some students really have very little understanding of math. After we completed those math lessons, the students started using the concepts to explain what was going on. I could tell they understood the concepts because they were using them within the context. The students understood why and how they had to use the math.

　　　　　　　　　　　　　　　Chapter 1/Critical Questions in Curriculum Decision Making

They were so engaged because they felt that they needed to know those concepts in order to complete the activity."

In addition to supplementing the curriculum by introducing relevant mathematical concepts, Lorena also designed some experiences to give her multicultural urban students access to information that might be more naturally a part of the lives of suburban or rural students. She says, "My students have a very urban experience. Before they could begin to explore groundwater contamination, they needed some background knowledge. They needed an understanding of what rocks look like, their textures, and their basic properties, how water moves, and all of that. So we began by looking at rocks. Then we took a plasticene model of a land formation and submerged that in water so we could actually see the formation of lakes and rivers. Then we read the story from the unit in class, and the kids were really devouring it."

Lorena's supplementation and adaptation of the materials to her students' experiences ensure that they can learn the science content in the groundwater contamination module, even when the materials do not reflect their immediate environment. In fact, without such tinkering, students might not be able to benefit fully from the module. Lorena notes, "The town that serves as the focus of the module is a suburban town, and my students don't understand the layout of a town like that. They don't live in towns, they don't even live in houses. They live in apartments in housing developments. It would be good to have the same unit on groundwater contamination set in an urban setting, so urban kids could better understand how it relates to their own community. I was able to introduce them to groundwater in another setting, and I think they got it. But if the materials helped us look at groundwater in an urban setting, it would be even more meaningful."

Two features of the modules that further facilitate Lorena's commitment to engage and challenge all students are the emphases on group work and problem solving. The emphasis on group work reflects research on student learning and the benefits of providing students with opportunities for peer interaction. Lorena uses the variety of language and mathematical skills students bring to her classes to help them learn from each other. "To address the range of reading levels, I might read the activities aloud for the class as a whole, or I take a few minutes to explain it.

> **"My students have a very urban experience. Before they could begin to explore groundwater contamination, they needed some background knowledge. They needed an understanding of what rocks look like, their textures, and their basic properties, [and] how water moves."**

I usually place students who are better readers within each group so they can help each other. The better readers are not usually the best math students. So I have the better reading students read to the group and the students who are more proficient in math help with the math."

Furthermore, in Lorena's classroom, group work and problem solving reinforce one another. Lorena says, "Each of the modules presents the kids with a problem that they have to solve. They have to solve this problem; the teacher is not telling them what the problem means. It's a problem that was posed by a story they've read. I think they are empowered by this."

Working in groups encourages students to persist in solving complex problems. Lorena says, "Because they are working in groups, whenever they are confused, they discuss their ideas together to find the solution to the problem or to find a way to clarify an idea. I see them having a lot of conversations, and they're trying to convince each other to follow their own ideas. They are teaching each other a lot and they're trying to convince each other. That's real learning. They're learning how to find answers to questions, and I think that's the most important thing about these materials. Kids are coming up with a lot of questions and trying to use evidence to find the answers.

"One of the students told me she felt like she was a scientist. They feel they are scientists, and they like the idea very much. Many of the students wanted to test the water in the school to see if it was polluted. I was very pleased that they started thinking about the water they drink. They are becoming more aware of their own environment."

They get pushed, but they get very engaged too

Solving complicated problems. Working with peers to resolve questions that have more than one right answer. Looking at situations from diverse perspectives. Experimenting with different materials. Sometimes the very features that expand opportunities to learn science for students who have struggled in traditional science classes are also those features that challenge students who are used to coming up with "the one right answer" and then moving on. Sometimes the messiness and uncertainty of standards-based curricula can be most discomforting for students who most easily fit in classrooms where teachers talk and students use textbooks as the only source of answers to homework and test questions.

With the new curricula, the answers aren't always found in the text or supplied by the teacher. Instead, students explore phenomena, collect and analyze data, and reach their own conclusions. Once they adjust to the new way of learning science, however, students generally respond to the challenge and can excel.

Teacher Albert Earle has been using a yearlong inquiry-based curriculum for several years in his suburban school on the eastern seaboard. He says, "The curriculum challenges students who have traditionally been the high achievers in science class. At first, it frustrates the heck out of them. They're used to figuring out the system. They're usually good readers, and they're accustomed to finding the boldfaced words in the textbook and copying the right answers. So a lot of times they're frustrated at first when I ask things like, 'What do you think?' or 'What would you predict?' With other materials, they tend to get bored and 'check out,' but with these materials, they really hang in there because the work is interesting. They really have to think. It's more work than they are used to because they get pushed. But they get very engaged too."

Albert adds, "I think that once they get used to the curriculum, the higher achieving students would say it gives them a chance to stretch. When they do independent soil research, for example, the sky's the limit. I find that they will put more into it than is even asked for."

Teachers like Lorena and Albert work to ensure access to the science curriculum for students who struggle with reading or mathematics. They are equally alert to opportunities to capitalize on the strengths of students who have done well with curricula based on reading and memorizing, and to ensure that these students successfully adapt to learning science in ways that require more than just reading about it.

Standards-based curriculum materials that offer students numerous opportunities for teamwork reflect the realities of working in laboratory, business, and technical settings. In particular, assignments that require teamwork among students with different skills and learning styles benefit everyone. Albert explains, "You have the kids that like to build, then you have the ones that like to organize the group, then you have the ones that like to talk, and then you have the ones that never like to talk and they're going to have to. These materials really give everybody an opportunity to

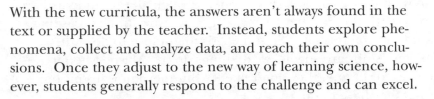

Standards-based curriculum materials that offer students numerous opportunities for teamwork reflect the realities of working in laboratory, business, and technical settings. In particular, assignments that require teamwork among students with different skills and learning styles benefit everyone.

do what they're best at. But sooner or later, all the students have to do each thing. They're challenged to grow in the areas that aren't so comfortable. So some kids might love to do stuff, explore stuff, investigate, write things down. Maybe when it comes to sharing, they don't like it. But they know it's part of what they have to do."

DEVELOPMENTAL APPROPRIATENESS

How will the curriculum engage and motivate middle-grades students to learn science successfully?

Making the science curriculum engaging for middle-grades students requires attention both to what fosters engagement for all learners and to the particular characteristics of young adolescents. Effective strategies for engaging students' interest in science include:

- Building learning around everyday phenomena and issues in which students are interested.
- Engaging students in explorations that have a genuine purpose and not a predetermined answer.
- Taking advantage of students' curiosity about the world beyond their families, schools, and neighborhoods, including the natural environment and society's impact on it.

The science curricula described in this guide engage students in examining phenomena from hurricanes to infectious disease, groundwater pollution to world hunger. Students investigate how things work and why they work the way they do. In doing so, they deepen their understanding of natural phenomena like atoms and molecules, leaves, lungs and gills, forests, clouds, and volcanoes. They also connect that learning to phenomena observable in the world humans have constructed, including vaccines and organ transplants, paper towels and computers.

When students engage in scientific investigations according to the processes that scientists use, they learn how to use important concepts as intellectual tools for solving problems that intrigue them. Standards-based curricula help students carry out those processes—posing questions, making hypotheses, designing experiments, gathering and interpreting data, reaching conclusions, and discussing and communicating their findings. Further, these curricula help students link their understanding of specific concepts—such as the relationship of the density of an object to the volume of water displaced—to practical and social problems ranging from preventing the bathtub from overflowing to predicting the effects of global warming. Even routine information found in traditional science texts and reference sources can become interesting to students who need the information to help them answer a question they care about.

Taking advantage of the intensity of middle-grades students' interest in interacting with their peers, standards-based science curricula offer opportunities for students to work in groups. Through such group work, students can:

- Become resources and sounding boards for one another as they work through the implications of their observations and hypotheses.
- Take advantage of complementary knowledge and expertise.
- Build skills in working collaboratively.

Group work, like other strategies for engaging students, is not an end in itself. Capturing students' interest is necessary but by no means sufficient. Standards-based curriculum materials employ group work to engage students in scientific investigations that advance their learning of key science content and processes, to enable students to master the knowledge and skills targeted in the science standards. In the following vignettes, teachers describe how standards-based curricula capitalize on middle-grades students' interests and capabilities in order to engage students in rigorous scientific inquiry.

Making science learning matter to students

Marilyn Prada teaches seventh-grade science in a small southwestern city. She has used a number of different curriculum materials and is particularly enthusiastic about those that "make science relevant to the kids, so that they can see the use for it in their own lives." Marilyn finds that students' engagement with the unit is a key to their actually learning the important scientific concepts it is built around. "When they get to the culminating activities, they don't feel like it's 'just something that we're doing for science class.' They can see how a lot of the concepts come together and are useful and necessary."

When students see how they can use scientific knowledge and understanding in their own lives, they also begin to take more responsibility for their own learning. The curriculum Marilyn uses "is always going back to something that's involved in students' own lives, something that they can see, something that affects them or their community." She says, "The kids get immersed in the question; they discuss it, they work on it, and it's all something that directly relates to them. And then I can hold them accountable for the content, because they've learned it in a context that they really care about. Not like some of the things we did in the past, where, truly, I couldn't say why they should care about it."

Connecting the individual to the larger social world

A number of standards-based curricula reflect young adolescents' interest in their own changing bodies and their place in the larger human society. Jennifer Phillips, who teaches in a small rural district in the South, elaborates, "A major theme of the curriculum we use for seventh grade is diversity. One of the first things students do is to look at human characteristics: shoe size and arm length, for example, and then they start talking about human vision. So we go from looking at these general human characteristics and their diversity in the human population to learning the specifics of how the human eye works.

"First, students do a series of experiments on how the eye works. In a couple of these, they use spinners and flip books to learn about persistence of vision; they figure out how long an image stays on your retina. Then they use what they learn in these experiments to understand how a television works. They see how the television tricks your eye into believing that you're watching continuous motion, when it's really an electron gun repeatedly tracing lines of pixels across the screen—so many screens per second. And in the final activities, students determine the ideal viewing distance for TV watching based on a survey of their classmates and then design a state-of-the-art TV for the 21st century."

In the course of the curriculum, students conduct measurements; collect, graph, and compare data; view and discuss videotapes; read and interpret articles and narratives; and learn and apply concepts such as limits, frequency, translucence, viscosity, conservation of energy, standards, and diversity. They have opportunities to work in pairs and groups as well as individually.

Jennifer continues, "While they're conducting these experiments in the context of studying human vision, the anatomy of the human eye, and how diverse populations are, students are also learning about controlled scientific investigation. They learn about variables and ways to control variables. But it all connects to television, which is relevant to kids' lives, and to their vision, which they also care about. It's also fun to do the experiments, to actually see how some people have greater peripheral vision than others, for example. So they're learning both these big concepts, big themes, and these important scientific processes while they're doing investigations on human vision that are interesting to them as individuals. The thing is, if the kids aren't invested in it, then I'm not going to be successful in teaching them. These materials really get them invested."

Addressing students' existing conceptions of scientific phenomena

Althea Bradley, a staff developer who works closely with science teachers in a large California district, applauds the way standards-based curricula engage students in developing their own explanations and models of scientific phenomena. However, she cautions teachers to be alert to the ideas students may already hold about difficult concepts, for they bring these ideas with them to the classroom. Althea asserts that curriculum materials should specifically address students' existing ideas about such phenomena as heat and temperature, force and motion, or photosynthesis if students are to transform their existing conceptions into more accurate understanding of science concepts.

Althea says, "You have to find materials that address the ideas about concepts (such as the kinetic theory of matter) that the cognitive research has shown us kids bring into their learning. Traditionally, when we teach about abstract things like molecules, kids really don't understand, they don't learn it even though we teach it. This makes it critical to construct curriculum units in a careful sequence, so that new ideas can develop. Curriculum is more than a collection of activities. The materials should alert the teacher to those ideas that need particular attention, and they should provide opportunities for kids to develop that conceptual understanding and to share their thinking so that teachers can address misconceptions. Teachers need to understand how students are thinking, even if they have the 'right' answer. This means you need to elicit students' ideas, get those ideas out, have kids think about their ideas."

Tuning the curriculum to the pitch of early adolescence

Gary Womack has been teaching long enough (in an urban district in the Northwest) to know what will engage his seventh- and

"The materials should alert the teacher to those ideas that need particular attention, and they should provide opportunities for kids to develop that conceptual understanding and to share their thinking so that teachers can address misconceptions."

"The middle school kid has a lot of energy. And [the curriculum designers] allowed that energy to be used. It's primarily a lab program. So the kids move around; they're up and moving and exploring. They've also realized that the child needs to talk. So, while the kids are working, they're talking about what they're doing."

eighth-grade students in learning. Describing how the design of his school's yearlong curriculum keeps young adolescents in mind, he explains, "The curriculum has been laid out from the perspective of a middle school student. From the start, you need a long-term, open-ended question that doesn't have a clear right or wrong answer, that gives students lots of possibilities they can get excited about. The designers of this curriculum also realized that the middle school kid has a lot of energy. And [the curriculum designers] allowed that energy to be used. It's primarily a lab program. So the kids move around; they're up and moving and exploring. They've also realized that the child needs to talk. So, while the kids are working, they're talking about what they're doing, and once they've collected their data, the curriculum allows them to discuss what they've found. We also put the data up on an overhead, so there's validation of what they did."

The standards-based curriculum in Gary's school also takes into account the developmental differences among students. He says, "The developers of the curriculum realized that kids are at different levels of abstract thinking. They're not all going to understand everything at the same time. Different concepts keep coming back at different places in the curriculum. So if kids don't understand something, there's an opportunity to go back and do it again, and work it out."

Gary recommends that teachers select curriculum materials that both recognize and take advantage of middle-grades students' strong interest in interacting with their classmates. The standards-based curriculum in his school offers many opportunities for students to work collaboratively in pairs and in groups. He describes how students work together to produce their own individual work: "Four students are together sharing the materials, kids are working in pairs to do the activity, but each one has his or her own product. The kids have their own journals and their own papers that they turn in."

Supporting students to work effectively in groups is a challenge of the curriculum, Gary notes. "To be honest, there is a little bit of socializing that goes on within the groups. But that's the middle school kid. That's something you're not going to stop, so you go along with it and try to channel it. Of course, you have to work to keep things under control and focused. Some kids do have trouble getting along with others, adjusting to working cooperatively.

But having the structure that the curriculum provides—the roles that get assigned when the kids work in groups, combined with specific kinds of tasks for each role—helps a lot. And when you do get to the point where students really use one another as resources, and build on each other's ideas, that's very gratifying."

If all students are to practice science in the way scientists do, simply putting standards-based curriculum materials in the hands of teachers is not enough. Teachers themselves must have solid understanding of the purpose, content, and pedagogical approaches built into new curricula. Ongoing professional development is essential to this understanding.

New standards-based curriculum packages typically include teacher guides that offer some assistance to teachers as they use new materials in their classrooms. The extent of the assistance offered by these guides varies, however, and, even with the best guides in hand, most teachers need professional development and support in order to become adept at working with new materials. In some cases, developers and publishers of standards-based curricula also offer professional development designed to help teachers use their specific materials. Like the teacher guides, the scope of these offerings varies, but they may provide resources or learning opportunities that can help jump-start or supplement the professional development that schools and districts provide.

Teachers and curriculum specialists using standards-based materials highlight several elements they look for in effective professional development. These fall into two main categories: pre-implementation professional development and ongoing support.

Pre-implementation professional development offers teachers opportunities to use the new materials themselves before they bring them into their classrooms. These formal professional development experiences are effective when they:

- Help teachers review and deepen their understanding of the science content and processes they will be teaching, using the same instructional approaches that the curriculum calls for in the classroom.
- Focus on how students develop their understanding of important science concepts.

What kind of professional development should the district provide that will enable teachers to implement standards-based curricula effectively?

Teachers using new curriculum materials benefit from opportunities to talk about what they are doing with other educators.

- Demonstrate how specific materials are designed to foster the development of this understanding.
- Guide teachers in shifting from a traditional approach of conveying science content to an inquiry-based approach that facilitates students' learning of science content and their mastery of science processes.
- Bring teachers who have successfully taught the curriculum together with teachers learning to teach it.

Ongoing support is a second essential component of effective professional development. Teachers using new curriculum materials benefit from opportunities to talk about what they are doing with other educators, both those who are knowledgeable about and experienced in using the curriculum and those who, like them, are just learning to use it. Such support, whether through visiting coaches, online or telephone conversations, peer consultation, or regular meetings of study groups, offers teachers help in solving problems as they come up. Effective ongoing support provides opportunities for teachers to:

- Share challenges and successes with other teachers who are using the curriculum.
- Develop a common understanding of what the curriculum expects of students through discussion and evaluation of student work.
- Learn to use guides for assessing student work (often called "rubrics" or "scoring guides").
- Use student assessment to guide teaching and learning.

Professional development for standards-based curricula is multi-faceted. The following vignettes illustrate how teachers benefit from professional development experiences in science content and processes; support in learning to facilitate inquiry-based learning; professional development and support offered by experienced teachers; follow-up support, networking, and peer consultation; and a coordinated approach that creates an infrastructure for multifaceted, sustained professional development.

Focusing on science content and processes

As Sandra Ciano describes the professional development her urban district in the Southwest offers to prepare middle-grades science teachers to use new curriculum materials, she emphasizes that both formal professional development opportunities and ongoing support are necessary to enable teachers to make the most of new curriculum. She explains, "One person I remember in particular came into the curriculum workshop, and toward the end of it, he said, 'You know, I've been teaching these units for ten years without professional development, and I didn't realize what I've been missing.' This teacher felt he'd been shoved into his classroom with the new materials by a district that said, 'Oh, well, you can just follow along with what some of the other teachers are doing.' So I would say that, in order to develop your skill, obviously practice is important, but the professional development is critical."

Pre-implementation professional development for teachers about to launch new science materials has a dual focus: it helps teachers master (or reacquaint themselves with) the content and it helps them prepare to use the materials with students. Attention to content is critical. Sandra explains, "This year we had a three-day, district-wide professional development workshop, focusing on the new unit we're teaching on biodiversity. The curriculum developers came. Part of the workshop focused on teaching the curriculum. But the other part—and I think the more important part—was focused on the actual science content and the process skills that we as teachers need to be comfortable with. How do you observe, really look closely? What is a dichotomous key? How do you use one? How do you collect bugs? Where are they? That kind of thing. Because that's something that middle-grades teachers haven't necessarily done, or haven't done for a long time. Especially at the middle grades, you have people with such diverse backgrounds. Some have worked in labs before they started teaching. Others just have an undergraduate degree. It's a wide variety of people, and skills, and strengths. And we don't stop with the one workshop. We'll be doing professional development on that unit throughout the year, continuing to focus on both the content of the curriculum and how you use it in the classroom."

In addition to focusing on science content, the intensive professional development session that precedes teachers' first use of the materials offers them opportunities to experience the same kind of scientific inquiry that they will ask their students to engage in. Such a session offers teachers an extended period of time to immerse themselves in and become comfortable with the curriculum's science content and understand its learning goals. As Sandra explains, "By working through an entire unit the way

The intensive professional development session that precedes teachers' first use of the materials offers them opportunities to experience the same kind of scientific inquiry that they will ask their students to engage in.

"One of the big challenges for teachers using a hands-on science program is to learn how to allow kids to take more responsibility for their own learning. How do you become the coach and 'guide on the side' instead of the person up in the front with all the answers?"

students will in class, we can see the philosophy behind it, and we can see how the beginning activities lead to greater understanding in the later activities."

Introducing teachers to new roles

Inquiry-based middle-grades science curricula call on teachers to know how to listen to students' ideas, to recognize how their understanding of important concepts is developing, and to guide them toward a deeper understanding. These curricula require teachers to be knowledgeable about how young adolescents learn scientific concepts as well as knowledgeable about the concepts themselves. As part of learning to use new curriculum materials, teachers need to become comfortable with an instructional role more compatible with inquiry-oriented learning. Sandra says, "One of the big challenges for teachers using a hands-on science program is to learn how to allow kids to take more responsibility for their own learning. How do you become the coach and 'guide on the side' instead of the person up in the front with all the answers? That's where the professional development comes in."

Making this shift from the person who tells students the answers to the person who helps students put together answers of their own is often difficult for a teacher who has been accustomed to being the sole authority and dispenser of knowledge in the classroom. Sandra cautions that this shift in roles "is a challenge to teachers. It really pushes teachers to start teaching the way the standards are asking them to teach—to be really tuned in to the kids and focused on their understanding. If you're worried about the kids asking a question you can't answer, you're out of luck, because some kid's always going to pop a question you can't answer. Teachers have to understand that they're going to have to give up the comfort of always having the answer. If they occasionally don't know something, they can model for their students ways to find out. After all, science is all about asking questions and then doing the research to discover the answers. Sometimes this research is in the lab, and sometimes it's in the library."

Sandra believes it's more satisfying to "be involved with the learning with the kids." She says that students are encouraged to do more thinking themselves when the teacher isn't the only person supplying the answers. She adds, "But that's why you need to have the professional development, have the support. If you have that, usually you can adjust." Opportunities for teachers to use the curriculum to engage in scientific inquiry themselves, and learn more about how student thinking develops, help teachers become comfortable with and adept at guiding student inquiry.

Teacher-to-teacher professional development

Professional development offered by classroom teachers who have successfully used the curriculum materials themselves is credible and compelling in ways that other approaches are not. Sandra says, "The professional development has to be with teachers who have taught the curriculum in the classroom. They know a lot of strategies for dealing with problems that might arise. The professional development we had was from two teachers who used the units last year—great teachers from a dual-language program. They worked with us, and they knew the material from top to bottom. They helped us anticipate exactly what kind of problems we would be likely to face. Teachers need to see how teaching the curriculum is done and hear from other people who have taught it that it's successful and that their classrooms are exciting places for learning."

Teachers who have first-hand experience with the materials can not only help first-time users anticipate problems that might arise but also communicate the rewards that await teachers who can address those problems. Any unit presents challenges initially. Sandra explains, "It's like anything else. The first time you do it, it's like walking down a dark tunnel and not knowing where you're going. Teachers who have used the curriculum before can tell you how excited the kids get and what a vibrant place the classroom becomes. So even when you are struggling with it, you know that once you've done a couple of the activities, you'll start to see the results. And by the second year, you really begin to mold it to your classroom, see how you want it to work."

Ongoing support, networking, and peer consultation

Once teachers start to use new materials, ongoing support and opportunities to continue to learn and share experiences with other teachers and with curriculum experts remain essential. For Louis Aponte, who has taught a very diverse eighth-grade population for over 15 years, ongoing support provided by the developers of the inquiry-based curriculum he uses is critical. He notes that teachers in his district benefit from being able to get expert advice when they run into problems or have questions: "We can access the curriculum developers; we can access the professional

Professional development offered by classroom teachers who have successfully used the curriculum materials themselves is credible and compelling in ways that other approaches are not.

Districts that are most successful in providing teachers with the appropriate professional development support to effectively implement standards-based curricula take a coordinated approach.

development providers that are in the area. That really makes the difference."

Teachers who successfully implement new materials also note the importance of having ongoing opportunities to meet with other teachers and discuss both the science content and teaching strategies. Teachers may meet in person, or may communicate online. Louis reports, "Following our introduction to the materials, we were divided into clusters of about five middle-grades science teachers, and we meet every month to talk about what we're doing and how it's going. 'Does this activity work? Doesn't it work? Why doesn't it work? What did you do to make it work?' We also have a little bit of flex time once a week in our schedule, so I can visit other people's classrooms, or they can visit mine."

Finally, communicating online is increasingly used to develop a network of teacher-learners. As Louis says, "Everyone in our school gets online, and we have e-mail, so that greatly enhances our ability to communicate. The developer runs an online discussion, so if we have questions about anything, we can send questions in online. We can get input from other teachers, and we found this to be very helpful with some of the activities."

Building an infrastructure to support professional development

Districts that are most successful in providing teachers with the appropriate professional development support to effectively implement standards-based curricula take a coordinated approach. They create an infrastructure that facilitates each of the components of effective professional development: pre-implementation professional development, including opportunities to review science content and become acquainted with new approaches to teaching and learning; connections with teachers who have experience with the curriculum materials; and ongoing support, networking, and peer consultation. Such an infrastructure includes advance planning for a balanced program of professional development opportunities, sufficient resources to pay for professional development, time for teachers to participate in pre-implementation and ongoing professional development, knowledgeable and supportive district and school leadership, support for development of teacher leaders, and assessment that is aligned with curriculum goals. The development of such a professional development infrastructure is a key outcome of a thoughtful curriculum selection process (as described in Chapter 2).

The experiences described by Carl Briscoe, a veteran middle-grades teacher in the South, and Elaine Green, the science coordinator in Carl's district, illustrate how their district's coordinated approach to professional development has supported implementation of an inquiry-based science curriculum. The district has been creative in finding funds from existing sources, such as Title II, to support its professional development program. In this context, Carl and a group of colleagues who were among the first in the district to use the curriculum have been able to develop a supportive community of teacher leaders who have become expert in using assessment to guide their teaching and now serve as resources to new teachers.

Carl, who has taught middle-grades science for 17 years, says, "What has made this new program so exciting is that the district is providing us with the materials and with the professional development. I think professional development is the most important aspect of a new program. I had tried doing this kind of thing before by buying kits: I bought a food chain kit, I bought an ecology kit, and I bought a pond life kit. Those were nice, but I was using them just as kits—you know, following the teacher's manual step by step, doing all the activities. I wasn't really engaging the kids in inquiry, and I wasn't doing the assessment. I think that the biggest help in the professional development we've had now is with the assessment. You have to use the rubrics and think about what it is kids need to do to demonstrate that they have met the science standards."

Carl believes that the time teachers in his district spent learning about the curriculum and becoming comfortable teaching it has been critical to their success. "It's hard, and you need the time. Everyone has the best of intentions, but unless you get the time and the professional development, you may try to do it, but you just won't fine-tune it. I know the professional development has made me a much better teacher."

Elaine, the district science coordinator, talks about the support system that the district has put in place to assist teachers just beginning to use the curriculum. "After the first year, new teachers, or teachers who are new to the program, really like it. The first year, just figuring out the system is difficult. But we have a

The district has been creative in finding funds from existing sources, such as Title II, to support its professional development program.

network of teachers, very experienced teachers, who have been in on this since the very beginning, to help support the teachers who are new to it. We also have what's known as the Middle School Science Alliance that provides a lot of support." The Alliance is a network of middle-grades science teachers across the district who serve as resources to other teachers. It supports ongoing study groups for teachers on particular aspects of the curriculum. Elaine describes the Alliance as "a collegial group" and adds that, "using Title II funds, we've been able to set up alliances at all of the grade levels and in three high school content areas."

Carl, now one of the Middle School Science Alliance's teacher leaders, was one of a small group of teachers who piloted the new curriculum before the district officially adopted it. He describes how the pilot teachers have taken on the challenge of implementing the assessment component of the curriculum. "We have five teachers who are really focusing on assessment. We ask whether the assessment is indeed testing what we think we are testing, looking at samples of student work, and going through a moderation process that is designed to assure that all of us are scoring consistently.

"We meet monthly for the moderation process. Everyone brings four or five examples, trying to get the full range of performance. We all grade them, using the rubrics. Then we discuss and try to come to consensus on what score we would give each paper. And then we try to find benchmarks within our sets of papers—ones that are really good examples of the different scores. So with five of us, we look at 25 papers, and we try to get the span from a score of 1 to a score of 4. Out of the 25, we're usually able to come up with a 1, a 2, a 3, and a 4 to use as the benchmarks. And having had that experience over the course of a year, our group is now teaching the moderation techniques to other teachers who are using the curriculum."

Carl describes how the professional development experience with moderation techniques has directly contributed to his students' learning. "We also learned to use the rubrics with the kids in the classroom. If you just score what they hand in, give their papers back, and that's it, I don't think it sinks in. But I actually use the moderation process with the kids. I give them the rubrics, and we look at the papers, and we discuss them.

"There are rubrics for different aspects of the curriculum. One focus of the curriculum is to help kids make tradeoffs, to think about weighing one side against another, and recognizing that there's not always a single answer, which is important for middle school kids to begin to recognize. The curriculum also teaches them to really recognize evidence: to know how to collect evidence and to distinguish what is evidence and what isn't. So, for example, one rubric that we use focuses on their evidence. You look for their ability to set up an experiment; you look for their data collection.

"Over time, the kids start to see the relationship between the scoring guide and their papers. 'Well, this is a 3 because . . . and you could make it a 4 if you did . . .' That really hits home, and then you give the kids a chance to redo their papers. And they'll say, 'Oh, now I know what I need to do.' They really begin to absorb that knowledge and can apply it again the next time we have to design and conduct an investigation."

Standards-based science curricula can challenge a wide range of school "regularities," requiring teachers—and administrators—to consider alternative ways of organizing their classrooms and schools so that they can successfully facilitate inquiry-oriented teaching and learning. The most common challenges involve the use of materials and equipment, preparation time, classroom management, and scheduling.

Materials and equipment: The curricula described in this guide assume the use of a variety of materials and equipment that depart from the norms in textbook-only classes. Some curricula call on students and teachers to use materials like water, rocks, corks, citric acid, vinegar, balloons, and bacteria. Others require equipment, including batteries, rulers, flashlights, handheld fans, microscopes, calculators, and computers. Some materials may need to be replaced after each use.

Preparation time: Many curriculum units require teachers to set up materials for five or six classes a day, and for six or seven groups of students in each class. Activities that engage students in using computers, whether to conduct simulations, record data in spreadsheets, or gather information from the Internet, may also require extra set-up time. Teachers may also need to allow for extra time to address any equipment or software malfunctions.

IMPLEMENTATION

What implementation challenges do standards-based science curriculum materials present, and how do teachers and schools address them?

Activities that engage students in observation and experimentation with new materials can seem messy at first. Students' group discussions can seem noisy compared to discussions managed by the teacher.

Classroom management: As teachers and students move from traditional seatwork to classroom assignments that involve hands-on inquiry, classroom management challenges may arise. Activities that engage students in observation and experimentation with new materials can seem messy at first. Students' group discussions can seem noisy compared to discussions managed by the teacher. In addition, student groups may need to move around the classroom as they do lab work, or they may move in and out of the classroom as they complete outdoor assignments.

Scheduling: Standards-based science experiments and observation activities are complex, and teachers cannot always count on completing their lessons at the conclusion of a 45-, 50-, or even 90-minute period. Schools adopting new curricula may ultimately need to review and revise daily and weekly schedules to accommodate extended inquiry-oriented teaching and learning.

Despite the challenges, most teachers using standards-based science materials report that the excitement and learning that result from inquiry activities make dealing with implementation challenges worth the effort. Teachers experienced with new curricula have a variety of suggestions for colleagues who want to adopt standards-based curricula while also minimizing the difficulties of using them. These suggestions include:

- *Gather information about the curricula.*
  Because different curricula present different degrees of challenge to implement, school and district leaders should carefully investigate beforehand the particular configurations, and demands, of the materials they are considering. Talking with colleagues who have used the materials in comparable circumstances can illuminate the requirements of a specific set of materials. Engaging a small number of teachers to pilot materials before they are adopted for an entire school or grade can allow any difficulties to surface and be addressed. (See the overview of the curriculum selection process in Chapter 2 of this guide and the profiles of particular curricula in Chapter 3.) In some schools, curricula that provide complete kits, including all of the materials, teacher guides, and student texts, are the best choice. Other schools find that curricula requiring the collection of common materials are equally manageable and offer cost benefits.

• *Invest sufficiently in necessary resources and professional development.*
Teachers who experience the most frustration are those in districts that have adopted curricula but have not invested sufficiently in buying materials and supporting implementation. In districts where teachers are required to share kits or where budgets do not include funds for "consumables" (materials such as graph paper, chemicals, and filter paper that need to be replenished after each use), standards-based curriculum units may fall by the wayside. Professional development is also essential so that teachers become familiar with the different kinds of teaching strategies required by inquiry-based science curricula and gain confidence in their content knowledge.

• *Think in terms of both immediate steps and long-term planning.*
Teachers and district leaders who have minimized implementation challenges recommend some practical strategies to improve the chances of successful implementation. In the short term, they suggest:
* Secure special grants to support the purchase of new materials or time for professional development, or redirect funds from existing grants (such as Eisenhower funds) to provide professional development and support to teachers.
* Pool district resources so that ordering of consumables can be done more efficiently.
* Reconfigure schedules to allocate planning time for teachers and allow for longer class periods.
* Engage students in collecting and setting up materials.

In the long run, consider renovation of school facilities, including:
* Creating classroom space that can easily be rearranged.
* Providing facilities that include at least a sink, multiple electrical outlets, and adequate storage space.

The following vignettes illustrate some of the challenges of implementing inquiry-based science curricula and some ways that teachers and schools have found to cope effectively.

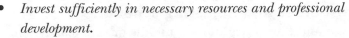

Teachers who experience the most frustration are those in districts that have adopted curricula but have not invested sufficiently in buying materials and supporting implementation.

Pooling resources and adjusting schedules

Rich Sorenson and Karen Argiulo are middle-grades teachers in different, but similarly sized, districts. Both use the same kit-based curriculum, but have had very different experiences. In Rich's school, three teachers share two kits for each unit. Rich says, "We're still struggling to get all the kits; we don't own them all yet. We have two kits and three classrooms, and I volunteered this year to be the one who doesn't have a kit in the room. So it was really hard to set up, on my lunch break, for an experiment that needed 12 or 15 items for each group. The kids would be coming in from recess, and I'd still be running back and forth.

"I really think every classroom that is using the curriculum should have a complete set of the kits. Sometimes one kit doesn't have everything, and you need to borrow something from another kit. So you need to track down that kit, and if someone else is using those materials, then you can't even get them.

"Also, there's a certain amount of money that needs to be budgeted for replacing consumables. Our district was one of the poorest in the state; we used be at something like $3300 per student. Other districts had $9000. Now we're up closer to $5,000, but it's still tough. Our new science coordinator has been terrific at getting grants, though, which is starting to make a difference."

By contrast, in Karen's district, all teachers have their own kits in their classrooms. Karen says, "The great thing is that everything you need comes in the kit. So you don't have to go out and buy the Epsom salts, for example, if that's part of the activity. It's all part of the kit. It makes it much easier to teach. Also, our district belongs to a collaborative of six towns which applied for and received a National Science Foundation grant to train teachers. I was one of the teachers who volunteered for the first round of the program. We looked at different kits available at our grade level. And we chose two to pilot, based on how they aligned with our state standards and with the *New Standards,* which we're moving toward. Since then, we've added a third and fourth kit, and in the second year we started training other teachers. Several of us are now specialists in one of the kits.

"We also don't have any problem with replenishing supplies. The collaborative now has what they call a Materials Resource Center, which is in an old factory building, where all the supplies are kept, and we have access to that. We can just call the Resource

Center and say, for example, 'We have two broken microscopes. Can we get them replaced?' And then we can pick them up or they'll be delivered to us.

"We also have block scheduling in our school, which gives us a great deal of flexibility. I see two classes on Monday and Wednesday, two classes on Tuesday and Thursday, and all four of them on Friday. So I have two hours at a time with my kids. And that really works great. But before we went to block scheduling, we had 50-minute classes, and the program worked with those too. I've even run workshops for people who teach it in 45 minutes. You can do that, since it's written so that you can really easily divide up the activities. You can do a pre-lab investigation one day, the lab the second day, and then the post-lab discussion the third day. There are good places to stop and start within the course.

"As far as facilities go, physical facilities, you really don't need anything special. It helps to have running water, it helps to have lab tables. But I've taught it on chair desks; when I've been working with other teachers, I've even taught it in a motel meeting room with no running water, where we had to fill up buckets. It's the kind of course where you can really teach it anywhere if you have some water.

"The only problem we had that we couldn't solve was with the solar unit where you need sunlight. We tried to teach that one in the fall, and we just have very little constant sunshine that time of the year. We had a lot of partly cloudy days, when I'd get the class prepared, with their experiments all ready, and then we'd go outside. They'd just be getting started and after a minute the sun would go behind a cloud. So we'd play a game while we waited, and the sun would finally come back out, and we'd get back to it, and then the sun would disappear again. That's a really difficult kind of unit to do with this climate. Probably designed in California! We don't use that unit anymore; we've found something else that addresses the same content, but doesn't require the sun to be out to do the experiments."

Sharing the burden

Curricula that require teachers both to set up and acquire materials, rather than packaging all necessary materials into kits, can be especially challenging. Districts need to take steps to reduce the burdens imposed on teachers by providing resources to assist them. Still, in the absence of district assistance, teachers often

"One day when I was in the middle of setting up it occurred to me to enlist the kids to help me get stuff together, and actually they liked that."

find new curricula sufficiently rewarding to justify the effort of additional preparation time. Jessica Hoffmann, a young teacher in a large urban district in the Northeast, describes the first time she used an earth science unit that involves an extended investigation. "The problem I had was gathering the materials. There was an extensive amount of material and preparation involved in getting the whole unit set up for the kids. I have 180 kids I see every day. So I'm thinking, 'How am I going to do this four times a day, and then turn around and do a completely different set of labs for my other two classes?' I really couldn't imagine doing that day after day after day. After a while, I think you'd just want to have the kids sitting and filling in the blanks again, because you would be totally exhausted.

"But one day when I was in the middle of setting up it occurred to me to enlist the kids to help me get stuff together, and actually they liked that. So I'll definitely do that again. And it is worth it. Because the whole unit is really laid out nicely. So once you do have it set up, it's very easy to use. Also, in retrospect, once you get all these things out, the kids are then engaged for several weeks in the explorations. So if you average the time out, it really isn't much more preparation. And the truth is, the materials are common things. Cranberry juice, window cleaner, cotton balls—things you might have at home or certainly can get in the grocery store.

"The one other thing you need to think about is storage space. It's essential to have a good storage space for materials. But you can also be creative about how you keep things in the classroom. I hang a lot of things up with tape. So even a wall can become a storage space just with some masking tape. I've hung things everywhere. Just make sure everyone puts their name on their project."

CHAPTER 2

Overview of the Curriculum Selection Process[1]

Much of this guide focuses on curriculum materials: ways to think about them, ways that people have been using them in their classrooms, and descriptions of the materials themselves. This chapter shifts the focus from the materials to the process of selecting them. The chapter outlines the steps involved in a thoughtful curriculum selection process. Though it is geared toward selection at the district level, the process described can also serve as a model (with some modifications) for smaller-scale selections—for schools, for example, or even for individual teachers. While some of the details may vary, the steps in the process are similar.

This chapter assumes (as does the whole guide) that your district has clarified goals for student learning, and that the district is operating from a set of standards or frameworks specifying expectations for student learning and performance that emphasize gaining conceptual knowledge as well as important skills.

Step 1: Create a Curriculum Selection Committee

Overview

Your selection committee will allow you to share the work involved in choosing a new curriculum. Depending on how you put the committee together, it can also create links to the larger community, and help to build community support, during the adoption process. Traditionally, selection committees meet for a relatively short time to look through the newest editions of familiar textbooks that differ very little from one another. When a district reviews standards-based curricula for possible adoption, the

Assemble the Committee

- Determine the function of the committee
- Determine the diversity of perspectives needed within the committee

Get Started as a Committee

- Design orientation activities for the committee

---

[1]This chapter has been adapted from *Choosing a Standards-Based Mathematics Curriculum* by Lynn T. Goldsmith, June Mark, and Ilene Kantrov. ©1998 by Education Development Center, Inc., K-12 Mathematics Curriculum Center. Published by Heinemann, a division of Reed Elsevier, Inc., Portsmouth, NH.

work of the selection committee can expand considerably. Committee members will have to examine candidate curricula in greater depth in order to become aware of important differences in structure and organization, treatment of content, instructional approaches, and teacher support materials. The committee will also need to decide whether to select a comprehensive (usually grades 6–8) curriculum for the middle grades, select from among the yearlong programs available, or combine different materials at each grade level to develop a comprehensive program of their own. In addition, the committee may have to decide what proportion of curriculum materials to mandate, and what portion can be teacher developed or context specific. (Magnet or theme schools, for example, may use locally developed interdisciplinary units.) The committee will also want to consider how likely the district is to welcome a new curriculum and how confident teachers will feel about implementing it.

Committee members may be called on to be spokespeople for the selection process itself, and for the choice to adopt standards-based materials. The committee, therefore, serves a variety of purposes, which include:

- Furnishing scientific and instructional expertise for curriculum review.
- Providing accountability to the community.
- Building community trust and support.
- Promoting understanding about standards-based curricula.

Main Ideas

◆ Establish a selection committee including representatives from different stakeholder groups within the school district and broader community.

◆ Make sure the committee includes diverse perspectives.

◆ Orient the group to the goals of standards-based science education.

1.1: Assemble the Committee

Determine the function of the committee

- *Decide who will make the final curriculum decision.*
  Will the committee make the final selection decision, or will it be advisory?

  Committees that make decisions may reach their conclusions by different means: some vote, while others seek consensus.

    Chapter 2/Overview of the Curriculum Selection Process

Voting can be efficient, but may not build a strong commitment to the chosen curriculum. Reaching consensus takes more time, but achieves a greater commitment to the curriculum from committee members. Committees that make selection decisions tend to be smaller than advisory groups, since large groups often make the decision-making process unwieldy and inefficient.

When the selection committee serves an advisory capacity, it helps the administration collect information and review potential curricula, but does not participate in the formal selection decision itself. Because advisory committee members don't make the selection decision, they need not be involved in all aspects of the process. More people can therefore participate, serving on subcommittees or working groups that report to the committee chair.

Determine the diversity of perspectives needed within the committee

* *Include committee members who represent different parts of the community*
  Positioning the committee to encourage buy-in within the district's various constituencies is a very important task. The more you can think strategically from the outset about ways to assemble a group of people who represent different stakeholders and will help advocate for standards-based curricula with the groups they represent, the greater your chances of a successful adoption.

Committee members from different parts of the community will be able to examine materials from their own perspectives and think about the potential strengths and weaknesses of the different curricula from their particular vantage points. (For example, consider including a scientist, laboratory technician, engineer, and/or others who use science intensively in their work.) A diverse committee will ensure that different groups feel they have a voice in the process, and can promote their sense of investment in the resulting selection.

* *Include committee members who represent the various needs of the students*
  A selection committee that represents diverse viewpoints and expertise can offer a fuller, more balanced assessment of different curricula on behalf of the teachers and students who

will be using them. Classroom teachers will examine materials with a different eye than the school counselor or teachers who serve students with limited English proficiency; a science curriculum coordinator and a special education teacher will be sensitive to different aspects of the curriculum. Including committee members from the K–5 and 9–12 levels can help to ensure that the middle-grades curriculum selection will coordinate with curricula at those grades.

1.2: Get Started as a Committee

Design orientation activities for the committee

- *Provide an overview of the ideas behind standards-based instruction*
  Many districts have found it useful to offer a half-day or full-day orientation for committee members. Such overviews introduce the ideas behind standards-based instruction.

- *Spend time focusing directly on learning science*
  Another way to orient the committee is to focus directly on science content, either by doing some short investigations and discussions as a group, or by analyzing student work. Both of these activities can provide committee members with shared experiences as science learners that can serve as common reference points. They can also help members build a greater personal appreciation for the kinds of learning and teaching promoted by standards-based curriculum and instruction.

- *Choose an experienced, enthusiastic workshop leader*
  Teacher leaders or content area supervisors in your own district may feel comfortable leading content area workshops for committee members. If not, you may be able to call on teacher educators from local colleges or universities. Another resource may be other school districts that have been involved in science education reform efforts through National Science Foundation (NSF) programs such as Local Systemic Change (LSC) grants, Urban Systemic Initiatives (USIs), and Rural Systemic Initiatives (RSIs). You may also contact one of the NSF-funded science curriculum dissemination and implementation centers which offer seminars to familiarize districts with standards-based curriculum materials. (See Chapter 4 of this guide for descriptions of these centers.) Some publishers and developers of science curricula also offer introductory workshops, though these are curriculum specific.

Step 2: Assess Resources and Needs

Overview

Part of a thorough review process will include some form of resources and needs assessment. Such an assessment will give you an accurate reading of current district policy and practice, a projection of future needs, and a sense of the resources you can enlist (or need to find) to move toward your vision of standards-based science education.

You may want to engage in a formal assessment process, collecting information through focus groups, questionnaires, school visits, or other means. On the other hand, you might decide to forgo organized data collection in favor of a more informal approach. Your decision about the rigor of your assessment process can depend on a number of factors such as the size and diversity of your district, the time and staff available for this task, and the mechanisms for communication that already exist in the district. The purpose of the assessment, regardless of the form it takes, is to provide information to help you make informed and strategic decisions about the interest, motivation, and readiness of constituents in your district to adopt standards-based curricula.

Assess the current state of curriculum and instruction in your district

- Current curriculum materials
- Current district policies
- District leadership
- Teachers' readiness
- Students' achievement and attitudes
- Parents' opinions and concerns

Assess financial costs and resources in your district

- Financial costs
- Current and potential resources

Main Ideas

◆ Assess the current state of curriculum and instruction in your district and consider the extent to which it supports your goals and standards for students' science learning.

◆ Assess the resources you have, and those you will need, to achieve your goals.

2.1: Assess the Current State of Curriculum and Instruction in Your District

Assess your current curriculum materials

When you have a clear idea of the strengths and limitations of the current materials in light of your goals and standards, you can be more focused in the ways you review potential replacements. You can use the critical questions in Chapter 1 of this guide as a framework for reviewing your current curriculum materials.

ACTION

Be sure to attend particularly to the first three categories of questions:

- academic rigor (including coherence and alignment with state and district standards and curriculum frameworks)
- equity
- developmental appropriateness

Reflect on how previous efforts to introduce new curriculum materials have fared, and ask yourselves what lessons you can learn from past experiences.

Assess your current policies and practices

District and state policies shape the curriculum selection and implementation process in a number of ways. Some, like new open-ended assessments, will support the use of standards-based materials, while others, like lack of common preparation times for teachers, may be more of a hindrance. After assessing the relevant district practices and policies, you will have a better idea of which will support the adoption of standards-based materials and which you may have to work around or seek to revise.

Talk with colleagues from other districts about their experiences with adoption and implementation to get ideas about how district policies and practices can affect the process. In assessing your own situation, consider the following:

- *Student Assessment*
  How does your current science curriculum prepare students for your local and/or state assessments? How would choosing a standards-based curriculum affect your current assessments?

- *Grouping of Students*
  How is your current policy working? What are parents' and teachers' expectations about tracking and grouping? What would be gained/lost by changing your policy?

- *Professional Development for Teachers*
  What is your current strategy for providing professional development in science? Are teachers provided with release time for professional development? What opportunities do teachers currently have to work together (e.g., common preparation times, co-teaching opportunities, study groups)? What are your current resources for professional development (financial

and in terms of expertise)? What kind of professional development will be needed to successfully implement a standards-based curriculum, and how well does this correspond to the current approach to professional development in your school or district?

- *School Structure and Organization*
  How will the structure of the school day accommodate a more exploratory science curriculum? Might changes in school structure and organization be needed to implement the new curriculum (e.g., longer class periods to accommodate extended projects and investigations, renegotiating with the teachers' union to provide additional time for teacher planning)?

- *Technology*
  What is your policy about integrating technology into the science curriculum? Do students have access to technology required by standards-based curricula? Is your projected budget adequate to supply the necessary technology? How strong is teacher leadership for integrating technology into the classroom? What other resources do you have to increase access to technology?

Assess your district leadership

District leadership is critical to successful curriculum selection and implementation. Administrators, including the director of curriculum and instruction, science specialists, principals, and the district superintendent, play important roles in the process. Their backing is necessary to maintain a steady course toward district goals and to support teachers' implementation efforts. To provide such support, they need to understand the implications of science standards for curriculum and teaching.

Teacher leaders are another critical component of district leadership. They can serve as mentors for other teachers, speak from experience about the benefits and difficulties of using new materials, and act as advocates with administrators and the larger community.

When assessing your district leadership, do not forget those individuals who serve as liaisons with the larger community, such as school board members.

Among the questions you should ask when assessing district leadership are the following:

- What do the leaders know about standards-based curriculum reform?
- What are the leaders' positions on standards-based curriculum reform?
- What resources are available to provide professional development to the leadership?
- What issues, roles, and responsibilities will be created for district leaders with the adoption of a standards-based approach to science education?

Assess teachers' readiness

Ultimately, the success of a curriculum lies in the work that teachers and students do together in the classroom each day. Because teachers' commitment to the principles and methods of a curriculum is a major part of the equation, it's important to know about teachers' readiness to use standards-based materials. These curricula may challenge teachers in a number of ways.

You will need to find out how prepared teachers feel they are to implement a standards-based curriculum in terms of several factors:

- science content
- instructional approaches
- assessment strategies
- classroom management

Assess students' achievement and attitudes

Look at information about student achievement in science to determine those areas in which students are already performing well and those concepts and skills that need improvement. This analysis will help you focus your review of the science content of different curricula.

Students who are unaccustomed to taking active roles in the classroom often need some time to adjust to the expectations of standards-based curricula. You will want to consider how adopting a standards-based curriculum will challenge your students in terms of these aspects of learning:

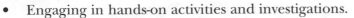

- Engaging in hands-on activities and investigations.
- Working collaboratively.
- Reading and writing in science class.
- Explaining their thinking.
- Participating in class discussions.

Assess parents' opinions and concerns

Learning about how parents are thinking about their children's education in science will help you plan ways to encourage parents' participation in their children's learning. Ask the following questions:

- What are parents' hopes for their children's learning in science?
- What satisfies parents about the current curriculum?
- What are parents' concerns about the current curriculum?
- In what ways would parents like to learn more about standards-based education in the district (for example, parent nights, short seminars, print and online resources)?[2]

2.2: Assess the Financial Costs of New Materials and the Resources in Your District

Assess the financial costs associated with new curriculum materials

New curriculum materials can be expensive, and the selection and implementation of a standards-based curriculum may involve costs that are not associated with traditional textbook adoptions. Ask about costs for:

- Equipment to support the curriculum (for example, computers, laser disks, and CD-ROM players).
- Supplementary materials, laboratory supplies, and consumables (for example, glassware, chemicals, live specimens, lab notebooks).
- Professional development.
- Reconfiguring classroom space and installing facilities (for example, sinks, gas jets, and multiple electric outlets) to accommodate science activities.

---

[2] You might consider sharing with parents the introduction to this guide as well as excerpts from Chapter 1. Some of the resources described in Chapter 4 are also appropriate for parents.

ACTION ⇨

Assess current and potential district resources

To offset costs, determine the kinds of resources that are currently available to your community, and also investigate future sources of support. Ask the following questions:

- What federal, state, and/or local grants are available?
- What Entitlement funds are available—for example, Title I, Title II (Eisenhower), Title VI funds?
- What publisher incentives are available?
- What private or community foundations and corporate support can you draw upon?
- What kinds of funds can you raise locally?
- What local, in-kind contributions can you solicit (for example, professional development, substitutes for teachers to attend in-service meetings, technology, supplies)?

Step 3: Choose Curricula for Review

Overview

Early in the selection process, you will begin to sort through potential curricula to review. As you proceed, you will work to narrow down your initial list of possible curricula to a short list that you can review more thoroughly. With a wide range of materials on the market, it can be challenging to pare down the choices to a manageable number.

As you sort through the options, you will need to decide whether to select a comprehensive middle grades curriculum, select from among the yearlong programs available, or combine different materials at each grade level to develop a comprehensive program. You will also need to select from different approaches to science teaching and learning: inquiry-based, social issues-oriented, and technology-focused. You may want to examine some materials of each type, and consult with districts that have recently gone through a similar process, before making these decisions.

This guide, supplemented by some of the resources described in Chapter 4, can help you identify standards-based curricula and assist you in selecting curriculum materials to review in depth.

Collect information about available standards-based curricula

Make an initial list of curricula for review

Create a short list of science materials to review thoroughly

---

Main Idea

◆ Use this guide and the resources described in Chapter 4 to help you identify and learn about standards-based curricula.

3.1: Explore the Variety of Curriculum Materials and Teaching Approaches

Identify and collect information about available standards-based curricula

Some strategies and resources to assist you in this phase include the following:

- Read the curriculum profiles in Chapter 3 of this guide.
- Consult Chapter 4 for additional resources that describe and/or evaluate science curricula.
- Contact the NSF-funded science curriculum dissemination and implementation centers (also described in Chapter 4) for information about the curriculum materials they support and for seminars and print resources. While these centers do not support all available standards-based curricula, many of their resources are generally applicable to selecting and implementing standards-based materials.
- Talk with people in other districts about their experiences with different curricula.
- Get recommendations from teachers in your district who have been active in science education reform.
- Attend state, regional, and national conferences of professional organizations such as the National Science Teachers Association (NSTA) to view presentations and meet publishers.
- Contact publishers for catalogues, sample materials, and initial sales presentations.

3.2: Select Curricula for Review

Make an initial list of curricula for review

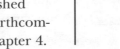

Your initial list can contain more materials than you will be able to review in depth. Don't neglect to consider newly published curricula, or new editions of existing curricula. Several forthcoming standards-based science curricula are previewed in Chapter 4.

ACTION
⇨

Narrow down your list to a short list of curricula to be reviewed thoroughly

Some curricula included on your initial list may be easy to eliminate on first review because of cost, technology requirements, lack of alignment with your district or state standards and assessments, or other obvious incompatibilities. The strategies suggested above for collecting information about standards-based curricula will help you sort through your list. You can also use the discussion of your selection criteria (see Step 4, below) to help you narrow the list further. As you assemble these criteria, you may find that some curricula can be ruled out without much further consideration.

Step 4: Assemble and Apply Selection Criteria

Overview

The selection criteria you use will guide your review of curricula. When you assemble criteria that reflect your goals and address your needs, you will have a powerful tool to use in your selection process. Much of the work you have already done to articulate your goals and assess community needs and resources will be useful in assembling your selection criteria.

The criteria help focus and standardize your review process. They reflect your district's particular needs and goals, focusing your evaluation on how the different curricula will help you achieve these goals. Criteria help standardize the process by providing a common set of questions to ask of each curriculum. You can use these questions to compare the different curricula and also to compare different reviewers' evaluations of the same curriculum.

There are a variety of critiquing instruments available, as described in Chapter 4, to help make your selection process rigorous and thoughtful. Because it takes a great deal of time and thought to construct the selection criteria in these instruments, it makes sense, if possible, to use one of these existing tools. However, you will want to review them to ensure that they reflect your district's needs and goals. If no single set of criteria does fit the bill, you can adapt one or combine elements from different instruments.

Assemble criteria for evaluating each curriculum in terms of:

- Academic rigor of science content/process
- Equity and developmental appropriateness of student experiences
- Instructional approaches
- Support for implementation and professional development
- Organization and presentation of materials

Design your evaluation tool

- Choose the method you will use to collect information on each curriculum
- Practice using the evaluation tool on some of the curricula

---

Main Ideas

◆ Selection criteria help standardize the process by providing a set of common questions to ask of each candidate curriculum.

◆ Use selection criteria that reflect your district's particular goals and needs as determined by your resources and needs assessment (see Step 2).

◆ If possible, use or adapt existing evaluation instruments, or combine elements of different ones.

4.1: Assemble Criteria for Evaluating Each Curriculum

The critical questions in Chapter 1 provide a framework for assembling appropriate selection criteria. The actual criteria will be more specific and may also need to be tailored to your particular district, schools, teachers, and student population. The introductions to the vignettes in Chapter 1 can help you identify the kinds of questions your evaluation instrument should address. You can find examples of selection criteria in some of the resources described in Chapter 4. The curriculum profiles in Chapter 3 also indicate how the profiled curricula address the critical questions and provide some information to address specific criteria, such as those concerning the structure and presentation of the materials.

Assemble criteria for evaluating the academic rigor of each curriculum

Assessing academic rigor is at the heart of a curriculum review. It is important to determine whether the curricula you are considering address the science your students need to learn, and whether the content is presented in a manner consistent with your approaches to teaching and learning. Some examples of the kinds of questions you will want to ask are:

• How completely and explicitly does the curriculum address state and local content and performance standards?

• How does the curriculum help students learn skills, understand scientific concepts and their interconnections, reason scientifically, and communicate their ideas?

• What is the balance between concepts and process skills in the curriculum, and how does it match the district's goals and standards?

- How does the curriculum help students see connections among scientific disciplines and between science and its applications in the world?
- Is the science in the curriculum accurate?
- Do the assessments used reflect the learning goals and experiences of the curriculum?
- How does the curriculum support the state and district assessments?

Assemble criteria for evaluating students' experience in terms of equity and developmental appropriateness

You will want to select curriculum materials that are engaging and comprehensible to a wide range of students, with lessons that offer multiple points of entry. Some of these offer students with varying learning styles and intellectual strengths different ways to think about the content. Others connect with students' different interests and backgrounds.

A fundamental premise of standards-based curricula is that students are actively involved in the construction of their own understanding. As you review curricula, look for ways that they involve students in developing ideas, testing them, defending them, and sharing their thinking with others. Examine the curricula in terms of:

- The ways each curriculum helps students with a range of abilities, learning styles, interests, and backgrounds to build skills and develop conceptual understanding.
- The ways each curriculum helps teachers engage students in active learning.

Assemble criteria for evaluating the teaching approach of each curriculum and the accompanying implementation and professional development challenges and supports

Standards-based curricula require teachers to take an active role. Teachers are brokers of the curriculum, providing a link between the written materials and the students. As you assemble your selection criteria, ask whether the curricula you are considering take the teaching approaches you are seeking with respect to:

- opportunities for student inquiry (for example, designing their own experiments, pursuing questions that arise in an investigation)

- classroom communication
- use of physical materials and technology
- assessment
  * individual projects
  * group projects
  * student self-assessments
  * in-class performance assessments
  * portfolios

You should also ask how the different materials you are considering, and their publishers or developers, support teachers in implementing these approaches.

Assemble criteria for evaluating the organization and presentation of each curriculum.

You will find a lot of variability in the organization, layout, and packaging of standards-based curricula. As reflected in the materials profiled in Chapter 3, you will find some yearlong or multi-year texts, some series of modular units, and some stand-alone units. Teacher guides differ in the type and amount of ancillary material they include—for example, samples of student work, solutions, tips about organizing and implementing lessons, and descriptions of primary learning goals for units.

The curriculum profiles in Chapter 3 can help you begin to assess the presentation and organization of the materials profiled. When designing selection criteria, be sure to ask about:

- What materials are included.
- What are the advantages of the way the materials are packaged.
- Whether the directions are clear (to teachers and to students).
- Whether required materials are readily available.

The critical issues considered by these criteria are addressed in the implementation vignettes in Chapter 1.

4.2: Choose or Adapt Your Evaluation Instrument

Most evaluation instruments are in the form of a questionnaire or table that allows reviewers to record their thoughts and impressions of different curricula. Organizing the information in this way makes it easier to compare and discuss different curricula. As you examine and consider choosing among or adapting the available instruments, you will need to consider what method(s) to use and try out the instrument(s), as outlined below.

Choose the method you will use to collect information about each curriculum

- *A quantitative approach*
  With this approach, selection criteria are phrased as yes/no questions or as questions that ask "How much?" and "How often?" You assign numerical values or low/medium/high ratings to your questions that you can then tally and use to compare curricula.

- *A qualitative approach*
  Using a qualitative approach, you will answer your selection questions by writing a series of brief answers. With this approach, selection criteria are phrased as questions that ask "How?" "Why?" or "Where?" and you answer these questions by synthesizing your impressions of the curriculum, supporting your evaluation with examples from the materials.

- *A combination approach*
  For those parts of the evaluation that are relatively straightforward (for example, review of the organization and presentation of the curricula), a quantitative approach will work fine. We recommend taking a qualitative approach to issues that require judgment (e.g., an evaluation of opportunities for student inquiry) because we think you will achieve a richer, more nuanced sense of each curriculum.

Practice using the evaluation instrument on some of the curricula

- *Practice together as a whole committee*
  You may want to practice applying the criteria together as a whole committee to make the process explicit, talking out your individual judgments and reasoning. Be sure to discuss the places where you disagree so you can reach consensus about what you are looking for when you use the selection criteria.

- *Practice individually, then get together to discuss*
  You may want to apply the criteria individually, and then get together to talk about questions that were difficult. In discussion, disagreements may also emerge that committee members need to resolve.

- *Get the committee to use the criteria reliably and consistently*
  The purpose of practicing is to get people feeling comfortable using the criteria as they look through the materials. You also want to get the committee to use the criteria as reliably and consistently as possible.

Step 5: Pilot Test the Curricula
Overview

After you have narrowed your choices to a few curricula, you will want to get better acquainted with these. You should have a good idea of the materials that look best on paper, but you also need to know how they fare when transformed into classroom instruction. As one curriculum specialist put it, "Our committee can identify materials that look best to us, but we still need to ask, 'Will these materials work with our students, and how will teachers react?'"

Many districts include a phase in their selection process in which some teachers use the candidate materials on a trial basis and provide feedback about their classroom experiences. Selection committees then use the results of this pilot test to make an official selection.

This strategy of piloting new curricula serves a variety of purposes. It allows you to do the following:

- See the materials in action.
- Build teachers' commitment to a new curriculum.
- Increase district familiarity with the materials.
- Identify professional development needs.
- Create a cadre of experienced lead teachers.

There are several advantages to including a pilot phase in your process. One is that it provides information about how teachers and students in your district actually work with the curricula you are considering. You will be able to find out whether the materials function in the classroom in the ways you imagined they would. Piloting can give you information about how comfortable

---

Design a piloting strategy
- Determine a strategy for piloting candidate curricula

Select pilot teachers
- Determine which schools and grades will be involved in the pilot phase
- Determine the number of teachers to be involved in the pilot phase
- Determine which teachers will be involved in the pilot phase

Provide professional development for pilot phase teachers
- Provide professional development prior to the pilot phase
- Provide professional development and support for teachers during the pilot phase

your teachers will be with implementing the new materials, and piloting can reveal unforeseen problems or pleasant surprises. In addition, you can compare the different materials based on how well they promote student achievement of district goals and standards.

The pilot phase also serves as a trial run, helping prepare the district for a full-scale implementation. It offers the opportunity for teachers to become familiar with the materials and develop a sense of ownership. When teacher interest helps to drive decisions about curriculum, commitment to successful implementation is greater.

Main Ideas

A pilot phase can have the following benefits:

◆ Teachers become familiar with standards-based curricula.

◆ The strengths and weaknesses of candidate curricula are assessed.

◆ District-wide awareness and support for a new curriculum increase.

◆ Teachers' professional development needs are identified.

5.1: Design a Piloting Strategy

Determine a strategy and timeline for piloting candidate curricula

Following are a number of different piloting methods. Generally, districts select one method to use.

- *Different pilot groups for each finalist curriculum*
  One strategy is to select a group of teachers to pilot each one of the finalist curricula for some extended period of time— a year or even two if possible. These pilot teachers can meet together over the year and report to the committee about their experiences. One disadvantage of separate pilot groups is that it may be difficult for teachers to compare their experiences.

- *Teachers pilot all contenders*
  Another strategy is to ask interested teachers to pilot all of the finalist curricula. This eliminates the problem of teachers becoming attached to the particular curriculum that they have piloted. Disadvantages to this approach are that teachers have

less time to spend working with individual curricula and therefore have less time to compare student performance.

- *Piloting a class of materials, not a particular curriculum*
Sometimes districts offer teachers the opportunity to use a variety of curricula for the year prior to selection. The purpose is less to pinpoint particular curricula than to provide teachers with some experience working with standards-based materials. In this case, the pilot phase is used as a way to familiarize teachers with standards-based curricula. If a district is considering different types of curricula—e.g., inquiry-based, social issues-oriented, and technology-focused—one set of teachers might use an extended investigation and another set could try one or two examples of each kind of modular unit.

5.2: Select Pilot Teachers

Determine which schools will be involved in the pilot phase

Some districts focus their pilot phase on a single school. One advantage of this approach is that the teachers can work as a team, meeting to discuss their experiences and to work together to iron out kinks they may encounter. Other districts open up the piloting process to any interested teachers in the district. This approach can help to ensure that the information gathered from piloting is more representative of the district as a whole.

Some districts try to have teachers from every grade level pilot materials, while others pilot in only one or two grades. The advantage of piloting in all the middle grades is that you can learn how the curriculum unfolds across the different levels.

Some districts make sure that teachers on the selection committee participate in piloting, while in other districts the pilot teachers may report to the committee but not be members.

Determine the number of teachers to be involved in the pilot phase

Some districts have piloted materials with as few as 2 or 3 teachers; large districts may use more than 100 pilot teachers. How many you choose will depend, among other factors, on the size of your district, your need to cultivate stakeholder support, and the number of teachers who are ready and willing to bring a new curriculum into the classroom. The potential drawback of a very small pilot effort is that your information may be more about the particular successes and difficulties of specific teachers rather than the robustness and power of the curriculum materials themselves.

Determine which teachers will be involved in the pilot phase

Your choice of pilot teachers depends on your particular goals. By including pilot teachers who subscribe to the goals of standards-based reform, are strong in the science content, and are versed in new pedagogical approaches, you can gather information about how effective the curriculum can be. On the other hand, you may want to learn how other teachers will use the materials and what kind of support teachers in the district will need to implement the different curricula.

5.3: Provide Professional Development for Pilot Teachers

Provide professional development for teachers prior to the pilot phase

No matter which piloting strategy you use, you will want to make sure that teachers receive some professional development prior to piloting new curricula. Many of the science curriculum publishers and developers offer orientations, institutes, workshops, or other training opportunities specifically for their materials. Chapter 1 offers discussion and examples of effective professional development strategies. Chapter 4 also describes some resources for professional development support.

Provide professional development and support for teachers during the pilot phase

You should also plan for professional development and support for the pilot teachers during the pilot phase. Ongoing support might involve arranging common preparation time for teachers in the same building and holding regular meetings for teachers across the district facilitated by a staff developer. Such meetings offer teachers the opportunity to discuss the teaching and learning promoted by the materials and identify implementation challenges and strategies for addressing them. (See Chapter 1 for discussion and illustrations of implementation challenges and solutions.)

Summary

The processes outlined in this chapter represent a "soup to nuts" approach to choosing curriculum materials. It is time- and energy-consuming, but worth the effort. Purchasing curriculum materials is an expensive and relatively infrequent event. It's wise to spend the time "up front" to make sure that you've selected materials that will really help your students learn. It's a lot more expensive to find out after the fact that the materials you've selected aren't as promising as you hoped they would be. By being thoughtful, careful, and deliberate about your selection process, you increase the likelihood that you will pick materials that will meet your needs, serve your students well, and endure until it is time for a new selection process.

CHAPTER 3

Profiles of Exemplary Science Curricula

This chapter contains profiles of 11 middle-grades science programs that are currently available commercially. A number of these programs were developed before the publication of the National Research Council's *National Science Education Standards* and Project 2061's *Benchmarks for Science Literacy.* However, they all reflect the philosophy and approaches advocated by the *Standards* and *Benchmarks,* and they share some family resemblances. When we asked teachers to describe the distinctive features of the standards-based materials they were using, they often mentioned the same things, regardless of the particular program. They said that their curriculum used hands-on experiences to engage students in learning to carry out science processes and think scientifically, that more students were understanding the science concepts they were studying, that activities were rich and engaging for students, and that, although successful implementation required professional development and took some adjustment, the curriculum was very rewarding to teach. The teachers we spoke with tended not to compare the standards-based curricula to one another, but instead to focus on the differences between the standards-based materials they were using now and the science textbooks they had used in the past.

Despite the similarities among these curricula, they differ on a number of dimensions. Several are comprehensive, multiyear or yearlong middle-grades curricula; several are comprehensive elementary curricula with components that can be used in the early middle grades; and others focus on particular subject matter across several grade levels. As noted in the introduction to this guide, the science curricula profiled in this chapter overall represent two different types of middle-grades materials currently used by reform-minded school districts. These are (1) yearlong and multiyear materials that constitute comprehensive, core instructional programs, and (2) modular materials that can be used over shorter periods, either as supplements to a core curriculum or as part of a tapestry of modular units that are woven together to create a comprehensive program.

The curricula profiled also differ in their entry points and content focus. Inquiry-based programs generally use science as the door to learning; modular units often use social issues or everyday phenomena as the door into the study of the science. Among the materials profiled are examples of social issues-focused curricula, curricula that highlight the study of design technology, and curricula that involve extended investigations. This chapter does not include activity books, CD-ROMs, or curriculum units that are published individually, rather than as part of a series or a larger science program. Some of these other kinds of materials are, however, described briefly in the annotated list of resources included in Chapter 4. Also described in Chapter 4 are some science curricula that were not yet published at the time this guide was written. Among these forthcoming programs are comprehensive, multiyear curricula that were designed specifically in accordance with the *Standards* and *Benchmarks* and have undergone field testing. As your selection process proceeds, you may want to examine some of these newer curricula and also consider additional modular materials described in Chapter 4, looking at them through the same lenses that we have used to profile the examples of high-quality curricula in this chapter.

Because districts and schools often combine modular units or supplement a core curriculum in order to meet the requirements of state and local standards and frameworks, we have tried to include in these profiles sufficient information to give you a sense of the content as well as the structure and organization of the curricula. The profiles themselves are divided into eight main sections:

- *Overview:* Summary of the main features of the curriculum.
- *Curriculum Focus:* Content of the curriculum, organized by major strands.
- *Curriculum Format:* Structure and organization of the curriculum.
- *Academic Rigor:* How the curriculum specifically addresses rigor; also how it makes connections across disciplines and approaches assessment.
- *Equity:* How the curriculum specifically addresses equity.
- *Developmental Appropriateness:* How the curriculum specifically addresses developmental appropriateness.

- *Teaching Resources and Support:* Contents of teacher's guides and other print materials, and professional development available from the publisher and/or developer.
- *Teacher Hints and Guidance:* Suggestions from teachers who have taught the curriculum.

In addition to the information we have provided about the curriculum, each profile concludes with an excerpt from a lesson. These lessons offer a more concrete sense of the approaches different curricula take. Because they are only brief excerpts, they cannot offer a complete view of the ways the curriculum develops a concept—it's not possible from these short illustrations to tell what preceded the work, or what followed. However, we do think that the lessons give you a feel for the ways the different programs approach the science and science instruction. When you examine different programs more carefully yourselves, we strongly recommend that you trace the development of concepts and their related skills throughout the curriculum. Ask yourselves what kind of work students will do, how the curriculum develops and reinforces concepts and skills, how deeply the curriculum develops ideas, and how the ideas and skills are interconnected and applied.

We hope that these profiles will help you think about how different materials might fit with the specific needs and circumstances of individual schools or districts. However, the profiles are *not* intended to take the place of careful review and piloting of materials, as described in Chapter 2. Instead, they can offer a general introduction to the different curricula and a first step toward developing a better sense of which materials will merit further consideration.

BSCS Middle School Science and Technology

Publisher:	Kendall/Hunt Publishing Co. 4050 Westmark Drive P.O. Box 1840 Dubuque, IA 52004-1840 (800) KH-BOOKS
Website:	http://www.kendallhunt.com
Years Published:	1994, 1999
Developer:	Biology and Science Curriculum Studies (BSCS), Colorado Springs, CO
Website:	http://www.bscs.org
Grade Levels:	6–8
Science Domains:	Earth science, life science, and physical science

Overview

BSCS Middle School Science and Technology is a comprehensive middle-grades program. The curriculum integrates the major areas of science and technology and organizes each grade level around a broad theme. Concepts build upon each other, and students apply concepts across different domains of knowledge— earth, life, and physical sciences. The curriculum requires students to work cooperatively, engage in a large number of hands-on activities, and read challenging text. The curriculum is published as three hardbound student texts made up of investigations, readings, and "connections."

> "This is a standards-based science curriculum. It's also research-based. I think the pedagogy and the topics are inherently interesting. . . . A lot of times people have this polarizing debate between content and process, and it took me a while to see that content and process are not mutually exclusive. *BSCS* uses content as a vehicle to teach process. My experience is that the content they pick is engaging, things that are relevant to kids' lives. . . . The developers have written something layered and conceptual, and that would be really hard [for a teacher] to make up."
> — Science teacher

Characteristic features of the program include:

- The "5Es" instructional model. In each chapter, students *engage* (think about a new idea), *explore* (through one or several activities), *explain* (construct an explanation for the idea), *elaborate* (through additional activities), and *evaluate* (demonstrate understanding of the idea).
- Use of cooperative learning strategies. The student book and teacher's guide offer specific directions and recommendations so that students learn how to work effectively with their peers and understand what specific skills each activity requires.
- Focus on process. The program pays strong attention to the development of general science procedures.
- Hands-on activities. An estimated 60 percent of the activities are described as hands-on.
- Readings to support the development of concepts. All chapters include readings designed either to reinforce what is learned through hands-on activities or to introduce concepts or processes.

Curriculum Focus

The curriculum for each grade is organized into three levels of study: Patterns of Change, Diversity and Limits, and Systems and Change. There are four units within each level. Science and technology concepts are integrated throughout the curriculum. The technology concepts include design process, efficiency, costs, benefits, criteria, constraints, and decision making. The topics addressed within the three levels are as follows:

Level A, Patterns of Change: Key topics include patterns in the natural world, such as the phases of the moon, water and wind movement on the earth, and plant growth. The curriculum also includes topics related to the impact of humans on the environment, for example, the size of the human population and the accumulation of garbage. Within the context of these topics, the curriculum develops physical science concepts (e.g., convection).

Level B, Diversity and Limits: Student activities include collecting data on human limits, graphing data to produce normal curves, designing toys, testing a scientific model about particles, and finding out about human diversity in relationship to genetics. Concepts developed include the chromosomal theory of inheritance and the particulate model of matter.

Level C, Systems and Change: Student activities focus on learning about the different systems in the body through reading texts, manipulating batteries and electrical circuits, designing and constructing a water heating system, and observing the growth of a *Daphnia* population. The program develops a number of the concepts and scientific processes through reading of specially selected texts.

The same four themes cut across levels A, B, and C, and a broad question related to the theme serves as the focus for each unit at each level, as summarized below.

		Unit 1	Unit 2	Unit 3	Unit 4
Theme		*Personal dimensions of science and technology*	*The nature of scientific explanation*	*Technological problem solving*	*Science and technology in society (STS)*
Focus Question	**Level A** *Patterns of Change*	How does my world change?	How do we explain patterns of change on the earth?	How do we adjust to patterns of change?	How can we change patterns?
	Level B *Diversity and Limits*	What is normal?	How does technology account for my limits?	Why are things different?	Why are we different?
	Level C *Systems and Change*	How much can things change and still remain the same?	How do things change?	How can we improve our use of energy?	What are the limits to growth?

Curriculum Format

Each level is a one-year program that makes connections across units and with the other two levels. The activities and the concepts in each unit and level build on those in previous units and levels. This program does not, therefore, lend itself to selective use of particular sections but requires teachers to use the entire program.

Each of the four units at each level has a particular focus.

- Unit 1 uses activities relevant to students' lives to connect concepts of science and technology to their everyday environment.
- Unit 2 of Levels A and C and Unit 3 of Level B emphasize scientific explanations, such as the theory of plate tectonics, evolution, and the particulate model of matter.
- Unit 3 of Levels A and C and Unit 2 of Level B provide students with opportunities to learn about the principles of technology, such as the design process and the efficient use of energy resources.
- Unit 4 requires students to consider the impact of science and technology on society, focusing on issues such as recycling, genetic engineering, and the problems of overpopulation.

The number of chapters varies within a unit. However, each chapter follows the five-stage instructional model (engage, explore, explain, elaborate, and evaluate) and contains the following components:

Investigations: Present students with a problem or question and challenge them to use materials to solve it. Questions called "Wrap Ups" appear at the end of each investigation.

Readings: Include explanations of concepts, science content, and connections between ideas and investigations. "Stop and Think" questions are a critical component of the readings.

Connections: Ask students and teachers to reflect on and discuss their work and to make connections among key ideas.

Academic Rigor

The first edition of this curriculum program preceded the final publication of the National Research Council's *National Science Education Standards* and Project 2061's *Benchmarks for Science Literacy.* Therefore, the first edition has no information about alignment of the curriculum with the standards for the middle grades. However, the second edition of the teacher's edition provides a detailed correlation with the *National Science Education Standards* and indicates which activities are aligned with specific standards.

The curriculum aims to build students' understanding of basic science and technology concepts and skills, to promote critical thinking and problem solving, and to help students see the connections between science and technology and their own lives. As students use the curriculum, they are expected to take increasing responsibility for their own learning. The program encourages teachers to use open-ended and "what if" questions.

The curriculum builds on previous learning and stresses understanding and application rather than rote memorization. The activities in each chapter develop concepts, skills, and themes in an orderly, coherent way. The activities afford many opportunities for students to reveal their preconceptions and to discuss what they have learned. Readings are generally in service of the activities and are not encyclopedic or traditional textbook materials.

Students are expected to make connections between concepts as they play out in particular contexts and in terms of their broader significance in science and technology. Students are also expected to make connections between concepts and the overall theme of the curriculum level. For example, in one of the design projects, students make a toy boat. In order to make the boat function properly, they need to figure out how to use the air pressure in a balloon to propel the boat. This requires some understanding of the scientific concepts of air pressure and momentum. Having students create and test designs as they do with the toy boat promotes an understanding of the design process as a way of solving problems and develops ideas about constraints and diversity. While these ideas have meaning within the context of the project, they also contribute to the development of the overall theme of *Diversity and Limits*.

Connections to Other Disciplines

Many of the program's activities require students to solve problems or design products or services that cut across the science disciplines and various aspects of technology. For example, in *Diversity and Limits*, students explore a number of concepts: distribution of characteristics of living things, limits of living things, diversity of materials and products available for technological design, and genetic diversity. The program also provides opportunities for teachers to make connections with mathematics and social studies.

Assessment

The curriculum encourages ongoing assessment. It lists learning outcomes for each of the four units within each level. These address the more general and abstract concepts developed throughout the level. The teacher's edition includes specific outcomes for skills and concepts for each of the subsections within a chapter. These outcomes relate to particular activities or readings that students have completed. For instance, in one activity students are asked to set speed limits for cars on the highway. They must use data tables to determine stopping distances for cars. This information must also be coordinated with perception experiments that students conduct. The teacher can assess performance by observing how well students understand and use a graph they are given and how they are able to use and interpret a normal curve. The program also provides suggestions for assessing how well students have made connections from these specific skills and concepts to the broader concept of diversity.

An activity at the end of each unit is designed to help the teacher evaluate students' understanding of the entire unit. This activity requires students to apply the concepts and skills they have learned. For example, in one Level B investigation students evaluate paper towels. At the end of the investigation is a follow-up assignment for students to design a trash can for their classroom. This assignment is used to assess their understanding of the design concepts of criteria and constraints. By the end of each year of the curriculum, teachers have assessed student progress and growth through student self-evaluations, teacher checklists, team feedback, portfolios, chapter evaluations, and homework.

Equity

The program explicitly addresses different learning styles. In some instances, plays are used to introduce new concepts. Other strategies include use of charts, logs, data tables, hands-on materials, reference materials, games and simulations, research, outdoor activities, and both individual and collaborative work. Cartoon characters representing different learning styles appear throughout all three levels, and represent a mix of male and female characters as well as racial groups and physical challenges. The resource book for teachers also discusses issues related to diverse learning styles.

Nonetheless, this program relies heavily on the readings, and students must interpret and understand text introducing or explaining concepts. For instance, in Level A, several chapters have few activities, so students must rely on the text to develop an understanding of concepts. Students who struggle with reading may have difficulty with these sections and will need assistance to understand and interpret the readings.

Developmental Appropriateness

At each level, the first unit begins with activities that have a real-world connection, followed by related investigations and discussions. Often these beginning activities address personal characteristics of students. For example, one of the first activities at the beginning of Level C introduces the concept of balance by having students stand on one foot. The student book includes readings with topics likely to interest middle-grades students (for example, a discussion of clothing sizes for teenagers in America).

The curriculum continually emphasizes group work. The student book includes specific directions that tell student how to work cooperatively with their partners. One teacher provided this example:

> "The curriculum might ask students to draw a 'T chart' . . . and then ask them about listening to each other talk about their T charts. It asks what good listening sounds like and looks like, and how you know someone is listening to you."

Teaching Resources and Support

Print Materials

Teacher's Edition: Follows the development of each chapter and provides an overview describing the sequence of activities in the unit, cooperative learning skills for the unit, lesson preparation (including strategies for teaching each activity and answers to "Wrap Up" questions), and science content and background. At the end of the teacher's edition, a series of reference pages entitled "Strategies for Teaching How To" include strategies for teaching students graphing techniques, methods for constructing data tables, and brainstorming methods. The teacher's edition also includes reduced facsimile student pages, lists of educational technology resources, and a list of websites that supplement the concepts addressed in the materials.

Teacher's Guide and Resources: Designed for teachers to use daily or weekly, and as background for better understanding the program's approach to teaching and learning. The guide includes an introductory unit to get the students started in cooperative learning. It also includes safety procedures, blackline masters for the entire program, and a wide assortment of information to facilitate the teaching of the program (e.g., strategies for assessment and extension activities).

Implementation Guide: Provides strategies for implementing the curriculum in the classroom and in schools. The information in the guide is based on case studies of schools that field tested the program. The guide identifies the kind of staff development that is essential for schools and districts implementing the curriculum, including fairly comprehensive and detailed suggestions (e.g., outlines of activities for each day of a professional development workshop).

Student Book: Contains readings, investigations, and connections sections that comprise the primary learning activities of the curriculum. It provides complete instructions for students to carry out the investigations and includes readings that explain and expand on concepts.

Minds-on Science Videotape Series: Includes a set of inquiry-based video activities for each level.

Materials Kits: Available from Science Kit–Boreal, 77 East Park Drive, P.O. Box 5003, Tonawanda, NY 14151, (800) 828-7777.

Professional Development

Several options for professional development are available from the publisher. Teachers can participate in a weeklong "train the trainer" model. This option works best when the entire school has adopted the program. Districts can also take advantage of one- and two-day sessions offered by grade level, which focus primarily on classroom use of the curriculum. For more information about or to schedule professional development, contact Kendall/Hunt Publishing at (800) KH-BOOKS or visit the website <www.kendallhunt.com>.

Teacher Hints and Guidance

Materials: The materials used in this curriculum are common items that can be found at local discount stores. They are easily accessible, but the monthly cost can be substantial. The curriculum suggests the use of supplemental books, videos, and newspapers, but these are not part of the curriculum package.

Integration of Science Disciplines: Because the curriculum cuts across the three science disciplines and technology, teachers accustomed to specializing in one discipline often have to teach unfamiliar content. This requires additional study on their part.

Rigorous Reading: Depending upon students' reading levels, teachers find the text either on level or too difficult. For struggling readers, some teachers use Title I resources or employ strategies such as group readings and teacher reading to give students access to the text.

Students Working Independently: Students need the maturity to work on their own and follow directions. Teachers commented that sometimes middle-grades students have the capacity, but frequently not the discipline. Therefore, teachers often find they have to do a lot of explaining and "hand-holding" at the beginning of the year. Such support is especially necessary when students have previously used only traditional textbook programs.

Scheduling: Because the content and processes are demanding, some teachers find it difficult to implement the curriculum in short class periods. A block schedule or another type of alternative schedule seems most conducive to effective use of this program.

Making Connections: Students may find it challenging to make connections between concepts in different contexts and use different sets of materials within a few sessions. Students have to become acquainted with each set of materials, learn how to assemble them quickly to achieve a certain effect, come to understand the manner in which the system operates, develop a concept of how it works, and relate the particular concept to a broader one that makes the connection among this diverse set of experiences.

Use as a Comprehensive Program: Since the program spans three years, the concepts in each subsequent year build on the previous year's work. Teachers need to develop strategies for working with students who did not achieve grade level in the previous year or come from schools that do not use the program.

Professional Development: Experienced teachers report that on-going support from science coordinators or other specialists is essential for implementation, and that it takes several years for teachers to feel successful. Professional development and support need to focus both on subject knowledge and pedagogy. Science coordinators or teachers with questions about the curriculum can also contact the developer.

Sample Lesson

The following is an excerpt from the teacher's edition of *Change Through Time*. Copyright 1999. Reproduced with permission from Biology and Science Curriculum Studies (BSCS).

Discussion Questions

1. The students might develop an explanation similar to the following: When the tree trunks were light-colored from the gray-green lichen, the birds couldn't see the light-colored moths on the tree trunks. The dark moths were more conspicuous, so the birds ate them, keeping their numbers low. When the tree trunks became dark, the light-colored moths were more conspicuous, so the birds ate them, decreasing their numbers. The dark moths could now blend in with the dark tree trunk. Because the birds couldn't see them, their numbers increased. Accept any explanation that uses the evidence and that demonstrates some effort by the students to understand change in populations.

2. Students should recognize that if the trees were to return to their light color, the environment again would favor the survival of light-colored moths, and their numbers would increase. The birds would be able to spot the dark moths, and the number of dark moths would decrease as the birds ate them. This is what actually happened when pollution controls curbed the production of soot. Scientists currently disagree about whether or not the peppered moths actually evolved; the change in numbers might not reflect a change in gene frequency. Accept any answers that the students can justify with the evidence.

Investigation:
Breakfast for the Birds

explore

Outcomes and Indicators of Success

By the end of this investigation, the students should understand the difference between and the significance of specialization and generalization.

They will demonstrate their knowledge by

- identifying which tools were best suited for picking up particular foods,
- comparing the tools they use in the investigation to actual bird beaks, and
- listing an advantage and a disadvantage for a bird with a specialized beak and for a bird with a generalized beak.

Opportunity for Assessment

During this activity, you will have an opportunity to assess the students' understanding of the significance of specialization and generalization.

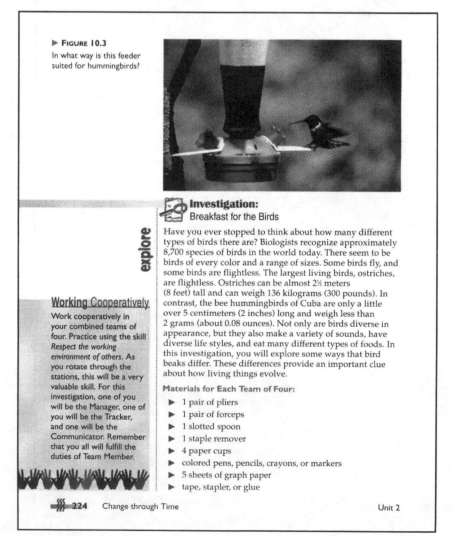

▶ FIGURE 10.3
In what way is this feeder suited for hummingbirds?

Investigation:
Breakfast for the Birds

explore

Have you ever stopped to think about how many different types of birds there are? Biologists recognize approximately 8,700 species of birds in the world today. There seem to be birds of every color and a range of sizes. Some birds fly, and some birds are flightless. The largest living birds, ostriches, are flightless. Ostriches can be almost 2½ meters (8 feet) tall and can weigh 136 kilograms (300 pounds). In contrast, the bee hummingbirds of Cuba are only a little over 5 centimeters (2 inches) long and weigh less than 2 grams (about 0.08 ounces). Not only are birds diverse in appearance, but they also make a variety of sounds, have diverse life styles, and eat many different types of foods. In this investigation, you will explore some ways that bird beaks differ. These differences provide an important clue about how living things evolve.

Materials for Each Team of Four:

▶ 1 pair of pliers
▶ 1 pair of forceps
▶ 1 slotted spoon
▶ 1 staple remover
▶ 4 paper cups
▶ colored pens, pencils, crayons, or markers
▶ 5 sheets of graph paper
▶ tape, stapler, or glue

Working Cooperatively

Work cooperatively in your combined teams of four. Practice using the skill *Respect the working environment of others.* As you rotate through the stations, this will be a very valuable skill. For this investigation, one of you will be the Manager, one of you will be the Tracker, and one will be the Communicator. Remember that you all will fulfill the duties of Team Member.

Advance Preparation

Copy and cut apart BLM 10.1, Description of the 5 Stations, which provides directions for the five stations. (Although you only will need one copy, an extra one will come in handy.) Copy BLM 10.2, Rabbit Outline, to use as a template when you cut out the rabbit silhouettes. In addition to the materials in the student pages, you will need to prepare the following materials and "foods" for each station.

1. Station 1: Prepare a log or piece of firewood with 12 or more holes.

2. Station 2: Prepare a tub or bowl of water with poly- styrene foam pieces floating in it.

3. Station 3: Prepare a tray of 200 mL of sunflower seeds (bird food), enough to cover the tray.

4. Station 4: Cut four rabbit silhouettes from file folders or other heavy paper and put staples all over them about 1 cm apart.

5. Station 5: Prepare a tub full of shredded paper interspersed with roughly 20 rubber fishing worms. You can purchase rubber worms at some fishing tackle stores. You also might substitute large, thick rubber bands for the worms.

You can conduct this investigation in several ways. One way is to set up the five stations and duplicate as many stations as you need to accommodate the number of teams in your class. If you have 32 students in teams of four, you will need eight stations. The easiest stations to duplicate are Stations 3 and 4—the sunflower seeds and the stapled rabbit silhouettes.

Materials

For the entire class:

1 copy of Description of the 5 Stations, BLM 10.1

1 copy of Rabbit Outline, BLM 10.2

For each team of four students:

1 pair of pliers

1 pair of forceps

1 slotted spoon

1 staple remover

4 paper cups

colored pens, pencils, crayons, or markers

5 sheets of graph paper

staplers, tape, or glue

For Station 1:

1 copy of the Station 1 description from BLM 10.1

1 log, or a piece of firewood, with 12 or more holes (1/4" diameter, approximately 1" deep) drilled on one side along the length of the log

2 tbs of rice

For Station 2:

1 copy of the Station 2 description from BLM 10.1

1 tub or large bowl of water

▲ FIGURE 10.4
What kind of advantages might this ostrich have because of its size? What might the disadvantages be?

Process and Procedure

1. Collect the first materials and distribute one tool and one cup to each Team Member.
   These tools will be your "bird beaks." Each person also will need a paper cup to use as a "stomach" at each station.

2. Practice using your bird beak according to the description shown in Figure 10.5.

3. Read the instructions for each of the five stations listed in Figure 10.6.
   At each station you will count the pieces of food you can gather using your tool.

4. Draw a data table in your notebook to record the information you will collect at each station.
   Remember to read the whole procedure to determine how you should construct your data table. Leave space to add information that you might find you need later on.

5. Go to your first station and read the instructions that are posted there.
   Your teacher will assign your team to this station. The Tracker will read aloud the rules for each station you will visit.

Pliers
Use just one hand and close the pliers. Do not use them as a spear. If anything sticks to the pliers, you may remove it with your free hand.

Forceps
Use just one hand to open and close the forceps. Do not use them as a spear.

Slotted Spoon
Hold the handle of the spoon in one hand and use the spoon like a scoop. You can not use your other hand to push things onto the spoon.

Staple Remover
Use just one hand to open and close the staple remover. If anything sticks to the staple remover, you may remove it with your free hand.

▶ FIGURE 10.5
Before you begin this investigation, read the rules for how to operate your bird beak tool.

Chapter 10   How Do Living Systems Change?   **225** ▼

---

600 mL of polystyrene foam pieces (packing material) to cover the surface of the water (Be sure that you don't have the type that dissolves in water.)

4 bowls or 600-mL beakers labeled "stomach"

For Station 3:

1 copy of the Station 3 description from BLM 10.1

1 tray or similar flat vessel to hold sunflower seeds

200 mL of sunflower seeds (bird-feed variety)

1 paper cup labeled "crushed seed"

For Station 4:

1 copy of the Station 4 description from BLM 10.1

4 rabbit silhouettes, cut from file folders, with staples spaced approximately 1 cm apart

1 paper cup marked "used staples"

For Station 5:

1 copy of the Station 5 description from BLM 10.1

1 large tub full of shredded paper (or comparable medium)

20 rubber fishing worms

1 clock, watch, or timer with a second hand

1 paper cutter

Strategies

Getting Started

The purpose of this investigation is to provide the students with a concrete experience that will help them appreciate and explore adaptation and its role in the evolution of organisms by natural selection. By seeing the advantages and dis-advantages of different kinds of bird beaks, students will better understand the mechanism of natural selection.

Process and Procedure

The students should begin by reading through the entire procedure so that they will be able to figure out how to construct their data tables. Each student should construct a data table in his or her notebook for recording the number of pieces of each kind of food (rice, foam pieces, seeds, staples, worms) that each tool (pliers, staple remover, forceps, slotted spoon) collects. You can provide a BLM of a data table or draw a sample data table on the board or on an overhead transparency for the classes that require extra help.

During the active portion of this investigation, you can time the students, telling them when to begin and when to stop collecting food. If you choose this strategy, you also will need to tell the students when to rotate to the next station. In that case, give them roughly three minutes to count their pieces of food and record their teammates' data. Or, instead of setting up stations, you could provide all of the teams with the materials for each station, one at a time. In that case, the students can tell themselves when to begin, and they can continue gathering

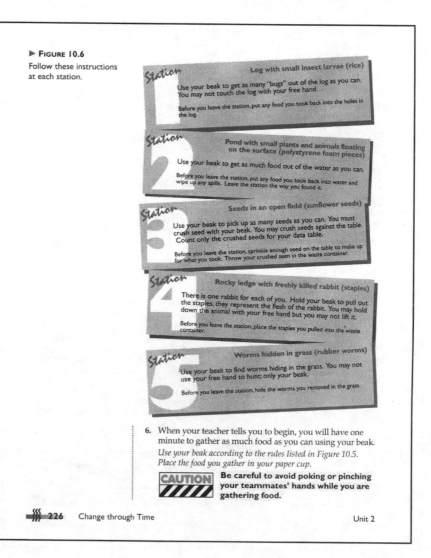

▶ FIGURE 10.6
Follow these instructions at each station.

Station 1 — Log with small insect larvae (rice)
Use your beak to get as many "bugs" out of the log as you can. You may not touch the log with your free hand.
Before you leave the station, put any food you took back into the holes in the log.

Station 2 — Pond with small plants and animals floating on the surface (polystyrene foam pieces)
Use your beak to get as much food out of the water as you can.
Before you leave the station, put any food you took back into water and wipe up any spills. Leave the station the way you found it.

Station 3 — Seeds in an open field (sunflower seeds)
Use your beak to pick up as many seeds as you can. You must crush seed with your beak. You may crush seeds against the table. Count only the crushed seeds for your data table.
Before you leave the station, sprinkle enough seed on the table to make up for what you took. Throw your crushed seen in the waste container.

Station 4 — Rocky ledge with freshly killed rabbit (staples)
There is one rabbit for each of you. Hold your beak to pull out the staples; they represent the flesh of the rabbit. You may hold down the animal with your free hand but you may not lift it.
Before you leave the station, place the staples you pulled into the waste container.

Station 5 — Worms hidden in grass (rubber worms)
Use your beak to find worms hiding in the grass. You may not use your free hand to hunt; only your beak.
Before you leave the station, hide the worms you removed in the grass.

6. When your teacher tells you to begin, you will have one minute to gather as much food as you can using your beak. *Use your beak according to the rules listed in Figure 10.5. Place the food you gather in your paper cup.*

CAUTION Be careful to avoid poking or pinching your teammates' hands while you are gathering food.

Change through Time

Unit 2

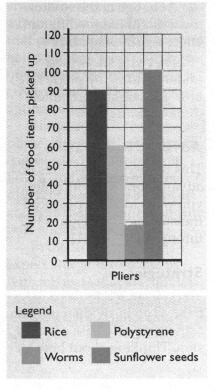

▶ **FIGURE T10.1** The students' bar graphs should look something like the one shown here.

Legend

■ Rice ■ Polystyrene

■ Worms ■ Sunflower seeds

food until there is none left. (Do not give the students a lot of food.) Then let the students ask for the materials for the next station. In either case, have the students set up the stations again after they have recorded their data.

Each Team Member will construct a bar graph that shows the number of pieces of each food that he or she collected. If you are able to provide colored pencils or crayons, students may color the bars on their graphs. Each graph must include a key or a legend for identifying the bars.

While you circulate around the room, check the students' graphs. The graphs should look something like the graph in Figure T10.1. When they have completed their own graphs, have the Team Members combine their team data to make another graph. Give teams time to present their results during a class discussion.

≋ **Wrap Up**

Have the students record their own answers in their notebooks.

1. Answers may vary depending on the teams' results. Based on their data, however, most teams probably will agree with the following: (a) the slotted spoon was the best tool for getting the polystyrene foam pieces; (b) the pair of pliers was the best tool for crushing the bird seed; (c-d) the pair of forceps was the best tool for getting the rice from the log and the worms; and (e) the staple remover was the

7. After each turn, count the number of pieces of food you gathered.

   Notebook entry: Record this number in your data table.

8. Share your data with your teammates.

   Notebook entry: You should record the data for each Team Member.

9. Clean up your station.

   Each station will have instructions that tell you how to leave the food for the next team.

10. Go to the next station and repeat Steps 5 through 9.

    Your teacher will tell the teams when to change stations. If you just completed Station 1, go to Station 2. If you just completed Station 2, go to Station 3, and so on. If you have just completed Station 5, go to Station 1.

    STOP: As you rotate among stations, be sure to respect the working environment of others.

11. Construct a bar graph of the data from your completed data table.

    Each Team Member will make a graph for the tool that he or she used. Label the vertical axis "Number of food pieces," and the horizontal axis "Type of food." With your teammates, decide on a numbering scale for these axes so that you all use the same scale. Also consult with your teammates to decide on a color for making the bars for each type of food. If you have questions about bar graphs, you might review How to Construct a Bar Graph (How To #10).

    Notebook entry: Attach your graphs to your notebook.

12. Combine your team data to make a single graph of all the data.

    Notebook entry: Each Team Member should construct his or her own team graph and attach it to his or her own notebook.

≋ **Wrap Up**

Discuss the following questions with your team and record your own answers in your notebook.

1. Which tool picked up the most of each "food" listed below?

   a. polystyrene foam pieces

   b. sunflower seeds

   c. rice

   d. worms

   e. staples

best tool for pulling the staples (tearing flesh).

2. Many students probably will say that the pair of forceps was the best, because they could pick up more of each kind of food, on average. Accept all answers the students can support with their data.

3. Answers may vary, but they should reflect the data from the graph. The staple remover and slotted spoon probably picked up a lot of only one type of food.

4. Some combined teams might have met with more success because they had practiced once before and because they had more strategies to use. Others might have felt that the larger group was less cohesive, so the temptation to stray was greater. Reward the teams that you observed to be the best at staying with their groups. Have these teams choose a class reward or offer other forms of recognition.

Further Opportunities for Learning

You can extend this activity by providing time for your students to explore using different items to simulate different types of beaks and food sources—for example, a straw or a tea strainer for beaks and water or rice for food sources.

Connections:
Birds and the Environment

explore

Outcomes and Indicators of Success

By the end of this connections, the students should understand the following:

1. Different bird beaks are specialized for different tasks.

They will show their understanding by comparing the beaks of five birds to the four tools they used in the investigation Breakfast for the Birds.

2. A change in the environment might have a different effect on different birds.

They will show their understanding by predicting how a drought might affect different birds.

Advance Preparation

This connections requires no advance preparation, unless you want to make overhead transparencies of Figure 10.7 through Figure 10.11.

Strategies

You can conduct this connections as an individual or team activity, or as a class discussion. Thinking about how an

2. Which tool or tools picked up large amounts of many types of food?

3. Which tool or tools picked up a large amount of only one type of food?

4. Why was it important during this activity to respect the working environment of others?

Connections:
Birds and the Environment

Different bird beaks work like different tools. Examine the birds shown in Figures 10.7 through 10.11 and read the descriptions. Then decide which of the tools that your team used in Breakfast for the Birds most closely resembles each bird's beak.

Imagine that a bird has a beak that is **specialized**, or useful, for getting only one type of food. How might such a beak be an advantage? How might it be a disadvantage?

Imagine that a bird has a **generalized** beak that is useful for getting many types of food. What might be some advantages and disadvantages of such a beak?

Now that you have more knowledge about how some birds eat, see whether you can predict how a change in the environment might affect the different birds. Read the following questions, and then share your ideas in a class discussion.

1. During a drought, many bodies of water become dry. Which of the birds shown in Figures 10.7 through 10.11 might not be able to gather food if the bodies of water and mud flats dry up?

2. During some droughts, many flowering and fruit-bearing plants die as well. Which birds would this probably affect first?

3. Imagine that during one drought a young snipe hatches. Unlike the other snipes in the population, this young bird develops a short beak. This snipe is able to crack open some seeds. How might this beak be a disadvantage or an advantage to the bird?

▲ FIGURE 10.7
A grosbeak uses its strong beak to crack open seeds.

▶ FIGURE 10.8
A bald eagle uses its curved beak to tear flesh from fish and other animals.

228   Change through Time

Unit 2

Event-Based Science (EBS)

Publisher:	**Dale Seymour Publications**
	Pearson Learning
	299 Jefferson Road
	P.O. Box 480
	Parsippany, NJ 07054
	(800) 526-9907
Website:	**http://www.pearsonlearning.com/ dsp-publications/**
Year Published:	**1995**
Developer:	**Montgomery County Public Schools, Rockville, MD**
Website:	**http://www.mcps.k12.md.us/ departments/eventscience**
Grade Levels:	**6–9**
Science Domains:	**Earth science, life science, and physical science**

Overview

The *Event-Based Science (EBS)* series is a modular program with a focus on current events. The *EBS* design emphasizes the role and importance of science in the lives of ordinary people. Students are expected to learn scientific concepts and content, as well as the skills to analyze problems, ask critical questions, explain events, and develop a final product involving applications of the science they have learned. Each *EBS* module creates interdisciplinary linkages. The real-event focus, coupled with a social issues orientation, allows for connections with language arts, social studies, and mathematics.

> "*Event-Based Science* is unlike any science program I've ever used. It truly involves the kids in real-world situations. Kids have to become a paleontologist or a roller coaster designer, or whatever it is, and they have to do jobs in that field. They have to brief their teammates about their particular jobs. The program really develops awareness about the subject like no other curriculum I've seen."
> — Science teacher

EBS is not a stand-alone curriculum. Teachers generally use one or two of these modules a year, selecting particular units based on the district's science standards, their students' interests, and their own knowledge of the specific topics addressed in the modules. In conjunction with other instructional materials, *EBS* modules can be used to create a comprehensive middle-grades science program. By design, teachers and students have to supplement each module with additional data about a specific event from various resources included as part of the materials, or suggested by the program.

Curriculum Focus

The *EBS* series has 18 modules, each of which focuses on different themes and concepts across the domains of earth, life, and physical sciences. The modules can be used at all middle-grades levels.

Earth Science

Asteroids!: An asteroid impact 65 million years ago is the context for studying solar system astronomy. Students explore solar system orbits and develop an understanding of earth's place in the solar system. The unit also focuses on collisions with asteroids, comets, and other bodies, and creates opportunities for correlation of mass extinctions with asteroid impacts throughout geologic time.

Earthquakes!: The 1989 Loma Prieta earthquake serves as the context for studying concepts of faults, earth structure, plate tectonics, liquefaction, and landslides.

Flood!: The Great Flood of 1993 is the context for studying concepts related to river and stream dynamics, erosion, deposition, and floods.

Gold Rush!: The California Gold Rush of 1849 provides the context for the study of rocks and minerals, including concepts of density, solubility, and magnetism; crystal properties and crystallization; igneous, metamorphic, and sedimentary rocks; and physical and chemical separation techniques.

Hurricane!: Hurricane Andrew is the context for studying air pressure, humidity, wind, hurricane formation, and the hydrologic cycle.

Oil Spill!: The Exxon Valdez oil spill provides the context for exploration of oceanographic concepts, including the study of tides, currents, marine life, and ocean-floor topography.

Tornado!: The context for exploring weather concepts in this module is the tornado that destroyed a Piedmont, Alabama, church in 1994. Students study concepts related to severe weather events and conditions.

Toxic Leak!: This module involves the study of geological concepts related to groundwater, including permeability and porosity of soils, subsurface layering, surface and subsurface profiles, wells, and water supply.

Volcano!: This module uses the Mount Pinatubo eruption in the Philippine Islands to study the forces that shape the earth, such as earth structure, plate tectonics, volcanoes, and volcanic hazards.

Physical Science

First Flight!: Study of aviation firsts such as the Wright brothers' first flight at Kitty Hawk and the round-the-world flight of the Voyager provide the contexts for studying the physics of flight.

Fraud!: This module sets the study of chemistry within the context of investigations of art forgeries. Over the course of the module, students develop a set of protocols for authenticating works of art.

Thrill Ride!: The context for this module is the opening of a new thrill ride at an amusement park. Students investigate inertia, force, potential and kinetic energy, energy transformations, friction, weight, velocity, acceleration, centripetal force, free fall, and action/reaction.

Life Science

Blight!: The study of plants is set within the context of the Irish potato famine. Students work in teams to produce television shows about plants and plant diseases. Teams focus on crops and diseases in different regions of the United States.

Gold Medal!: Wilma Rudolph's battle with polio and her victory at the 1960 Rome Olympics set the context for the study of the muscular and skeletal systems, including the structure and function of muscles, bones, and joints.

Outbreak!: This module uses the 1995 outbreak of the Ebola virus in Zaire to study diseases and immunity, including infectious diseases, microorganisms, transmission of diseases, adaptation, environmental interactions, and natural and acquired immunity.

The following modules are currently under development.

Survive!: The context for this module is the discovery of deformed frogs in a small Minnesota pond. Students study animals, animal diversity, and adaptation. They study the effects of environmental changes on the various animal populations on a fictitious island. At the end of the module, they create a museum display about the island and its changing animal populations.

Blackout!: Power blackouts in the West and Northeast set the context for the study of electricity and solar activity. Students work together in power-company teams, recreating and analyzing the events that occurred on the day the blackout struck their fictitious companies.

Fire!: The Yellowstone National Park Fires of 1988 and the controversial issue of fire suppression policy provide the context for studies of the chemical nature of fire and the role of fire in the natural environment. Students study the components of fires, fire prevention, and fire retardants.

Curriculum Format

Similar activities and instructional strategies are used in each *EBS* module. These include open-ended and hands-on activities, statistical analysis, performance assessments, cooperative groups, and guided discussions. Modules generally take between four and six weeks to complete. Each module includes the following sections:

Story: Gives accounts of a real event and introduces students to the work of the module.

Discovery File: Provides background information about the scientific concept(s) involved.

In the News: Supplies articles about the current event(s) being studied.

On the Job: Includes information about job responsibilities represented in the module tasks and interviews with professionals in the field.

Student Voices: Provides personal accounts from students who actually experienced the event.

Every module follows the following instructional steps:

Hook: Captures and holds student interest in the event and the scientific concepts involved.

Discussion of the Event: Promotes students' participation and elicits their current knowledge of the related scientific concepts.

Task: Invites students to investigate a particular role related to the event under investigation. Students in their cooperative groups must refine their knowledge and explore new concepts and processes related to each other's roles.

Hands-on Instructional Activities: Provide students with strategies to search for the information they need to complete the task.

Final Product: Represents students' applications of the science learned in the module.

For instance, in the *Earthquake!* module, the hook used to generate interest in earthquakes is videotape of news coverage of the Loma Prieta earthquake in California. The video allows students to observe the swift and devastating force of a major earthquake and encourages them to think about the power unleashed by this natural event. Students then have small group discussions and read newspaper articles providing some additional information about the earthquake. The discussion sessions are intended to uncover some of students' major preconceptions and allow teachers to assess their current knowledge.

Students investigate the science through a series of hands-on activities that may be interdisciplinary in nature. Students choose "expert" roles for their work on the final team product. As they research their task, students simulate the kind of teamwork and problem solving that occurs in workplaces and communities.

Academic Rigor

The *EBS* program targets concepts from standards for "Science in Personal and Social Perspectives." Its website describes the program's alignment with selected standards. Each module supplies background information students need in order to understand the targeted concepts and provides hands-on opportunities to compile the data needed to answer emerging questions. A major part of the work requires students to predict, make inferences, draw conclusions, and justify their conclusions. The *EBS* approach fosters understanding of the nature of science and encourages students to develop habits of mind common to scientists.

Connections to Other Disciplines

EBS materials suggest activities that encourage connections among technology, mathematics, social studies, and language arts. However, teachers have the flexibility to decide whether, and how, to collaborate with other subject-area teachers. In spite of the cross-disciplinary approach, teachers indicate that the science does not lose its integrity. One teacher who has used *EBS* observed,

> "It brings in social studies—where things happen and why they happen. Through its emphasis on current events, it makes connections with the outside world. It has math components, too, but it is basically based in good science."

Assessment

The modules suggest various strategies for assessing students' work. Each science activity has detailed, specifically designed assessments to explore students' growth and learning. Specific performance assessments are embedded within activities and tasks, and a general performance assessment is included as the final project at the end of the unit. Rubrics are available for these assessments.

One teacher described the culminating project from the *Thrill Ride!* module as follows:

> "The task is to create a ride and to show how each of Newton's laws are at work on the ride. To do this, students have to use all the associated terminology correctly and be able to explain it. And best, the kids are always so excited about it. It's amazing! We put all the rides together and create this big amusement park. The kids all demonstrate their rides for you and tell you how they work—where the potential energy and the kinetic energy are. It's a great culminating activity."

Equity

The curriculum materials address the needs of students with varied learning styles and backgrounds by offering students a range of activities that promote science learning. By assuming different roles and responsibilities in developing their final products, students are able to approach the science from different perspectives. The activities also allow students from typically underserved populations to simulate professional roles that are not typically part of their families' work experiences.

EBS modules offer a variety of opportunities for students to communicate their science understanding, both individually and within their task-based groups. Students present their findings in both oral and written form and create a final product. Additionally, the "News" section of the *EBS* website includes some guidance about modifications and extensions for use with special needs students.

Developmental Appropriateness

EBS seeks to place the study of science in a meaningful, interdisciplinary context in which students can see the role that science plays in everyday life. It does so by having students explore actual phenomena. Tasks designed for student work emphasize both scientific relevance and age-appropriate skills and experience, and create opportunities for cooperative learning and teamwork, as well as independent research. Students can make many of their own decisions about their work and get to work independently and in groups to collect, analyze, and synthesize information. Over the course of each module, students have the opportunity to build on their prior knowledge and develop new, deeper understanding.

Teaching Resources and Support

Print Materials

Teacher's Guide: The teacher's guide offers a detailed explanation of the philosophy and instructional approach of the program. The introduction provides information about the flow of the teaching and learning experiences. Each teacher's guide also includes the following information:

- Suggestions for classroom management.
- Suggestions for facilitating group work, addressing the needs of all students, creating a "student-centered" classroom, facilitating discussions, increasing student participation, and sustaining student interest.
- Strategies for supplementing activities.
- References to relevant organizations and other resources.

Student's Edition: The student's edition for each module explains the various components of the module, describes how to use them effectively, and explains the purpose of each section of the module. The student's edition also includes resources and background information, including copies of newspaper accounts of the event and profiles of professionals whose roles are relevant to the work of each module.

Professional Development

The Event-Based Science Institute, Inc. (EBSII) in Rockville, Maryland, offers professional development workshops for districts considering the purchase of *EBS* materials. EBSII, in collaboration with the Montgomery County Public Schools, is also developing a teacher training CD-ROM. For additional information, contact EBSII at (301) 806-7252. Upcoming professional development opportunities are listed on the "Event-Based Science Training" page on the *EBS* website.

Other Resources

The *EBS* website offers the following support for teachers:

- News coverage and updated information about each event, with suggestions for supplementing, modifying, or exchanging the activities according to current events.
- Links to organizations and resources relevant to each event.
- Teaching suggestions by practitioners who have used the modules.
- Correction alerts.
- Remote-sensing activities sponsored by NASA designed to augment selected modules.
- Information about new modules being developed.
- Information about alignment of the modules with standards.

Teacher Hints and Guidance

The activities in the *EBS* modules require few materials, engage students, and result in interesting, well-researched final products. Teachers' major caution to new users involves the need to find appropriate supplementary materials for the modules. Teachers made the following suggestions and observations.

Finding supplementary materials: Teachers generally do not mind having to supplement the materials because they believe "the information the *EBS* activities give you is good." There are many ways to supplement *EBS*, for example, with encyclopedias, digital lab materials, and information from archives.

Preparation: For novice teachers, the set-up of students' final products may be difficult. Teachers find that creating tight structures for students' work often helps to make the modules run more smoothly. The flexibility the program offers can be problematic or exhilarating, depending on the teacher's individual style and comfort with ambiguity.

Facilities/Schedule: Teachers commented on the need for a reasonable amount of physical space when students work on *EBS* modules. Classroom tables, rather than individual desks, facilitate group work. One veteran *EBS* teacher also observed, "It gets kind of messy. For certain activities, you've got to spread papers out."

Classroom Management: Students are engaged in many different activities at one time. This requires strong management skills on the part of the teacher.

Teacher Experience: For teachers who are experienced with open-ended processes, the instructional strategies used in *EBS* will be familiar. Teachers who want to move toward this approach to teaching will find *EBS* consistent with their efforts. One teacher observed, "*EBS* gives those of us who are a little more adventurous a license to do that." However, teachers who are not comfortable managing investigation-based activities may find these materials difficult.

Student Support: The *EBS* website provides additional information to students working on various tasks in the modules. It brings them more recent research data than is available in the modules, and refers them to real-life situations that can extend the material in their guide.

Sample Lesson

The following is an excerpt from the teacher's guide for the module *Earthquake!* Reproduced with permission of the Event-Based Science Project, Montgomery County Public Schools.

What Is Liquefaction?

Purpose
To investigate conditions that produce liquefaction during an earthquake.

Materials
- 2 large clear containers
- Tubing
- Water
- 2 rocks
- Sand
- Gravel

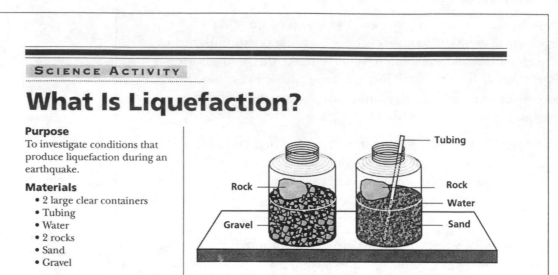

Activity

Background: You and your partners are experts on earthquakes. Your company just received a contract from the Alaskan state government to evaluate two possible building sites for a new state office building within Anchorage. Both sites are frequently shaken by earthquakes, but one site is located on sandy soil that is constantly saturated with water and the other site lies on bedrock. You and your partners decide to conduct an experiment before you write your recommendation.

1. Read Solid to Liquid in the Blink of an Eye, page 22.

San Francisco Marina District

2. Using the materials listed, construct a model of the two sites.

Note: When you add water to the sand, add it slowly and watch it fill the spaces between the grains. Keep adding water until it is just below the surface of the sand.

3. Wait a minute or two for everything to settle, then pound on the table with your fist to simulate an earthquake.

4. Pay particular attention to the rock. It represents a building or other heavy object on the surface.

Conclusions
Now prepare a brief memo for your supervisor in which you comment on the suitability of the two sites. Make your recommendation based on your understanding of liquefaction. State the reasons for your recommendation in words your supervisor will understand. (She is not a scientist.)

Objective

Apply knowledge of liquefaction in making a decision about appropriate building location.

Science Outcomes

- Processes of Science

- Applications of Science

Science Concepts

- Liquefaction

- Fluid mixture

- Saturation

Description

In this activity, task teams should be split into smaller groups of three students. Students will investigate liquefaction by completing a laboratory activity. The activity simulates what happens during an earthquake to unconsolidated soil that is saturated with water. This activity works best if the sand is saturated. Students use the knowledge gained from the laboratory activity and an article on liquefaction found in the text to advise the Alaskan state government on appropriate building site selection. A memorandum model should be provided before teams prepare their recommendation. Your principal probably has several from which you may choose.

Materials

For groups of three students:
- 2 large, clear containers

- Tubing

- Water

- 2 rocks

- Sand

- Gravel

- Solid to Liquid in the Blink of an Eye (student edition, page 22)

Scoring Rubric

Observation of students as they conduct the experiment, then a formal evaluation of the quality of their recommendations, will result in both individual and group assessment of this activity.

- memorandum is neat and well written, contains a logical recommendation supported by data = 2 points

- memorandum fails in one aspect but is complete = 1 point

- memorandum is incomplete = 0 points

Foundations and Challenges to Encourage Technology-Based Science (FACETS)

Developer/ Distributor:	**American Chemical Society** **1155 Sixteenth Street, NW** **Washington, DC 20036** **(800) 227-5558**
Website:	**http://www.acs.org/education/ curriculum/facets.html**
Year Published:	**1996**
Grade Levels:	**6–8**
Science Domains:	**Earth science, life science, and physical science**

Overview

Foundations and Challenges to Encourage Technology-Based Science (FACETS) is a set of 24 stand-alone, interdisciplinary investigation guides organized into three series of eight. Each guide introduces concepts and skills from science, mathematics, and other curricular areas on a "need to know" basis. The modules assume that science teachers will work with other content-area teachers in the school to design cross-curricular experiences for students. The reading level of Series 1 is suitable for grades 6 and 7, and Series 2 and 3 are suitable for grades 7 and 8.

> " *FACETS* works for a broad range of students. It's employing different skills and it's a much more hands-on oriented program. Some of the kids were accustomed to using traditional methods where they were reading and writing and using memorization skills and perhaps public speaking. But this program requires them to make inferences and analyze data and things like that. So it's a new ball game."
>
> — Science teacher

The curriculum engages students in scientific inquiry in the context of issues related to technology and society. Units focus on a set of problem-solving skills that reflect the processes and strategies used by scientists in investigative research: defining a problem, finding information, testing explanations, using models and simulations, collecting data, checking and analyzing data, drawing conclusions, communicating findings, and reflecting on and connecting ideas.

FACETS can be used as a complete curriculum package, or individual modules can be used to supplement other curriculum materials. Although each of the modules can stand alone as an instructional unit, they work best when used in the recommended order.

Curriculum Focus

Whatever the content focus of the modules, the curriculum always includes problem-solving skills. These comprise a series of strategies that are flagged throughout the individual activities, such as testing explanations, analyzing and checking data, and drawing conclusions. Brief descriptions of the content of the individual modules within each series follow.

Series 1

Keeping Fit: Students critically examine the question, "Does exercise make a difference in the health of a young adult?" They learn about their circulatory and respiratory systems as they collect heart and breathing rate data before and after exercise.

Food Substitutes: Students examine the properties of common food substitutes in terms of taste, texture, and behavior in a processed food product. They do a store survey to find out what substitutes are available and how they are used in food products.

Packaging: Students investigate the mathematics of package design, as well as the science behind the packaging materials. As a final project, students design and construct a package for a single serving "designer" cookie that will protect it and keep it fresh.

Weather and Health: Students examine the possible relationship between weather changes and human health changes. As students conduct a weather study, they also collect health information to try to pinpoint trends.

Investigating Buildings: Students investigate their own school building as a structure specially built to fit the needs of its occupants. They construct a plan of the school drawn to scale and interview students and staff. Based on their analysis, they redesign their school.

Earthquakes: Students learn about where earthquakes happen and how structures are built to withstand the shock waves that result. They play the roles of members of a building design company that wants to expand its market to earthquake-prone areas.

Changing Shorelines: Students investigate the causes of and the rate of erosion. They simulate what would happen to the shoreline if developers were allowed to develop an island for recreational purposes.

Shrinking Farmlands: Students examine the causes and effects of farmland erosion due to wind and water. They explore the total amount of arable land available in the world, then simulate what happens to topsoil when exposed to flooding, high winds, and rainfall.

Series 2

Communicable Diseases: Students engage in simulations and laboratory activities that illustrate how communicable diseases are spread and how they are controlled.

Growing Older: Students investigate what happens to people, both physically and mentally, as they age. Students work with an older partner as a data resource throughout the course of the module.

Structures and Behavior: Students learn about behavioral science by studying the behavior of their peers. They learn how to observe behavior, how to recognize patterns, and how to record them systematically.

What's in Our Food?: Students investigate food additives by analyzing product labels. They group additives according to function, then engage in laboratory activities to examine the effects of various thickening agents and mixing technologies on a common mixture.

Food from Our Land: Students investigate the ways in which farmers can maximize the yield on the land they have. Students grow plants to investigate the effects of overwatering and overplanting.

Cleaning Water: Students examine the types of impurities that can get into water systems. Role playing employees in a filtration company, they work with the company's research and development department to make sure that water filters are developed to suit the water problems of their marketing districts.

Acid Rain: Students learn about the causes and effects of acid rain problems. They learn about pH and how it is used to test for the presence of acid rain. They construct and carry out a long-term study to determine whether they have an acid rain problem in their area.

A Sunken Ship: Students figure out whether the cargo from a ship that sank 50 years ago is salvageable by determining what conditions are like at the depth of the ship. They conduct laboratory experiments to determine what parts of the cargo may be damaged and use the financial sections of local newspapers to look up the prices of gold, silver, and platinum. The end product is a proposal to a funding agency requesting support for the salvage effort.

Series 3

Threads: Students investigate the physical and chemical properties of a variety of common fibers from the perspective of what would be most appropriate for a school-related garment. They design a garment and explain why they selected particular fibers.

Oil Spills: Students explore the causes and effects of oil spills in a number of settings. They use laboratory simulations to determine the behavior of oil on the surface of water, what happens when dispersing agents are added to the oil and water mix, and how the oil can be skimmed or otherwise cleaned up.

Managing Crop Pests: Students investigate the types of pests that can destroy farmers' crops. They model what happens when pesticides leach into groundwater, test water for dissolved materials, and research pest management techniques.

Investigating Populations: Students learn how populations grow and decline, and the major effect that carrying capacity has on a population. They collect demographic information about their own local population, then compare these demographics to those of populations in other parts of the world.

Climate and Farming: Students learn about factors that affect climate in various parts of the world. They tie climatic conditions to the crops that are grown in different parts of the world and hypothesize about the effects of global warming on future crop distributions.

Energy for the Future: Students use their school as a test site, examining ways in which energy is used and energy sources are conserved in their building. They investigate alternative energy sources and use their data on energy to suggest methods to improve the energy efficiency of their school.

Transportation Systems: Students investigate ways in which people and goods get to and from their school building. They explore the role of energy in transportation systems, and the history of transportation. They suggest a way to redesign the school's transportation system.

Handling Information: Students find out the many ways in which information is communicated within and around their school. They explore the processes of encoding, transmission, and decoding of information in face-to-face and long-distance situations. The module focuses on the science behind the communication and the social implications of rapidly improving communication technology.

Curriculum Format

Modules typically begin with an introduction to the topic followed by approximately six activities. Each module takes two to four weeks to complete.

Every module follows this pattern:

Big Question: Provides the student with background information relevant to the topic under study.

Introduction: Sets the scene for the investigation.

Activities: Offer a set of hands-on experiences presented in four sections:

- How To Go About It—a range of processes and procedures to help students engage in scientific study in an organized way.
- Conclusions—key questions about the activity for students to consider.
- Reflections—a look back at the entire module that helps provide an answer to the big question.
- Looking At—information that teachers and students access as needed throughout the module.

The teacher's role is to be more of a facilitator, consultant, and organizer than provider of information. Students work in collaborative groups of three or four to explore questions and define problems. The activities offer suggestions to both the teacher and the students on strategies for successful group work.

Academic Rigor

FACETS aims at developing students' understanding of the relationship between science and technology, including the role of technology in the evolution of science as well as its role in learning science. Much of the program's focus is on "Standards for Science in Personal and Social Perspectives," but modules also address concepts related to other *National Science Education Standards,* including "Science as Inquiry" and "History and Nature of Science."

FACETS is built around student investigations that focus on particular topics and issues, involve hands-on activities, and evoke critical thinking skills. Each module places the responsibility for designing and carrying out investigations into students' hands. Investigations provide students with opportunities to explore questions in depth and involve a range of processes and procedures that help students to organize their work.

The curriculum uses these active investigations, problem solving, and open-ended tasks to develop conceptual understanding. The many different types of problems students investigate elicit a variety of problem-solving strategies. Students act as scientists during all of their investigations: they are continually asked to question, identify variables, and assess data. They need to justify conclusions and apply concepts to different circumstances. Investigations become increasingly more complex and open-ended. Students must frequently consider different points of view, and one module in each series asks students to conduct an in-depth investigation that specifically focuses on addressing an issue from different perspectives.

Connections to Other Disciplines

FACETS investigations offer opportunities to make connections between science and technology, mathematics, language arts, and social studies, and all subjects are seen as tools that teachers and students can use to carry out the investigations. For example, students must communicate their thoughts and reasoning through small group discussions, class presentations, and written and oral communication. Students employ various mathematical models, such as graphs, Venn diagrams, geometric models, scale drawings, and scale models. Students also have to apply what they have learned to contexts outside the classroom.

Assessment

Students are encouraged to track their own learning process. Reflecting and connecting sections at the end of each activity help students see how all the work they are doing fits together. These sections also give teachers a chance to assess how the investigations are progressing and guide them in adjusting instruction.

The modules also recommend that teachers use additional methods for assessing student progress, including portfolios, performance assessment, debates, and sets of questions (although the materials do not provide specific guidance for developing and carrying out these assessments).

A separate assessment guide that accompanies the curriculum provides teachers with information about embedding assessment into activities, developing scoring tools, scoring and grading, and involving students in assessment.

Equity

Students investigate real-world problems, which in some cases involve culturally diverse groups from around the world. Students are guided to include in their research the contributions that groups in different regions of the world have made to the history of science.

Teachers are also encouraged to take advantage of resources in the local community, including knowledgeable colleagues, representatives of the community, and parents, in order to enrich the experiences that students have in the classroom. A number of the learning activities provide opportunities for students to make connections in their community.

Modules support the learning of concepts and skills through a mixture of approaches that suit a variety of learning styles. Opportunities to draw pictures or diagrams, make graphs, design models, and create displays are integrated into every module. Students design their own investigations and formulate their own approaches and strategies.

The "Reflections" sections at the end of each activity and at the end of the module encourage students to consider how the work all students have done has contributed to their own learning.

Developmental Appropriateness

The curriculum places the responsibility for designing and carrying out investigations into the hands of the students. Each module's investigations provide students with a wide variety of choices for investigating the natural and designed world. Topics include very personal subjects as well as global issues and societal challenges. Proposed activities reflect situations relevant to students' lives and the materials encourage students to make connections to local community issues and concerns.

FACETS provides numerous opportunities for collaborative activities as well as independent work. Students often work in groups to explore questions and define problems.

Teaching Resources and Support

Print Materials

Teacher's Guide: The introduction to each teacher's guide provides information about the *FACETS* program as a whole—philosophy, curriculum connections, module collection (i.e., descriptions of the modules), and investigation strategies. A section entitled "Working with *FACETS*" describes *FACETS'* instructional style, explains the reflections on learning, and offers advice about time management.

Specific to each module are the following sections of the teacher's guide:

- Investigation Strategies: A range of processes and procedures to help students engage in scientific study in an organized way. Each activity suggests the relevant scientific strategies in a sequence that is specific to each investigation.
- Module Content: Description of the activities specific to each module.
- Module Time-Line: Chart that suggests the number of class periods and days needed for each activity.
- Materials: List of all the materials needed to teach the module. (Modules use everyday materials that teachers collect.)

- Background Information: Information for the teacher about the topic under study and tips about logistics.
- Sidebars: Tips and hints for particular activities and discussions.

Student Book: Each module includes a student book which contains the investigations and activities that students will do. The student book provides students with questions to investigate, ideas and suggestions about activities, sample charts, data tables, presentation formats, "special notes," and student readings.

Professional Development

FACETS Connections (a teacher support laser disk) and an assessment guide for teachers are available from the developer, the American Chemical Society (ACS). The Education Division of ACS also offers professional development. For more information about the laser disk, assessment guide, or professional development, contact the ACS or visit its website.

Teacher Hints and Guidance

Teacher Role: FACETS is designed to provide a framework for the teacher to take on a new role in the classroom. Students assume the lead in the investigations, and teachers guide them through this process. Taking on this role requires a shift away from traditional teaching strategies.

Instructional Strategies: Throughout the modules, activities are followed by discussion questions, but the materials do not always provide guidelines for written assignments to accompany the activities. Teachers who have used the curriculum suggest the following strategies to fill this and other gaps in the program:

- Students maintain their own record or log books which may include class notes, collected data and charts, answers to any discussion questions the group has completed, or a written explanation of what task or job within the group they completed each day.
- Each group or individual records additional research questions based on what they have learned.
- Students complete assessments that evaluate their participation.

- For oral presentations, provide clear directions or rubrics before students begin the task.
- Set up conference times for each group throughout the investigation and upon completion of a module.

Sample Lesson

The following is an excerpt from the teacher's edition of *Earthquakes*. Copyright 1996. Reproduced with permission from the American Chemical Society.

Pull resource materials from the library on buildings in earthquake zones around the world.

Some of the most fragile-looking buildings are those that can move with the ground as it shifts. Rigid structures can only take so much stress, then their materials have to give.

Skyscrapers that have a low center of gravity tend to withstand earthquake vibrations more successfully than other designs. More specifically, this means that the bulk of a building's weight is close to the ground, giving it a wide base and narrower peak.

Steel reinforced frames provide additional stability to skyscrapers, as well. The strongest points of these frames are where the cross members join one another. On soft, unconsolidated ground, a short, stiff building gets added rigidity with diagonal steel supports added to the framework.

Another way that buildings are designed to withstand earthquakes is by building them on floating platforms.

ACTIVITY 6	CAN THE RISKS OF EARTHQUAKE DAMAGE BE REDUCED?

If we cannot prevent earthquakes from happening, what can be done to minimize the risks to humans and the buildings they occupy? Today, seismologists, scientists who study movements in the Earth's crust, have learned a great deal about earthquakes. Their observations and measurements can sometimes help them to predict where earthquakes may happen. Buildings and other structures can be designed to cope better with tremors and shock waves caused by earthquakes. Emergency services and systems can be developed to swing into action at the first signs of an earthquake alert. But how are building designs tested before they are built?

You are going to work in a group of about 4 students.

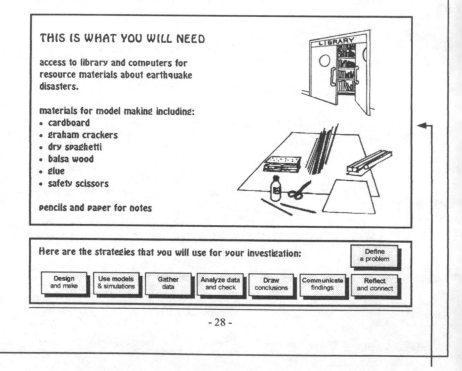

THIS IS WHAT YOU WILL NEED

access to library and computers for resource materials about earthquake disasters.

materials for model making including:
- cardboard
- graham crackers
- dry spaghetti
- balsa wood
- glue
- safety scissors

pencils and paper for notes

Here are the strategies that you will use for your investigation:

| Design and make | Use models & simulations | Gather data | Analyze data and check | Draw conclusions | Communicate findings | Reflect and connect | Define a problem |

- 28 -

Other materials that your students might want to use can include poster board, popsicle sticks, coffee stirrers, licorice sticks, etc. Encourage them to look around their houses to find and bring in as many of the materials that they want to use as possible.

Scale is an important consideration when your students are designing and testing their models of earthquake-resistant structures. You may need to take time to review how objects are scaled up and down and why.

Again, this is a place where the interrelationships between materials and design are important. A material such as balsa wood may be perfectly adequate for a very small scale structure. Once that same structure is scaled up, however, the mass of the entire structure increases proportionately, and the light balsa wood cannot provide sufficient support. The structure collapses.

Often, earthquake-resistant buildings are a combination of materials that provide support to the structure while maintaining their flexibility. They can keep a building up, yet allow it to move with the ground as the Earth quakes.

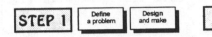

STEP 1 | Define a problem | Design and make

HOW TO GO ABOUT IT

An obvious way to protect lives and prevent injury from earthquakes is to avoid the construction of buildings in earthquake zones at all. But this can be very difficult and also very expensive. Imagine trying to move everyone out of San Francisco to a new San Francisco in another part of the country!

Predicting earthquakes also helps. If there is enough warning time, people can get away from buildings to safe areas before the earthquake hits. But seismology is a young science and it is still very difficult to make accurate predictions. Research needed is also very expensive.

Since most of the immediate deaths in earthquakes happen because of building collapse, there are two possibilities:

1   design the building so that it will absorb the shock waves;

2   make the buildings from materials that are lightweight, causing less injury to people when the buildings collapse.

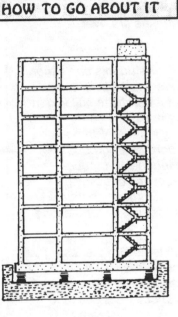

Architects and engineers designing buildings or bridges need to test how they will stand up to earthquakes. Obviously, they cannot do this with the real thing. Instead, they have to conduct design tests before construction begins.

There are several ways this can be done. One way is to build a model of the structure and test it. Another is to test parts of the real building before it is put together (such as door frames, ceiling beams or a foundation pile.)

Tests can also be done using computer simulations. These have been developed by studying all the data that have been collected about how structures behave during actual earthquakes.

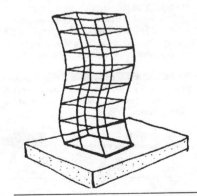

- 29 -

Before making their models, be sure that your students have done research on the various types of structures that have been successful in withstanding earthquakes. Japan, in particular, has experimented with a number of building designs and materials that are still standing when the quakes are over.

Your students can either design and build a model of a complete building to test, or they can collaborate with one or more other groups of students to produce sections of buildings, which they can then assemble before testing.

Videotaping the testing will provide a visual record of the events. The tapes of various tests could be edited by a team of students to document the best designes for the final reports to the company's chief executive officer.

To simulate earthquakes, you can either procure a shaker table (which will give you a side-to-side movement,) or suggest that your students test their structures atop a water filled rubber pillow or mattress. Although the water mattress will give waves that are more like the surface waves of an earthquake, it is difficult to control the strength of the waves produced by pressing down on one end of the mattress.

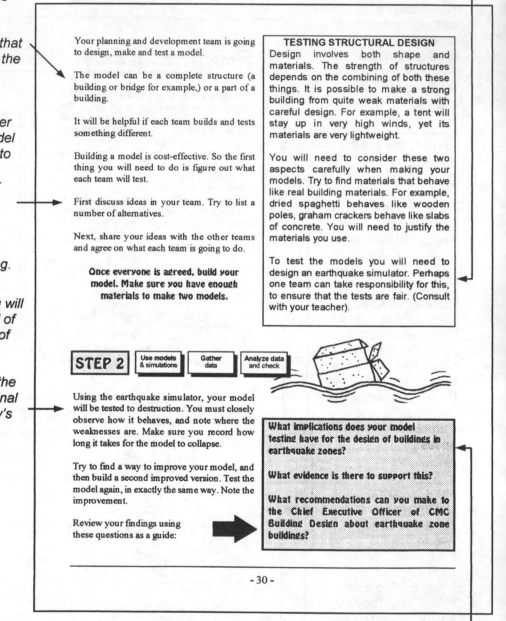

Your planning and development team is going to design, make and test a model.

The model can be a complete structure (a building or bridge for example,) or a part of a building.

It will be helpful if each team builds and tests something different.

Building a model is cost-effective. So the first thing you will need to do is figure out what each team will test.

First discuss ideas in your team. Try to list a number of alternatives.

Next, share your ideas with the other teams and agree on what each team is going to do.

Once everyone is agreed, build your model. Make sure you have enough materials to make two models.

TESTING STRUCTURAL DESIGN
Design involves both shape and materials. The strength of structures depends on the combining of both these things. It is possible to make a strong building from quite weak materials with careful design. For example, a tent will stay up in very high winds, yet its materials are very lightweight.

You will need to consider these two aspects carefully when making your models. Try to find materials that behave like real building materials. For example, dried spaghetti behaves like wooden poles, graham crackers behave like slabs of concrete. You will need to justify the materials you use.

To test the models you will need to design an earthquake simulator. Perhaps one team can take responsibility for this, to ensure that the tests are fair. (Consult with your teacher).

STEP 2 | Use models & simulations | Gather data | Analyze data and check

Using the earthquake simulator, your model will be tested to destruction. You must closely observe how it behaves, and note where the weaknesses are. Make sure you record how long it takes for the model to collapse.

Try to find a way to improve your model, and then build a second improved version. Test the model again, in exactly the same way. Note the improvement.

Review your findings using these questions as a guide:

What implications does your model testing have for the design of buildings in earthquake zones?

What evidence is there to support this?

What recommendations can you make to the Chief Executive Officer of CMC Building Design about earthquake zone buildings?

Be sure that your students know why they are making and testing two models. Remind them of the cost-effectiveness of models: much cheaper than testing out the real thing to destruction!

This last session will give your students the opportunity to pull together all of their information and findings over the course of the module. You may find it a good strategy to have them produce their plans for designing earthquake resistant buildings in the form of a report and presentation. They should also include a budget summary in their report, showing that they achieved the results requested while still remaining within budget.

Each team should demonstrate their building models and explain their testing procedure, as part of their demonstrations. They also need to defend why they chose particular materials and why they put them together in the way that they did.

All models should be tested in front of the class using the same earthquake tester.

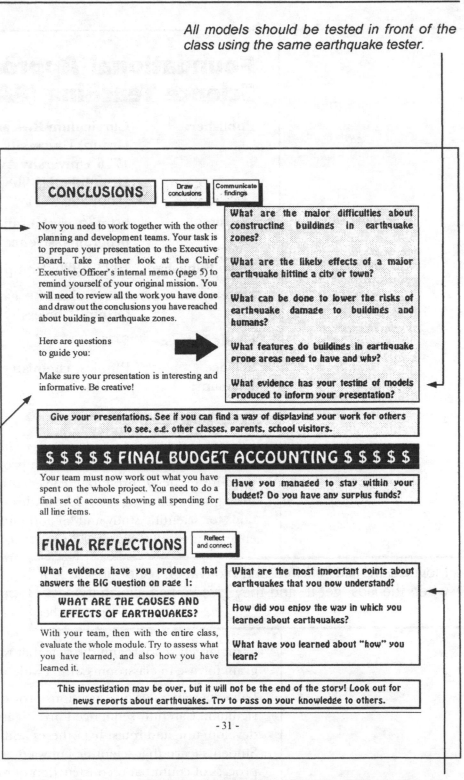

CONCLUSIONS

Draw conclusions | Communicate findings

Now you need to work together with the other planning and development teams. Your task is to prepare your presentation to the Executive Board. Take another look at the Chief Executive Officer's internal memo (page 5) to remind yourself of your original mission. You will need to review all the work you have done and draw out the conclusions you have reached about building in earthquake zones.

Here are questions to guide you:

Make sure your presentation is interesting and informative. Be creative!

> What are the major difficulties about constructing buildings in earthquake zones?
>
> What are the likely effects of a major earthquake hitting a city or town?
>
> What can be done to lower the risks of earthquake damage to buildings and humans?
>
> What features do buildings in earthquake prone areas need to have and why?
>
> What evidence has your testing of models produced to inform your presentation?

> Give your presentations. See if you can find a way of displaying your work for others to see. e.g. other classes, parents, school visitors.

$ $ $ $ $ FINAL BUDGET ACCOUNTING $ $ $ $ $

Your team must now work out what you have spent on the whole project. You need to do a final set of accounts showing all spending for all line items.

> Have you managed to stay within your budget? Do you have any surplus funds?

FINAL REFLECTIONS

Reflect and connect

What evidence have you produced that answers the BIG question on page 1:

> **WHAT ARE THE CAUSES AND EFFECTS OF EARTHQUAKES?**

With your team, then with the entire class, evaluate the whole module. Try to assess what you have learned, and also how you have learned it.

> What are the most important points about earthquakes that you now understand?
>
> How did you enjoy the way in which you learned about earthquakes?
>
> What have you learned about "how" you learn?

> This investigation may be over, but it will not be the end of the story! Look out for news reports about earthquakes. Try to pass on your knowledge to others.

- 31 -

Students can respond to the final questions as individuals, if you would like to use their final reflections as part of your assessment of the module.

Foundational Approaches in Science Teaching (FAST)

Publisher: Curriculum Research and Development Group, University of Hawaii
1776 University Avenue
Honolulu, HI 96822
(800) 799-8111

Website: http://www.hawaii.edu/crdg/programs/science/fast

Years Published: 1992–1996; first published in 1978

Developer: Curriculum Research and Development Group, University of Hawaii

Grade Levels: 6–10

Science Domains: Physics, chemistry, earth science, and biology

Overview

Foundational Approaches in Science Teaching (FAST) is a three-volume, comprehensive curriculum program. Originally developed for grades 7 through 9, *FAST* has been used successfully from grades 6 through 10. It provides students with the foundations for scientific study and an authentic experience of how science occurs in the real world. Students work collaboratively, and frequently encounter commonly held misconceptions which, by design, they later challenge through a series of investigations. The program targets schools and districts that want a multiyear core program for use in classrooms with a wide range of students.

> " I love seeing kids excited and motivated. And I just love it when the kids 'get it' and they give you an explanation."
> — Science teacher

Lab experiences or investigations provide the grist for this curriculum. Carefully sequenced investigations require students to develop, test, and retest hypotheses and reach conclusions. Students learn that scientific knowledge develops through a process of continual reconstruction of explanations in the light of new findings. The immediate application and reinforcement of concepts is a key program feature. Investigations help students build on their existing knowledge, and a return to concepts in a variety of contexts allows students to achieve a deep understanding of the ideas. Seventy to eighty percent of the time, students work on labs or field studies. The remaining time is devoted to data analysis, small group or classroom discussions, literature research, and report writing.

Instructionally, the program emphasizes the importance of the teacher's questioning strategies and other techniques that encourage students to think critically. Based heavily on laboratory experiences, *FAST* puts the teacher in the role of "director of research." Students develop skills in measurement and laboratory procedures as they develop concepts through their laboratory work. Students who experience *FAST* as a core curriculum over several years become comfortable and confident with its instructional approach and learning environment.

The *FAST* program requires professional development for teachers. Districts or schools that select this program must be willing to commit resources for professional development to introduce teachers to the curriculum and to help them as they implement it. Teacher leaders from the local area provide follow-up support, which is considered a key component of the professional development. Teachers who experience the professional development and implement the curriculum as designed can expect to improve their content knowledge and to change their instructional approaches substantially.

FAST is one of the few middle-grades curricula that have rich student achievement data (available from the developer). Studies indicate that students using *FAST* have higher science achievement (as measured by the California Test of Basic Skills (CTBS)/California Achievement Test), better performance on basic thinking and problem-solving skills (as measured by the CTBS), and increases in manipulative laboratory skills.

Curriculum Focus

The curriculum has three strands which appear in each level: physical science, ecology, and relational study. The teacher's guide suggests ways to teach the first two strands concurrently so that the two reinforce each other. The third strand requires students to apply what they have learned in the other two strands. Strands are organized into units that include investigations on topics common to all strands.

FAST 1: The Local Environment
(Grade 6, 7, or 8)

Physical Science: Properties of matter (mass, volume, density, buoyancy), physical and chemical properties of matter, changes of state in matter, pressure, fluid mechanics, heat, temperature, energy, metric measurement

Ecology: Plant and animal growth, weather and climate, field mapping, populations, sampling, water cycle, life cycles, ecosystems, propagation, experimental design

Relational Study: Air pollution, water resource management, technology, epistemology, energy usage, economics, interaction, interdependence, science as inquiry, disciplines of science

FAST 2: Matter and Energy in the Biosphere
(Grade 7, 8, or 9)

Physical Science: Newtonian physics of light, relationships of light and heat, evidence for an atomic theory, conservation of matter, elements and compounds, kinetic molecular theory

Ecology: Photosynthesis, respiration, decomposition, models in science, chromatography, interdependence, ecosystem, community, biosphere, cycling of matter, flow of energy

Relational Study: History of chemistry, use of models in science, systems, epistemology, world food production and distribution, interactions of science, technology, and society

FAST 3: Change Over Time
(Grade 8, 9, or 10)

Physical Science: Force, work, energy, gravity, Newton's laws, Kepler's laws, biochemistry of life, molecular evolution, plate tectonics, stellar evolution and formation of elements, history of chemistry and astronomy

Ecology: Earth origin and structure, weathering and erosion, origin and structure of the universe, organic molecular structure and function, diversity, adaptation, change in life forms and ecosystem, geologic time

Relational Study: Change, constancy, human impact on environments, land use, energy use, epistemology, interactions of science, technology and society, evolution, history of science

A new edition of *FAST 3* will be published in 2001.

Curriculum Format

FAST looks like a textbook series, but is more like a series of laboratory manuals. Its structure allows students to conduct concurrent investigations in physical science and ecology. For example, in *FAST 1*, while students carry out extended studies of seed germination and plant propagation, they concurrently conduct experiments related to properties of matter. *FAST* is distinctive in the connected set of experiments in each unit. Both the lab equipment and the procedures are used repeatedly in succeeding experiments. For instance, in *FAST 1*, students spend an extended period investigating the properties of density and buoyancy. In several of the experiments they use syringes to study fluid systems, developing concepts related to air and atmospheric pressure and changes of states in matter.

The third strand of the program, relational study, focuses on interconnections between scientific disciplines and the interactions among science, technology, and society. After students have concluded most of the physical science and ecology units, their work in the relational studies strand helps them to apply what they have learned to the solution of a real-world problem. For instance, in *FAST 1*, students conduct a study of their local environment which provides a context for applying some of the concepts and procedures they learned during the experiences in the first two strands.

The curriculum includes suggested outlines with alternative plans for using the units. For example, in *FAST 1*, one outline describes how to teach all the units in a single academic year by involving the students in two or three investigations concurrently. An alternative outline shows how to use the units over a two-year span. With this approach, there is less overlap between units.

Academic Rigor

Although this program was developed before the publication of the National Research Council's *National Science Education Standards* and Project 2061's *Benchmarks for Science Literacy*, it does align well with these standards. The publisher can supply information about alignment of the curriculum with the *Standards* and *Benchmarks* on request and expects to make this information available on its website. Information about alignment of the curriculum with selected state assessments is also available.

The lessons in each unit build upon the previous lesson or investigation. Concepts from previous lessons are reintroduced in a background section; skills taught previously are used throughout the units. According to one teacher who has used the curriculum:

> "I did a lot of really good inquiry before I used *FAST*, but it was never connected. The spiraling effect of seeing it happen over and over again—I never had that part of it. In *FAST* everything moves towards a final project, which pulls everything together. I used to have to devise those connections myself."

Each unit begins with an anomaly. Students confront an occurrence that appears to be inconsistent with their previous experiences. This approach piques students' interest. They then conduct a series of investigations to further explore the phenomenon illustrated by the anomaly.

FAST emphasizes science process; students learn how to problem-solve, collect data, and keep it organized. The curriculum requires very little reading, especially in the initial year (*FAST 1*). The second year of the program (*FAST 2*) includes more reading, and the final year (*FAST 3*) includes still more as the work requires more knowledge of historical science.

Connections to Other Disciplines

FAST is designed to highlight connections between the sciences. An end-of-the-year project also has the potential to involve content relevant to social studies. Because students must record their laboratory results and reflect in writing on their investigations, they have many opportunities to practice their writing skills. Students also use mathematical skills, performing calculations and making estimates, as well as graphing data. *FAST* also provides students with experiences in design technology through the design and construction of working models of various phenomena.

Assessment

FAST uses multiple assessment strategies to evaluate student learning and growth. The individual investigations offer many opportunities for assessment through a combination of performance tests and student self-evaluation. The tests cover the range from laboratory skills to conceptual understanding. An evaluation guide also provides teachers with the means to record class progress and keep track of individual students' mastery of laboratory skills and concepts.

Equity

Evaluations indicate *FAST*'s effectiveness with students regardless of race, gender, and disabilities. The teacher's guide offers suggestions for modifying materials for students of different ages and previous levels of achievement, and includes challenge problems and optional worksheets for use with advanced students. Effective use of the curriculum with a wide range of students hinges on teachers' professional development. The curriculum is available in Braille and has been translated into Japanese, Russian, and Slovak.

Developmental Appropriateness

FAST's emphasis on group work both introduces students to the importance of collaboration in scientific study and helps students learn to communicate their ideas to peers and work with others. Many students find the program's content interesting. Much of the curriculum focuses on environmental issues and allows students to develop alternative solutions to problems posed; to think about science in the context of politics, economics, and community; and to get out of the classroom and into the community. In addition, the heavy emphasis on laboratory work allows a wide range of students to participate. Teachers report that students who have previously struggled with science find *FAST* to be a particularly engaging program.

Teaching Resources and Support

Print Materials

Teacher's Guide: Explains the logic connecting strands and the investigations within them. The guide contains teaching suggestions, advice on classroom procedures, and detailed discussion of the conceptual and practical progression of the student investigations. In addition, it includes lists of equipment and chemicals, and suggested schedules. For most experiments, the guide provides detailed comments on classroom management and procedures. It also includes examples of what students might propose as explanations for the phenomena investigated.

Instructional Guide: Explains the philosophy, objectives, and design of the *FAST* program.

Evaluation Guide: Explains the program's approach to student evaluation and describes how to use the assessments to guide teaching and learning. This guide includes tests for assessing laboratory skills and understanding of concepts. Evaluations are also designed to involve students in self-evaluation. The guide provides a series of class progress records and an inventory of skills and concepts for use in recording individual progress.

Student Book: Contains background information, problem statements, procedures for the investigations, and questions related to the concepts to be developed. It resembles a laboratory manual.

Student Record Book: Records class activities. It contains data tables and space for notes.

Reference Booklets: Describe the use of laboratory instruments, outline experimental techniques, and suggest experimental designs.

Professional Development

Introduction to the Program: FAST offers a ten-day teacher institute during the summer or academic year at the local site. All institute staff are teachers who use the curriculum in their classrooms. The institute focuses on laboratory and field experiences, inquiry teaching strategies, classroom management and organization techniques, facilitation of classroom discussions, and methods for addressing mathematics, reading, and evaluation.

The institute is required for the implementation of *FAST*. Both the developers and participating teachers believe this support is the essential ingredient for effective use of the program. According to one teacher:

> "I think one of the significant values of the program is that the developers don't just sell you a package and say, 'I'll see you later.' You sign on for professional development, and the professional development is the key component."

The critical feature of the professional development is its emphasis on inquiry as a whole teaching philosophy, distinct from simply using hands-on activities. As one teacher said:

> "You have to learn how to teach this way. The professional development component is key because it requires the teacher to do all the labs in the entire program before they go off to teach it. Teachers have to experience scientific inquiry themselves."

Ongoing Support: Beyond the initial institute, the program's developers at the University of Hawaii and teachers using *FAST* in the local area provide further support. About 14 universities around the U.S. also offer support to teachers in implementing *FAST.* In addition, each school district that adopts the program designates a local coordinator who receives additional professional development and can eventually serve as an in-house resource person.

Teachers find this ongoing support to be critical to their effectiveness in the classroom. *FAST* recommends four to six follow-up sessions during the first year of the program. During these workshops and consultations, teachers are able to share their positive and negative experiences, and receive guidance from veteran teachers. These sessions also allow teachers to gain a deeper knowledge and understanding of the program, its philosophy, objectives, and teaching methods.

Teacher Hints and Guidance

Cooperative Group Skills: If students have had no experience with cooperative group work, they need to learn how to work together effectively. Teachers, therefore, need to be skilled and confident in establishing and supporting a cooperative learning environment. Cooperative learning strategies are addressed in the teacher institute and the instructional guide. One teacher reported:

> "If students haven't encountered group work before, their first difficulty is seeing themselves as authorities, and relying on each other as partners in learning. The first thing they want to do is have the teacher give them an answer. But they really like being given a certain amount of independence, and they really, really, really like being in labs."

Professional Development: The program requires a significant commitment on the part of the teachers, school, and district because of the required professional development.

Standards: For districts with standards that designate topics that must be covered but that are not addressed in the *FAST* curriculum, using the complete program can be problematic. Teachers may need to use some supplemental materials, but not at the expense of the program's careful sequence of concept development. Assistance in making adaptations is available from the developer's staff.

Materials: Most materials used in the investigations are easy to find and reasonably priced. Students and teachers frequently construct some of the needed equipment and supplies. Classrooms do need triple beam balances. The program has minimal requirements for use of heat, water, and lab benches.

Scheduling: The program's flexibility allows its use with a variety of school schedules.

Support: FAST has a toll-free number, a website, a "Question and Answer" e-mail address, and an electronic newsletter available to teachers using the program.

Sample Lesson

The following is an excerpt from *Changes of State in Matter.* ©University of Hawaii. These materials are reprinted with permission from the Foundational Approaches in Science Teaching (FAST) program.

27. HEIGHT OF LIQUID COLUMNS IN A TORRICELLI TUBE

Background
In an earlier investigation we removed air from a Torricelli tube containing water. After we closed the clamp, the water remained standing in the Torricelli tube.

Now let's see how high other liquids will rise when air is removed from a Torricelli tube.

Problem
How high do different liquids rise in a Torricelli tube when the same amount of air is removed?

Materials
- Torricelli tube
- 250-mL Erlenmeyer flask
- pinch clamp
- #6 two-hole stopper
- 6-cm length of glass tubing
- 15-cm length of glass tubing
- tubing connector
- 50-cc syringe
- meterstick
- graph paper
- liquid assigned by your teacher
- apron and goggles

Procedure

CAUTION: Wear an apron and goggles.

1. Assemble and adjust the equipment as shown in Figure 27–1.

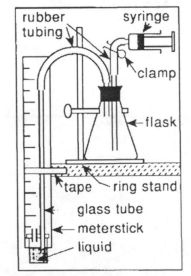

Figure 27–1 Equipment for measuring the height of liquid columns in a Torricelli tube

a. Fill the syringe 1/4-full with air and attach it to the equipment as shown.

b. Check for leaks in the system by opening the clamp and pushing the syringe plunger all the way in. If there are no leaks, air will bubble out of the tube through the liquid in the container.

c. Use the syringe plunger to adjust the level of the liquid in the tube to 0 cm on the meterstick. Close the clamp.

d. Remove the syringe from the tube and empty it of air.

e. Reconnect the empty syringe to the equipment. The apparatus is now ready for use.

NOTE: Do not strain the rubber when you operate the syringe.

2. Determine the height a liquid rises in a
   Torricelli tube when some air is removed
   from the tube. Record the name of the liquid
   in a table like Table 27–2.

Table 27–2 Data on height of liquids in a Torricelli tube

Name of Liquid:		
Height of Liquid (cm)	Volume of Air Removed (cm³)	Total Volume of Air Removed (cm³)*

*Total volume of air removed in each operation is added to the volume of air
removed in previous operations.

    a.   Open the clamp and pull the syringe
plunger back about 5 cm³.

    b.   Clamp the tube and release the plunger.
After you release the plunger, record the
volume of air removed and the height of
the liquid in the tube. The volume of air
removed is the volume of air in the
syringe after the plunger is released.

    c.   Repeat procedures 2.a. and 2.b. until the
liquid reaches the top of the meterstick
or until you have removed about 250 mL
of air, whichever happens first.

3. Using different liquids, repeat procedures 1
   and 2.

Unit 2. Changes of State in Matter

Summary

¶1. Graph your data. Plot the data for all the liquids on one graph. Identify the plotted points of each liquid with a different symbol. For each liquid, draw a line or curve through the points for that liquid.

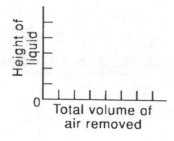

a. For every 10 cm that water rises in the tube, how much does each of the other liquids rise?

b. What properties of liquids might explain these results?

¶2. Compare the operation of the Torricelli tube in Figure 27–1 with the operation of the tube in Investigation 23, A Torricelli Tube and a Fountain.

a. How are the operations similar? How are they different?

b. What is your hypothesis to explain how a Torricelli tube operates?

¶3. Refer to your observations of a fountain in Investigation 23, A Torricelli Tube and a Fountain. What is your hypothesis to explain how fluids are moved in a fountain?

Challenge

1. Suppose that a Torricelli tube is 50 m tall. In the open air, what is the greatest height to which water can be raised in the tube using a vacuum pump?

2. An instrument that measures the pressure of a fluid is called a *manometer*. An instrument that measures air pressure is called a *barometer*. Air pressure is measured in centimeters (cm) or millimeters (mm) of mercury. The average air pressure at sea level is 76 cm (760 mm) of mercury. This means that, on the average, mercury stands 76 cm (760 mm) high in a Torricelli tube or barometer. Design and construct a barometer.

Full Option Science System (FOSS)

Publisher:	Delta Education 80 Northwest Boulevard P.O. Box 3000 Nashua, NH 03063 (800) 258-1302
Website:	http://www.delta-ed.com
Years Published:	1993; 2000 (revised)
Developer:	Lawrence Hall of Science, University of California, Berkeley
Website:	http://www.lhs.berkeley.edu/FOSS/ FOSS.html
Grade Levels:	3–6
Science Domains:	Earth science, life science, physical science, and technology

Overview

The *Full Option Science System (FOSS)* includes eight fifth- and sixth-grade modules organized into four strands: Life Science, Earth Science, Physical Science, and Scientific Reasoning and Technology. Between four and six lessons make up each module, and student activities take the form of investigations, simulations, and hands-on activities involving collection and examination of data.

The program suggests using four modules per school year; however, it is possible to use fewer and to supplement them with other curriculum materials. Since modules span two grade levels, teachers have the flexibility to move modules around in order to meet the needs of their students, or their school's or district's science standards and framework.

> " The students learn methods that they will be able to use for problem solving: not only science skills but measurement skills, ways of articulating with math, bringing out their understanding of the concepts through writing, and working in collaborative groups. It's all blending together for the students."
> — Science teacher

FOSS also includes modules for grades 3 and 4, and is widely used for the elementary grades in school districts that have moved away from textbook programs. All *FOSS* modules for grades 3 through 6 were revised in 1999; the revised versions are available as *FOSS 2000*. A new *FOSS* curriculum for grades 6 through 8 is scheduled for publication in Fall 2000. The forthcoming 6 to 8 program includes a new technology component. (For more information about the forthcoming middle-grades materials, see Chapter 4.)

Curriculum Focus

Each of the four strands contains two modules for grades 5 and 6. These modules are described briefly below.

Life Science Strand

Environments contains six investigations which expose students to a variety of different plants, animals, and their environments. Investigations in terrestrial and aquatic systems guide students through the development of concepts about behavioral response, tolerance range, environmental preference, and environmental range.

Food and Nutrition contains four investigations which provide students with the tools and techniques for testing foods, using indicators to determine acid, vitamin C, fat, and sugar content. The module gives students opportunities to explore concepts related to metabolism and nutrition by studying nutrients, chemical indicators and reactions, and the calorie.

Earth Science Strand

Landforms contains five investigations leading students through the development of concepts of physical geography and mapping (change over time, deposition, elevation, erosion, landform, map, model, slope, and viewpoint). Students use stream tables to investigate variables that influence erosion and deposition of earth materials (amount of water, steepness of slope, time) and the creation of landforms (valleys, canyons, river channels, deltas, alluvial fans). Students assemble models of mountains and create topographic maps.

Solar Energy has four investigations which introduce the concept of solar energy. Students explore the relationship between the sun, an object, and its shadow, and monitor the sun's apparent movement over a day, week, month, and year. They learn about orientation, reflection, shadows, and surface area. They design experiments to explore the variables (solar energy, reflection, absorption, insulation, and heat sink) that affect the transfer of energy from the sun to air, to water, and to earth materials, and the sun's influence on weather patterns.

Physical Science Strand

Levers and Pulleys consists of four investigations which introduce students to basic concepts of mechanics using two kinds of simple machines—levers and pulleys. Students have firsthand experience as they study advantage, effort, fixed and movable pulleys, fulcrums, lever classes, load, and simple machines. They set up systems, measure outcomes, and record results using conventional diagrams. They relate the force needed to lift a load to the advantage resulting from the simple machines, and then they graph data to organize and interpret results of investigations.

Mixtures and Solutions presents four investigations through which students explore concentration, saturation, and solubility. They investigate properties of mixtures and solutions, the dissolution of a solid in a solvent, the concentration and saturation of a solution, evidence of a chemical reaction, evaporation, and crystal formation. Students gain experience with laboratory tools and techniques.

Scientific Reasoning and Technology Strand

Models and Designs helps students explore technological design principles to propose solutions and evaluate products. In four investigations students create scientific models to help them think productively about complex problems, explain the relationships of parts in systems, and design and build model carts that respond to a series of engineering challenges.

Variables contains four investigations which engage students in scientific inquiry and introduce the ideas of variable, controlled experiment, capacity, cycles, energy, and system. Students identify and control variables and conduct controlled experiments using several multivariable systems: pendulums, airplanes, boats, and catapults. They observe and compare the outcomes of experiments, identify relationships between independent and dependent variables, graph relationships, and make predictions using the results of their experiments.

Curriculum Format

Investigations in each module include lesson plans and other supports to help the teacher and the students carry out specific activities. The format is highly structured.

Lesson Plans: Each lesson plan in the module includes the following three sections:

- Materials—lists the necessary items included as part of the curriculum kit (e.g., thermometers, balances, syringes, graduated cylinders, pitchers), and items the teacher needs to supply.
- Getting Ready—describes what the teacher needs to do or consider to prepare for the lesson.
- Guiding the Investigation— provides the teacher with a detailed description of the sequence of steps for teaching each part of the lesson. This section includes a rationale for each step and information about materials to use, instructional strategies for carrying out activities, and challenges students may encounter.

Support: This component of the curriculum provides the teacher with useful information, tips, and hints for each investigation. It includes the following elements:

- Purpose of the Investigation—describes what students will do in the investigation to develop understanding of the concepts.
- At a Glance Chart—summarizes the inquiry questions, investigation steps, science content, and assessment opportunities for each lesson or part of the investigation. It includes interdisciplinary extensions for language arts, mathematics, and social studies.
- Content Background for the Teacher—discusses the specific concepts addressed in the investigation.
- Teaching Children About…—provides a summary of scientific research relevant to the module. It suggests ways that the teacher can use this information to motivate students to think about new ideas and to make connections to other areas of study. It helps students advance their ideas from intuitive ones to scientific ones.
- Interdisciplinary Extensions—includes a list of suggested extensions based on reading and writing activities to help with language development; specific connections to other subject

areas; and recommendations for additional language, mathematics, science, social studies, and art projects to further the study of the topic and concepts in the module.

* *FOSS* for All Students—makes suggestions for adapting activities for diverse classrooms, with an emphasis on language development.

Academic Rigor

According to the program's developers, the central goals of the *FOSS* program are to promote scientific literacy and instructional efficiency, and support science education reform. Its approach to science teaching revolves around activities and investigations which involve collection and interpretation of data, and discussions and debates based on readings and findings. Throughout the modules, questions guide the investigations. Students begin their exploration of solar energy, for example, by considering questions such as, "What is a shadow?" and "What would happen to your shadow if you stood in the same place all day?" Later they consider, "What will happen to earth materials when they are placed in the sun?" "How is water heated?" and "How could solar energy be used to heat water?" They conclude by asking, "What kinds of energy do you use in a typical day?" and "What are some of the things that you use that energy for?" Students engage in hands-on learning—experimenting, gathering data, organizing results, and drawing conclusions based on their work. The process of conducting these investigations and the information students gather through experimentation support their development of scientific ways of thinking.

The program uses varied strategies to facilitate student reflection and discussion. Students discuss activities in collaborative groups and in question-and-answer sessions that summarize the lessons. In the *Models and Designs* module, when students work with self-propelled carts, they hold a "mini-convention" in which teams share one design modification they have tried or a problem they would like help with. Opportunities for reflection occur in inquiry sessions that wrap up each lesson, in the student sheets where students organize data and discuss results, and in the response sheets used for assessment purposes.

Teachers using *FOSS* materials at the middle-grades level believe it helps students prepare for high school. One teacher made the following observation:

> "It pays off in the future when students come to work in the higher grades. If they come across a problem, they don't just sit there and spin their wheels. They jump in and identify the problem, identify a way of solving that problem through developing a fair test or going through a sequence of steps to get to their data collection. They know how to set up tables of data. They know how to set up charts and graphs and then analyze the data. They can draw conclusions and make a presentation."

Connections to Other Disciplines

Throughout the investigations, teachers can find opportunities for students to read and write, to solve mathematics problems, to discuss applications of science to society, and to take on special projects that draw on skills from different disciplines. Some suggestions for cross-disciplinary connections appear directly in the investigations, or as extensions. Others are derived from readings in *Science Stories,* a series of student readers developed specifically to complement the modules. These stories create a context for integrating reading and language arts skills with the development of science concepts.

For example, as part of their study of mixtures and solutions, students read and discuss an article entitled "Decompression Sickness." They have been experimenting with solids dissolving in liquids, and this article tells how a gas (nitrogen) dissolves in a liquid (the bloodstream) and describes problems that arise if the gas comes out of solution too quickly. Other readings include narratives (e.g., folktales, descriptive writings, and journal notes); informational readings (e.g., encyclopedia articles); technical selections requiring students to follow a sequence of instructions; and historical documents (e.g., newspaper articles or letters).

One teacher shared an example of connections the program makes between science and mathematics.

> "Within each module, there is a lot of measurement, and a lot of math. Students use statistics—looking at mean, mode, and range. They take the data, analyze it, compare, and look for discrepancies. When groups report to the class, there are always going to be some calculations that don't match up with everybody else's. This allows the teacher to give the students an opportunity to analyze the 'outliers' in the data."

Another teacher noted how the skills students develop in language arts can help them in *FOSS* science.

> "I noticed that the kids that I had for language arts did much better in their science logs because they kept reading and writing logs in language arts. They had more experience with writing, and so they did a much better job in the science logs."

Assessment

The *FOSS* assessment materials include diagnostic assessments designed to guide instruction as well as assessments intended to evaluate student performance. Diagnostic assessments help teachers monitor student progress throughout each module. Teachers observe classroom activities, examine students' work, and assess particular tasks designed for both learning and assessment. End-of-module assessments and a portfolio of accumulated work provide an overall evaluation of learning outcomes.

FOSS centers its approach to assessment on three dimensions of learning, identified as "Assessment Variables."

Content Knowledge refers to the "facts" of science that students learn throughout the module.

Conducting Investigations focuses on skills needed for pursuing scientific investigations (e.g., systematic observations, experimentation, equipment design, data organization).

Building Explanations refers to skills needed to participate effectively in discussions (e.g., articulating experiences and using evidence to support ideas and conclusions).

Teachers find the assessment approach helpful and coherent. One teacher described the approach in the following way:

> "The curriculum has a good articulation of concepts, good strategies for teaching these concepts, a chance for revisiting concepts that are not understood, and assessments throughout the program. There are, I think, three different kinds of assessment styles: performance-based, multiple choice, and one free-response test. Having that all together is a real strength."

Equity

FOSS addresses the special needs of culturally and linguistically diverse populations and makes science accessible and meaningful by teaching students about traditional ways that science has been used to solve problems in a variety of cultures. Throughout the modules, there are opportunities for students to contribute their own cultural experiences, which enriches learning for all students.

The program's "multisensory" approach to science learning helps reach students with special needs and students from culturally and linguistically diverse groups. For example, the *FOSS* balance and tactile syringe were designed for students with visual impairments, but these tools proved to be effective not only for students with these and other forms of special needs, but for all students. *FOSS* provides these special items in its materials kits.

Teachers who use *FOSS* modules say that they work well with a wide range of students. However, for traditionally high-performing students, teachers may need to develop extensions. One teacher describes this challenge as follows:

> "I think the *FOSS* materials work extremely well for the average student and can challenge the students who traditionally have been 'turned off' to science. But I have a very academically strong group of students. My challenge is to make things more difficult for them, more interesting, more thought provoking."

Developmental Appropriateness

FOSS organizes scientific thinking processes into a developmental sequence which involves: observing (using the senses to get information); communicating (talking, drawing, acting); comparing (pairing, making one-to-one correspondences); organizing (grouping, sequencing); relating (classifying, determining, cause and effect): inferring (using if/then reasoning, developing scientific laws); and applying (developing strategic plans, inventing). Students use these processes when they engage in a variety of activities such as assembling models of mountains and creating topographic maps; designing experiments to explore independent and dependent variables and their relationships; setting up systems, measuring outcomes, recording outcomes using diagrams and graphs, organizing and interpreting results; creating scientific models to help them think about complex problems; observing and comparing outcomes of experiments and making predictions using results.

An important component of the investigations is the opportunity for students to explain and defend their thinking to others. Investigations foster the development of students' oral communication skills by creating opportunities for discussion and encouraging teachers and students to use questions to promote debate. Students work collaboratively in groups as well as keeping individual records and logs.

Teaching Resources and Support

Print Materials

Teacher's Guide: Each module guide contains the following sections:

- Module Overview: Provides science content background for the teacher and information to facilitate implementation (e.g., class organization, practical information about teaching the topic, interdisciplinary connections, scheduling of activities, materials management, and additional resources). A two-page module matrix includes synopses of the investigations, the concepts and themes relevant to each investigation, the thinking processes used in the module, extensions for investigations, *Science Stories* relevant to the module, and technology connections.
- Materials: Lists the materials included in the kit, materials the teacher needs to supply, and the one-time preparation needed to use the kit; also includes suggestions for kit maintenance.
- Investigation Folios: Provides detailed lesson plans. These include background information; materials list; preparation plans; discussions questions; math, language, social studies, and art extensions; home activities; and suggestions for adding a multicultural dimension to the lessons.
- Duplication Masters: Provides English and Spanish forms to assist students as they record, organize, and interpret their observations.
- Assessment Folio: Includes scoring guides for all assessment tools, a recording system, and guidance for turning assessment results into grades.
- *Science Stories* Folio: Describes the use of *FOSS* reading materials.
- Resources Section: Lists student trade books and additional readings (fiction and nonfiction) to support the hands-on experiences, multimedia materials that reinforce relevant concepts, and additional resources for teachers.

- The *FOSS* Website <www.fossweb.com>: Offers additional extension activities for home or school, such as interactive simulations, opportunities to communicate with other students and scientists, and teaching tips. The website also offers educators a place to share program information.

Science Stories: A series of original books developed to accompany the *FOSS* modules. Books include fiction and nonfiction, including biographies and, in many cases, technical readings. *Science Stories* are part of each kit for grades 3–6 and are also available separately.

Equipment Kit: Contains nearly all of the materials needed to conduct the investigations. A small amount of commonly available materials must be provided by the teacher. Replacements for consumable materials can be ordered in replacement kits or as individual items. Equipment inventory sheets provide descriptions of every item used in the investigations and categorize each as permanent, consumable, or supplied by the teacher.

Professional Development

Teacher Preparation Video: Provides an introduction to each module and includes a brief excursion into real classrooms to see the module in use. Lawrence Hall of Science, the developer of the program, also offers a variety of professional development opportunities. Contact the developer at (510) 642-8941 or see the listing of professional development opportunities at its website.

Other Resources

Optional parts of the *FOSS* program include the *Science Essentials* multimedia series (available in video, videodisc, and interactive videodisc formats) which encourages hands-on learning; and *Reading Resource Books* which include literature and trade books matched with the *FOSS* modules.

Teacher Hints and Guidance

Teachers with Little Science Background Knowledge: The modules guide teachers and students through step-by-step activities, which makes teaching science more comfortable for teachers with limited content knowledge and experience. One teacher described the materials as "teacher friendly."

Locale Specific: Teachers caution that particular units work better in certain parts of the country. One teacher had difficulty implementing a solar energy unit for lack of sunshine. Teachers should become familiar with all the lessons in advance and be prepared to make adaptations as necessary.

Materials: Kits are well organized, complete, and help expedite planning and setup. Districts and schools should factor in the costs of maintaining and refurbishing kits.

Professional Development: Teachers commented on the need for and easy availability of professional development when they are beginning to teach these modules. They found a good support network among the many teachers across the country who either provide professional development for *FOSS* or who are experienced in using the program in their classrooms and are available to support others.

Sample Lesson

The following is an excerpt from the teacher's edition of *Solar Energy.* Copyright 2000 by The Regents of the University of California. All rights reserved.

GUIDING THE INVESTIGATION
PART 1: SHADOW PLAY

1. DISCUSS SHADOWS

Find out what students know about shadows. You can help them along with questions.

- *What is a **shadow**?*

- *What do you need in order to have a shadow?*

- *Do you have one all the time?*

- *What would happen to your shadow if you stood in the same spot all day?*

NOTE: *This is an early-morning activity.*

2. PREPARE TO GO OUTSIDE

Tell students that today they will be going outside to observe their shadows. They'll go out now and again after lunch. Discuss rules for outside behavior.

Students will work in pairs, taking turns tracing the outline of their partner's shadow and their partner's feet. Each shadow should be labeled with the owner's name and the time of day it was drawn.

Ask one student from each pair to get a small piece of chalk.

MATERIALS FOR STEP 2:
2 Pieces of chalk

3. TRACE SHADOWS

Take the class outside to trace shadows. Ask students to spread out enough so their shadows will not overlap, and to think about buildings and trees that might overshadow their spot later in the day. Remind students to label their tracings inside the shadow outline with their name and the time of day.

NOTE: *Be sure students trace around their partner's feet so they can return to the same location later in the day.*

NOTE: *Students can also make up challenges for each other.*

4. PLAY SHADOW CHALLENGES

As students finish tracing their shadows, engage them in a game of shadow challenges. Tell them to concentrate on their shadows, and you will challenge them to make their shadows do something.

- *Use your shadow hand to touch your shadow head.*
- *Use your real hand to touch your shadow head.*
- *Make the smallest shadow you can.*
- *Separate yourself from your shadow.*
- *Touch your partner's shadow knee with your shadow hand.*
- *Make your shadow disappear.*
- *Slip into someone else's shadow.*
- *Make your shadows shake hands.*
- *Play shadow tag.*

MATERIALS FOR STEP 5:

4 Solar Energy Journals

5. DISCUSS OBSERVATIONS

When students have finished tracing their shadows and have tried some shadow challenges, return to the classroom. Distribute the *Solar Energy Journals.* Have students record their observations from the shadow challenges. Ask them to share their observations. Did they observe anything surprising?

6. THINK ABOUT WHAT WILL HAPPEN

Remind the students that they will go out again to observe their shadows, standing in the same spot they did the first time. Ask them what they think their shadows will look like at lunchtime. Have them record their ideas in their journals.

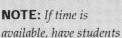

NOTE: *If time is available, have students observe their shadows again later in the day. Or suggest that they look at their shadows before leaving school at day's end.*

BREAKPOINT

7. LOOK AT SHADOWS AGAIN

Three or four hours later, take students out to look at their shadows again. They should stand in their own footprints and look to see where their shadow now falls. After groups have finished comparing their shadows, go back to the classroom for discussion.

8. TALK ABOUT CHANGING SHADOWS

Ask students what changes they saw in their shadows. Confirm that the shadows changed shape (what they look like) and **orientation** (direction they point). Ask,

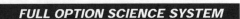

- *Why did your shadows change shape and orientation?*

Students should realize that the changing position of the Sun changed the shape and orientation of the shadows. Ask them to guess how the shadows would look right before sunset. Have them record their latest observations in their journals.

WRAPPING UP PART 1

9. START A WORD BANK

Start a list of key vocabulary words that relate to solar energy. Ask students to suggest words for the word bank. Review the meaning of each word as it is suggested. Make sure the words in bold below are added to the chart.

- A **shadow** is the dark area created by an object that stops light.

- **Orientation** is a position or arrangement in relation to another position or location.

10. START A CONTENT/INQUIRY CHART

A content/inquiry chart lists concept statements that summarize the knowledge acquired in the investigations. To generate the statements, ask students what they learned from the investigation. If they need prompting, ask questions related to the inquiry just completed, and write the answer on a sheet of chart paper, using students' words as much as possible.

- *How did you create a shadow when you were outside?* [Opaque objects, like bodies, block light from the Sun, creating a shadow behind the object.]

- *How did your afternoon shadow compare to your morning shadow?* [The shape and orientation of shadows change as the day progresses.]

- *Why did your shadows change shape and orientation?* [The orientation and shape of outdoor shadows change because the position of the Sun changes continuously.]

11. READ SCIENCE STORIES

Have you read the science stories called *The Sun* and *Shadows?* See the Science Stories folio for more information.

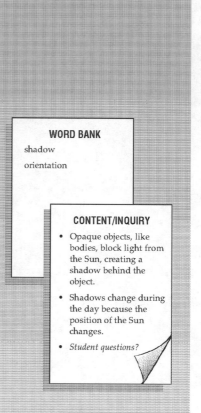

WORD BANK

shadow

orientation

CONTENT/INQUIRY

- Opaque objects, like bodies, block light from the Sun, creating a shadow behind the object.

- Shadows change during the day because the position of the Sun changes.

- *Student questions?*

Issues, Evidence and You: Science Education for Public Understanding Program (IEY)

Publisher:	**Lab-Aids, Inc.** **17 Colt Court** **Ronkonkoma, NY 11779** **(800) 381-8003**
Website:	**http://www.Lab-Aids.com**
Year Published:	**1996**
Developer:	**Lawrence Hall of Science,** **University of California, Berkeley**
Website:	**http://www.lhs.berkeley.edu/** **SEPUP/iey.html**
Grade Levels:	**8 or 9**
Science Domains:	**Biology, chemistry, physics, and earth science**

Overview

Issues, Evidence and You (IEY) is a comprehensive, yearlong curriculum that teaches science concepts, processes, and techniques relevant to the real-world experience of students. The focus is on environmental issues related to public health, pollution, waste management, and energy use. *IEY* builds upon the previously published *SEPUP Modules* (see separate profile in this chapter), and users of those modules will recognize some of the features and lessons from them. The curriculum uses a sequenced, interdisciplinary approach. Science coordinators and teachers view *IEY* as an alternative to using textbooks or constructing their own comprehensive science program from various modules, teacher-developed units, and reference books. *IEY* materials are bound as a hardcover book.

> " I think the majority of my kids really like *IEY* because it's active learning. They like being able to do hands-on work. They like the fact that there's discussion. They like the fact that there's not a lot of memorization for tests. They like the assessments because they know exactly what their score is based on."
>
> — Science teacher

IEY's most distinctive feature is its "Embedded Assessment System," which offers a comprehensive, integrated way to assess, interpret, and monitor student performance. The curriculum's assessment tools include tasks, scoring guides, and examples of student work. Assessment tasks vary in format (e.g., lab reports, town meetings, journal writing) and are an integral part of the curriculum. Teachers are encouraged to work in groups to determine their local standards of performance through "consensus moderation" (a process that is described later in this profile).

IEY engages students in careful investigation of scientific concepts and use of relevant evidence to make decisions about a range of social and environmental issues that young adolescent students should find interesting. The curriculum can accompany *Science and Life Issues (SALI)*, another *SEPUP* program being piloted at the time this guide was written. (See the description of *SALI* in Chapter 4.)

Curriculum Focus

The curriculum has four parts: *Water Usage and Safety, Materials Science, Energy Use,* and *Environmental Impact,* each of which focuses on a different issue.

Water Usage and Safety addresses the safety of the water supply and the problems, implications, and biological risks of waterborne diseases. Students explore alternative water treatment processes as methods to control risks. They learn about tradeoffs as they confront the health risks of exposure to the chemicals used to treat water, and learn to make decisions based on evidence. Students explore concepts about solutions, concentration, chemical interactions, risk assessment, and toxicity as they investigate water chlorination, water quality, and groundwater contamination. They practice data analysis and reporting. These skills and approaches form a "toolbox" which students use as they explore issues in the rest of the curriculum.

Materials Science helps students develop an understanding of the environmental impact of the production, use, and disposal of fabricated materials. Students investigate natural and synthetic materials. They explore the relationship of resource use to materials production, as well as disposal and potential impact on the environment. They conclude this part of the curriculum by developing an integrated waste management system for their community.

Energy introduces the concept of energy and its important role in society. Investigations lead students through the role that energy plays in decisions about economic, social, environmental, and political issues. Students explore their own use of energy and relate their consumption to the efficiency of energy transfer. They examine alternative sources of energy and apply what they learn about chemicals, materials, and energy to design an energy-efficient, cost-effective car.

Environmental Impact builds on concepts introduced earlier, asking students to make a decision about building a factory on an imaginary island. The factory construction sets the stage for investigating the diverse implications of this decision. Students consider economic, environmental, political, and social issues as they prepare an environmental impact report, and they discover tradeoffs at all levels of decision making.

Curriculum Format

The program consists of 65 investigations distributed among the four units described above. It is organized into sections which include a series of interconnected investigations presented in a logical sequence. Each investigation requires between one and three class periods.

Investigations are structured to follow a learning cycle that includes:

Introduction: Sets the stage and relates the activity to previous concepts.

Challenge: Focuses students' attention on the task at hand.

Procedure: Provides directions for the investigation and suggestions and examples (e.g., data tables) to help students record and process data.

Data Processing: Suggests questions for students to consider about the data collected and its implications in relation to the challenge of the investigation. Students respond to these questions in their journals.

Questions: Direct students to assigned readings that support the investigations. Students draw on the readings to write independently about these questions in their journals.

Academic Rigor

IEY includes a correlation of the curriculum content to Project 2061's *Benchmarks for Science Literacy* and *Science for All Americans*. (The curriculum was developed before the publication of the National Research Council's *National Science Education Standards*.) Because it is a full-year, comprehensive curriculum, careful consideration is given to how the concepts developed in each section support the concepts developed in later sections. One teacher explained how the process works.

> "The concepts are cyclical from the beginning to the end of the yearlong program. What we talk about on the first day of school, we'll talk about at the end of school—but with much greater understanding by the end. What's really neat about this course is that you collect data from student activities, student investigations, and from each one of the lab groups. Then you post it, and you can look at it and say, 'OK, I didn't quite get what you got, but if we take all of this together and analyze it, we can see a pattern here. And we can see that the more data we have, the closer we get to what we might theoretically expect to get.' . . . All the concepts are continued from one activity to the next so students can begin to understand what these concepts mean."

The curriculum is designed to build students' capacity to design and carry out investigations. Increasingly, towards the end of the unit, the investigations encourage students to work independently in their design, analysis, and written and oral reporting. For example, students' development of a scientific "toolbox" in the first section of the curriculum builds their operational understanding of chemical interactions, biological effects of chemicals, epidemiology, risk, qualitative and quantitative analysis, evidence-based decision making, and the difference between science and public policy. Students later use these ideas and those introduced in subsequent sections of the curriculum as a basis for their own investigation of social and environmental issues.

Connections to Other Disciplines

IEY includes concepts in biology, chemistry, physics, and earth science. It also connects to disciplines other than science. Mathematical skills are required when students calculate and use tables and graphs to organize and represent data. Students use many language arts skills as they keep journals; write letters to local authorities stating the pros and cons of a policy, rule, or practice;

and discuss and write about agreements, disagreements, or recommendations on a particular issue. Social studies concepts come into play when students sketch and interpret maps of the community and explore the global context for particular issues. Students also study the benefits and limitations of advances in technology.

The connections between science and writing are fundamental to *IEY*'s approach. One teacher described how writing is an integral part of the investigations.

> "There are a lot of opportunities for writing. For example, students have to write about the chlorine activity. They read two articles to gather information: one saying chlorine's bad; one saying chlorine is good. They have to use information from the articles as evidence to make their own decisions. Later, they're going to have to write an editorial or a letter to the London Health Department explaining about the spread of cholera. Before this, they will have had experience with different ways to write. So they can write in any mode. Then we do another lesson where we talk about cholera in our own city. They have to write something from the point of view of a cholera victim—as a poem, a diary entry, an editorial in a newspaper, or a format of their choice. Most recently, students tested water in the town for various characteristics, and I asked them to write up their results as a lab report to the water department."

Assessment

A fundamental principle of the *IEY* assessment system is that assessment has to be continuous and integral to the instructional experience in order to inform and facilitate effective teaching and learning. The features of the assessment system reflect this integrated approach, and the eight components described below guide the teacher in assessing student progress. The first three components define the core content to be assessed and set the standards for evaluating student performance.

SEPUP Variables are five performance areas that represent student learning in terms of the core concepts of *IEY*: Designing and Conducting Investigations, Evidence and Tradeoffs, Understanding Concepts, Communicating Scientific Information, and Group Interactions. These variables form the conceptual framework for *IEY* instruction and assessment, and the curriculum offers a developmental perspective from which to view student progress on each variable.

Assessment Tasks contain two components, Assessments and Quick Checks. Each component consists of student activities that can be used for regular instruction yet also serve as assessments. Teachers find these tasks far less intrusive on instructional time than typical end-of-chapter tests.

Scoring Guides are rubrics that establish baseline criteria for assessing different levels of student performance and interpreting student work.

The remaining five components of the assessment system help teachers with the assessment process.

Assessment Blueprints consist of sequential lists of *IEY* investigations, identifying timely points for assessing student learning.

Assessment Moderation outlines a process in which teachers meet, discuss, and reach consensus on local standards for scoring student work.

Exemplars are examples of student work that have been scored and moderated for each variable and score level.

Performance Maps are graphic representations of student development of the *SEPUP* variables.

Link Tests are additional assessment activities, based on the *SEPUP* variables, which can be used by teachers at major transition points in the curriculum.

Teachers who have used *IEY* report that they have learned a great deal about their students' perceptions and misperceptions from these assessments. The information provided by the assessments helps them to re-teach and change assignments that "don't work." Students themselves are better able to track their own learning. One teacher described the assessment process this way:

> "We talk about all the variables involved and why it's important to gather a lot of information. And eventually you start to see a pattern. That's one of the great things about the curriculum. You can gather all this information. It's like repeating a test. Well, we've done it over here, you know, 40 times in all of our classes and we have the whole team's data up, and they can see the patterns. It's right there in front of their eyes. That is so neat, because they are gathering all of this data. I guess you could do that with any course. But then to be able to use the scoring—the curriculum has five scoring guides that we use for everything that we score. All the concepts are continued from one activity to the next, so students can begin to understand what these concepts mean."

Equity

IEY is designed for use in classrooms with a wide range of students and challenges and supports all students in many ways. The curriculum addresses different learning styles by giving students varied opportunities to communicate their understanding, including orally sharing data, inferences, and conclusions; writing in journals; and designing and creating charts, graphics, and posters to illustrate their findings and conclusions. *IEY* emphasizes both individual and group work. Teachers report many examples of successes with *IEY* for students who had struggled in classes using traditional science materials.

The curriculum includes suggestions for alternative approaches to completing investigations, and recommends that teachers modify the printed materials to meet the needs and interests of their students. Teachers are encouraged to check all student work on specific items, or to sample student work to assess the class as a whole, in order to identify places where they need to make modifications.

The program focuses on issues that affect not only the students as individuals, but also extend to the community at large. These issues are global and of concern to communities of varied cultural backgrounds.

Developmental Appropriateness

IEY responds to the developmental needs of young adolescents by making the science in the curriculum personally relevant to students, focusing on social issues, capitalizing on students' increasing ability to think abstractly, and acknowledging their inclination toward peer interaction.

The personal, community, and global issues addressed by *IEY* provide a range of topics likely to be of interest to middle-grades students. The design of the investigations helps students make connections between science and their own lives. The issue-oriented approach of the program provides opportunities for parent and community involvement.

IEY encourages students to develop their own ideas about the issues under discussion. The teacher is encouraged to model objectivity and non-judgmental attitudes. *IEY* avoids telling or guiding students toward the "right" or "appropriate" decisions. Rather, through discussion and debate, it helps students to develop an understanding of the available evidence while guiding them to reach their own conclusions.

IEY provides students with opportunities to combine concrete experiences with practice in making inferences and decisions. These opportunities help foster the transition from concrete to abstract thinking. Students learn to listen to their peers' opinions and to evaluate and criticize arguments based on the soundness of the scientific evidence.

IEY proposes a "4–2–1" model for organizing student work in the classroom. That is, a group of four students shares materials, solutions and reagents, and dropping bottles; teams of two students share a tray and other items; and individual students have their own student books and keep personal journals of their work.

Teaching Resources and Support

Print Materials

Teacher's Guide: Provides support and guidance for introducing students to background information, using teaching and assessment strategies, and drawing on specific resources. The guide suggests ways to carry out investigations and to modify printed materials in order to meet the needs and interests of students. The guide has the following sections:

- Overview: Brief summary of each activity.
- Purpose: Rationale for each activity and its relationship to the performance areas described in the assessment system.
- Materials List: Outline of materials and information about advance preparation.
- Teaching Summary: Outline of each activity.
- Teaching Procedures: Detailed lesson plan in narrative form.
- Assessment Opportunities: "Quick checks" for understanding and more detailed investigations with accompanying scoring guides.

Student Book: Guides the investigations and provides related readings and sample data tables.

Assessment Resources Handbook: Provides support for using the assessment system. The handbook includes an overview section with helpful suggestions for getting started with the assessments and appendices that offer teachers assistance in implementing the assessment system. The appendices include a glossary of assessment icons and terms; scoring guides for each instructional sequence; assessment forms useful for grading purposes; scoring guides for all five variables; examples of student work at each scoring level for each variable; assessment blueprints (one for each of the four parts of the curriculum); and information about the moderation process, the performance maps, and the link tests.

Materials Kit: Contains materials for 32 students for the entire academic year. No special equipment or technology is needed.

Professional Development

The teacher support section in the teacher's guide includes information about professional development sessions that the developer of the curriculum offers throughout the year. The publisher provides on-site support for professional development related to implementation. Workshops are available for teachers, administrators, parents, or others on request. Initial professional development for teachers generally consists of a three- to five-day workshop and midyear follow-up. For small groups, professional development is provided on a regional basis.

Teacher Hints and Guidance

Because *IEY* was a relatively new curriculum when this guide was prepared, teachers had not had extensive experience with its use. However, some of their early insights may be helpful for others who plan to use the curriculum.

Preparation: Teachers find that the already assembled kits are useful and make preparation time reasonable.

Facilities and Scheduling: Teachers find they can use this curriculum in almost any type of space. According to one teacher, "As far as facilities go, you don't really need anything special. You can really teach it anywhere if you have water." The same is true of schedules. While block scheduling is helpful, teachers report that 45-minute sessions are workable. Teachers have to sequence the work carefully: pre-labs one day followed by the lab session, then a discussion the next day.

Meeting District Standards: Because the curriculum is yearlong, some teachers need to figure out how to supplement *IEY* with activities or units that address particular district or state standards. Teachers who have used the curriculum have shown creativity in meeting local standards. For example, one teacher who has the same students for two years uses the curriculum for half of each year.

Instructional Approach: Teachers need to be comfortable and skilled in guiding student inquiry. Professional development is critical if teachers are going to use the curriculum as intended. Teachers with past *SEPUP* experience are poised to be successful with the *IEY* materials, but they are likely to need ongoing support and assistance with the curriculum's assessment component. Teachers new to this type of instructional approach, as well as these materials, should attend professional development workshops.

Student Discussions: A strength of the program is the potential for thoughtful discussion among students. Frequently, teachers find it difficult to facilitate these conversations; they need help with questioning strategies and techniques for facilitating productive discussions.

Sample Lesson

The following is an excerpt from the teacher's edition of *Investigating Energy Transfer.* Copyright 1996 by The Regents of the University of California. All rights reserved.

Activity 50 — Investigating Energy Transfer

Overview   Students broaden their operational definition of energy as they are introduced to the concepts of *potential* (stored) and *kinetic* (motion) *energy*. First they build a multi-story building out of cards. Next, they drop weights of different masses from two different heights to drive nails into foam blocks. The two investigations in this activity provide students with the opportunity to explore the concepts of potential (stored) and kinetic (motion) energy, the relationship in this situation of stored energy to mass and height, and the conversion in this system of stored energy to energy of motion.

Purpose   *The students will:*

1. Broaden and refine their operational definition of energy (DESIGNING AND CONDUCTING INVESTIGATIONS).

2. Discuss how energy can be stored (potential energy) and then used (kinetic energy) in various ways (UNDERSTANDING CONCEPTS).

3. Investigate the variables involved in the transfer of potential to kinetic energy in a mechanical system (DESIGNING AND CONDUCTING INVESTIGATIONS[A]).

4. Discuss energy sources, transfer, and receivers in relation to examples of mechanical energy (UNDERSTANDING CONCEPTS).

[A]*Assessment*

Teacher's Guide

Materials

For the teacher:

- Assorted nails★ (optional)

For each group of four students:

- 80 "Building Cards" (3x5 index cards)

- One foam cup

- One 5-cm aluminum cylinder

- One 10-cm aluminum cylinder

- One 5-cm steel cylinder

- One 10-cm steel cylinder

- Two short plastic tubes

- Two long plastic tubes

- Two foam blocks

- Two sixpenny galvanized steel nails

- Two sixpenny aluminum nails

For each student:

- One copy of Student Sheet 50 (optional)

Teaching Summary	**Day One**

1. Introduce the "House of Cards" game and explain the rules.

2. Teams play "House of Cards" and record their data.

3. Students discuss the "House of Cards" game and the energy relationships involved.

Day Two

4. Introduce the "Drive a Nail" activity.

a
5. Students plan to carry out the "Drive a Nail" activity and predict the effect of different variables on the outcome (DESIGNING AND CONDUCTING INVESTIGATIONS—ALL ELEMENTS).

Day Three

a
6. Students carry out the "Drive a Nail" activity to investigate the effect of different variables on the outcome (DESIGNING AND CONDUCTING INVESTIGATIONS—ALL ELEMENTS, *continued*).

7. Students report and discuss the outcomes of the "Drive a Nail" activity.

8. Highlight and discuss the reproducibility of outcomes in the "Drive a Nail" activity.

9. Students identify and discuss potential and kinetic energy in various everyday occurrences.

Advance Preparation and Safety Note on other side of this page→

Teacher's Guide

Teaching Procedure

Day One

1. Introducing and Explaining the Rules for the "House of Cards" Game

Explain to students that working in groups of four, they will have the opportunity to try to build up to a five-story building using 3x5 index cards. Give a brief demonstration of what you mean. Using the six cards illustrated below, build a simple two-story building.

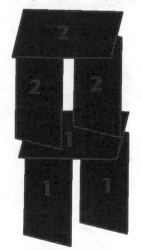

Use your building and the rules on page 28 of the Student Book to introduce the procedures for playing the game as well as the definition of *story* in the "House of Cards" game. Form the groups of four and distribute a set of 80 cards and a foam cup to each group.

As you distribute the cards, tell each group that they will have about 5 minutes to discuss the challenge on Student Book page 27 and to try out different approaches to solving it.

2. Playing the "House of Cards" Game and Recording the Data

After the 5 minutes of practice time are up, tell each group to stack all of their cards in separate piles arranged by number (or color). Remind students that each group will have only 10 minutes to cooperatively build one structure following all of the rules on page 28. Once you start the official game, call out the remaining time after each minute. After 10 minutes, stop all construction and ask each group to place the foam cup on top of their building. Count off the required one minute that the cup must remain supported for a structure to be official. At that point record on the board, or a piece of chart paper, the number of stories successfully built by each group. Discuss with students the fact that it took energy (not much) to lift a card and put it on a story. The fact that a card is part of a story means it possesses stored energy it can release when it falls down. The higher the story, the more stored energy in the card.

Next, challenge each group to see how many cards the group can remove from the first story before the structure collapses and releases its stored energy. Have each group follow the instructions for "Calculating Energy Costs," on page 29 to determine the amount of energy stored in their finished structure. When each group has computed the total stored energy for their structure, you

Teacher's Guide

should record it on the chart next to the number that shows the number of stories successfully built by that group.

3. Discussing the "House of Cards" Game and the Energy Relationships Involved

Identify the winning group as the group that was able to build the highest structure using the least amount of stored energy. Give students a chance to discuss why they think different approaches were more or less successful in building the structure. At this point ask students to discuss the energy needed to build a real multi-story building as well as the stored energy that results from the construction.

As students identify energy transfers involved in constructing a building, mention how energy of motion (digging, lifting, etc.) is used to raise, or build, the building. The building itself is the energy receiver and has a lot of energy stored in it. We call this kind of stored energy *potential energy*. We don't expect to ever convert this potential energy to energy of motion, or *kinetic energy*, but unfortunately that is what happens in a natural disaster, like an earthquake, when a building falls down. Motivate a discussion about examples of

potential and kinetic energy familiar to your students. For example, a skier at the top of the mountain has potential energy. However, as the skier comes down the mountain, this potential energy converts to kinetic energy. A compressed or stretched spring has potential energy that is converted to kinetic energy when the spring is released. Fuel oil has potential energy and can be burned in the furnace to produce heat (another kind of kinetic energy) for heating the home. Students will think of many other examples.

Summarize the discussion by emphasizing the difference between energy of position, or stored energy (potential energy), and energy of motion (kinetic energy). Potential energy, or stored energy, is frequently referred to as *energy of position* because the energy stored depends upon the position of an object or particle. For example, the energy stored by the water in a dam partially depends upon the height of the dam. The energy stored in a card depended upon what story the card was on. This will be more easily explained after students do the "Drive a Nail" activity.

If you have time, you may wish to have students complete Student Sheet 50 as a way for them to reflect on their group's interaction.

Insights

Publisher:	**Kendall/Hunt Publishing Company** **450 Westmark Drive** **P.O. BOX 1840** **Dubuque, IA 52004-1840** **(800) KH-BOOKS**
Website:	**http://www.kendallhunt.com**
Year Published:	**1994**
Developer:	**Education Development Center, Inc., Newton, MA**
Website:	**http://www.edc.org/cse**
Grade Levels:	**K–6**
Science Domains:	**Earth science, life science, and physical science**

Overview

Insights is a comprehensive curriculum for grades K–6 that is designed to develop students' understanding of key science concepts, improve their critical thinking skills, encourage investigation and problem solving though direct experiences, and connect science with other subject areas. The *Insights* curriculum consists of 17 modules, three of which have been designed to meet the needs of middle-grades students: *Human Body Systems* (life science), *Structures* (physical science), and *There is No Away* (earth science). Each of the grade 6 modules contains 13 to 16 sequenced learning experiences through which teachers guide students as they explore new concepts. The teacher's guide promotes hands-on, inquiry learning. The curriculum provides students with science experiences that build upon their natural curiosity about the world and enable them to learn skills and concepts upon which to build further science understanding.

> "*Insights* is a hands-on program, but it is more than that. It really does get kids to talk about what it is they've learned, so that it is not just about having them handle materials. The program gets kids thinking in a deeper way than if it's just hands-on, or if it's just me delivering facts to kids. It is a combination of using their hands and their minds."
> — Science teacher

Curriculum Focus

Human Body Systems develops the concepts of structure and function in a living system; it also addresses regulation and behavior. This module focuses on the human body as an interactive system of smaller, interdependent body systems. Students learn that cells are the building blocks of all living things and that cell specialization is necessary to carry on the many functions needed to sustain life. Students also learn about the interactive nature of the circulatory, digestive, and respiratory systems, and develop a sense of the size, location, and function of some of their internal organs. They explore how these three different body systems work together to meet the body's needs. To learn about cells, students follow a red blood cell on its journey through the circulatory system and discover how it interacts with the digestive and respiratory systems to supply the body with oxygen and nutrients.

The *Structures* module develops the "big ideas" of forces and transfer of energy, focusing on concepts of live load and dead load, compression and tension, and the relationship of materials and shape to structure and strength. In this module, students begin to explore some of the basic principles that help them answer the question, "Why do structures stand up?" They look at structures in the school neighborhood and record the variety of sizes, shapes, materials, and structural designs they find. Students explore the basics of building structures by building with straws, index cards, and other classroom materials. As they find solutions to the challenges of building structures that will stand, students learn how design is influenced by the need to support loads, the relationship between structure and function, building materials, and aesthetic factors.

There is No Away targets standards of "Science in Personal and Social Perspectives," focusing on land-use decisions and waste disposal. Students learn about decomposition—the concepts of organic and inorganic matter, and biodegradable and non-biodegradable material—and factors that affect the rate of decomposition. They also learn about solutions, suspension, and diffusion; the role of water in waste disposal; and waste control systems. *There Is No Away* introduces the topic of waste and examines why waste has become an overwhelming problem with no easy solution. Students learn that although matter as we know it changes form, it is neither created nor destroyed. Students set up controlled experiments that yield information about what happens to organic and inorganic wastes over time. They look at the kinds of materials that are discarded and consider what happens to them once they are thrown "away." This unit helps students understand the impact that waste and its disposal have on their lives.

Curriculum Format

The lessons in the *Insights* curriculum are called "Learning Experiences." Each includes the following information:

Overview: Briefly summarizes what students will do.

Objectives: Details the concepts and skills addressed.

Suggested Time: Gives information about pacing.

Science Terms: Defines key words that students learn in the context of their explorations.

Materials: Lists the materials needed for each student, for each group of students, and for the whole class.

Advance Preparation: Indicates exactly what needs to be prepared beforehand, including special materials, recording charts, and arrangement of the classroom.

Assessment: Lists strategies to help teachers make instructional decisions, tailor the module to student needs, and determine how well students have met the objectives of the learning experience.

Academic Rigor

Insights addresses the National Research Council's *National Science Education Standards* for the relevant content areas and for inquiry, science and technology, science in personal and social perspectives, and history and nature of science.

Insights modules develop scientific concepts and process skills through carefully designed and sequenced learning experiences. The modules provide opportunities for students to ask questions, plan and conduct simple investigations, use simple equipment and tools to gather data and extend the reach of their senses, use data to construct a reasonable explanation, and communicate about their investigations and explanations. Exploration of an idea or concept begins with students' sharing their ideas and understandings about a targeted concept. Student's existing knowledge, preconceptions, and misconceptions about the concept are used to organize the investigations. During these investigations, students work in small groups to collect and record data, discuss their results, and draw conclusions. Small groups share their data with each other and discuss what they understand.

One teacher's comment suggests how the curriculum carefully develops concepts over time.

> "*Insights* stands alone because it includes not just activities and some concepts but also helps students to get involved in inquiry. The other materials that I use usually have a bunch of activities that are based on a theme or topics. But they are not necessarily sequenced to teach concepts over time; they might, but there is no guarantee. There is nothing built into those activities to help you look at how kids are learning, the way you do with *Insights*."

Connections to Other Disciplines

All *Insights* modules offer opportunities to use skills developed in language arts. Small and large group discussion is emphasized. Class charts, science notebooks, and home–school activities all encourage students to communicate their findings in writing. Each learning experience concludes with extension activities that provide ways to expand the basic activity through reading, writing, social studies, and additional science explorations.

For example, in *Structures* students can further their explorations by looking at structures that animals build and inhabit or by inspecting other structures created by nature. They can extend the neighborhood focus of this module to their city or state, or to the country, and learn about the economic, political, and socio-logical structure of their environment by exploring housing patterns, building permits, and construction regulations. Students can also apply their mathematical problem-solving skills by dealing with the economics of building and the measurement of load.

Assessment

Assessment materials for each module include an introductory questionnaire, daily assessment strategies, embedded assessments (i.e., entire learning experiences that constitute an assessment), and a final assessment consisting of written and performance components. The introductory questionnaire is a pre-test designed to give teachers information about what students already know about the concepts taught in the module. Daily assessment strategies provide ongoing information about how students are making meaning of their science experiences. One or two learning experiences in each module have been designated embedded assessments. These activities are designed so that students can work with minimal guidance from the teacher. The teacher is free to move about the classroom to observe and listen to students as they work in cooperative groups. The final assessment is designed to measure students' growth over the course of the module. It consists of a performance assessment and a final questionnaire. The performance assessment is a hands-on task in which students demonstrate their thinking and process skills and their understanding of concepts. The final questionnaire includes questions from the introductory questionnaire for comparison purposes. It assesses how students have grown in their understanding of the concepts addressed in the module.

One teacher commented on the strengths of the program's assessment component.

> "There are all kinds of assessment strategies that make the program much more comprehensive because teachers don't have to make up their own tests. . . . I don't get the sense that the materials are telling me that this is the only way to do things. I can come up with my own way to assess, and that will be fine also. So I do come up with other challenges from time to time when I think that they are appropriate. . . . But, for the most part, 'the end of the unit' assessments ask questions specifically geared to the way you have taught, and the material also gives you suggestions as to how to use the assessment strategies every day."

Equity

Insights modules are well suited for students with a variety of learning needs and styles. Each learning experience provides students with multiple learning opportunities, including discussing ideas together, engaging in hands-on inquiry, recording and interpreting observations, making informal sketches and notes, and writing reports. Extension activities suggested at the end of each learning experience provide ways to expand on the basic activities.

One teacher described how the materials make science learning accessible to a wide range of students.

> "The materials present strategies to reach students with different learning styles. One of the things I've noticed is that all the kids seem really into it. In other words, these materials allow kids who might not be so confident in terms of reading the chance to do hands-on activities, so they start out relatively at the same level as the other kids."

Insights modules were developed, piloted, and field tested in urban classrooms. They reflect an understanding of what is important for science teaching and learning to reach diverse student populations. Lessons are designed so that students share their prior experiences, and students from any linguistic background can engage effectively in the hands-on investigations. The materials are readily adaptable to draw on students' varied experiences and cultures and to match students' knowledge and interests.

Developmental Appropriateness

Each *Insights* module is designed around a topic of interest to adolescents. Students explore societal issues such as waste reduction in *There Is No Away,* in which they build their own sanitary landfill. In *Human Body Systems* they study their own bodies and apply what they have learned in the module about the circulatory, respiratory, and digestive systems to analyzing case studies. And in *Structures* students are challenged to design and construct a unique piece of playground equipment after a series of learning experiences centered on tension and compression.

All three modules engage students in working individually and in pairs or groups of four. Other cooperative group strategies are suggested depending on the module and learning experience. The modules suggest ways to assign each student in a group a role or task to perform. The curriculum suggests a set of generic roles for all modules (e.g., principal investigator, recorder, reporter); other roles are specific to group work in a particular module. For example, in the *Structures* module, students take on the roles of architect, structural engineer, contractor, and draftsperson. Students learn the roles, responsibilities, and preparation necessary to perform these jobs. Having assigned roles encourages productive group interaction and fosters responsibility.

Teaching Resources and Support

Print Materials

Teacher's Guide: Includes an overview of the module, suggested teaching and management strategies, an explanation of the program's frameworks for teaching and learning, a description of the science thinking and process skills addressed in the module, and suggested assessment strategies. The guide also contains a section on science background and annotated lists of related age-appropriate books, teacher reference books, and technological aids. For each learning experience, the guide provides an overview of the activity, objectives, suggested time frame, detailed teaching sequence, materials list, and information about advance preparation.

Student Notebook Pages: There is no student book. Each teacher's guide includes reproducible masters for student notebook pages, group recording sheets, and home–school work assignments. The student and group pages are available in Spanish as well as English.

Materials Kit: Contains consumable and permanent items for a class of 30 students. The module overview in each teacher's guide includes a "Summary of Materials" list, as well as a "Specific Materials" list for each cooperative group of students in each learning experience. Not all materials necessary to teach the module are included in the publisher's kit. Some are easily obtainable or are common school supplies. A module kit contains the entire materials kit plus the teacher's guide; the teacher's guide can also be purchased separately.

Professional Development

Kendall/Hunt Publishing offers on-site in-service for schools and districts, and provides a toll-free hotline to handle questions about implementing the curriculum. Call (800) KH-BOOKS or visit the website <www.kendallhunt.com> for information about professional development.

Teacher Hints and Guidance

Frameworks: The *Insights* modules are organized around three explicit frameworks: a teaching and learning framework, an assessment framework, and a thinking and process skills framework. These frameworks address a teacher's need to understand and feel comfortable teaching science and have the potential to assist teachers with different levels of experience to develop their skills and understanding of inquiry-based science teaching.

Teacher Preparation: Teachers need to be prepared to deal with the materials, the variety of classroom activities, and the amount of information contained in the teacher's guide. One teacher described the necessary preparation in the following way:

> "*Insights* demands a lot of work at the beginning of the unit, especially the first time you teach it. There are lots of materials, and there are lots of good instructions for kids. It's not just me giving information to kids. Sometimes it is, but often it is me leading a whole group discussion, or kids working in small groups, or individuals working. For example, *Structures* in particular has a lot of materials. If you make sure that the kids have all the right stuff and know how to access it, then there's not a problem. I can imagine there could be a problem with the materials if you didn't have a place to store things from day to day; if you didn't have enough classroom space. Also there is a lot to read. The teacher's guides are a couple of hundred pages long, so they are not something you can just pick up the day before. You really have to look at them and think about what you are going to do. And again, the first time it takes a lot longer than the next times."

Professional Development: Feedback from districts using *Insights* indicates that professional development tied to specific modules and ongoing study groups greatly facilitate the implementation process. One teacher described the importance of professional development for teachers inexperienced in using an inquiry-based approach to teaching science.

> "If you are a teacher who knows a lot about science content and has done a lot of science with kids, you might not need as much preparation. Some things—not just the content, but how the teacher's guide suggests teaching—are really hard. If you have taught that way before, then it is not such a big deal; but it is very different from using textbooks, so if that is the only way you know how to teach science, then you should spend some time on professional development in one way or another. It's really important for the district to give teachers time to do that."

Materials: The cost of the *Insights* materials is comparable to that of other modular science programs. Some school districts purchase only the teacher's guide and build their own kits to reduce costs. Materials need to be replenished after each use, so a district should establish a strategy to accomplish this promptly. Districts that plan to provide their own kits can tie kit development and maintenance into their professional development design.

Sample Lesson

The following is an excerpt from *There is No Away.* Reproduced with permission from Kendall/Hunt Publishing Company, Inc.

Learning Experience 7

Overview

In this learning experience, students are challenged to use what they have learned thus far to design and construct a model of a landfill. The purpose of the exercise is for students to figure out the best ways to prevent or slow down the movement of potentially toxic materials through a sanitary landfill to a water reservoir.

Objectives

Students observe the lateral movement of water and solutes through soil.

Students determine the best landfill lining material for slowing the movement of water through soil.

Suggested Time

One 50-minute session and one 20-minute session

Science Terms

- *lateral*
- *hydrology*

Challenge—Keeping the Water from Escaping

Materials

For each student:
Home-School Worksheet

For each group of four students:
1 waterproof box, approximately 7" x 5" x 2 1/2" (see Advance Preparation)
1 cup of each of three of the following: gravel, sand, soil, clay, pebbles (see Advance Preparation)
1/2 sheet of paper toweling, stained with red food coloring (see Advance Preparation)
1 insulated cup (8-ounce size)
1 pushpin
1 timer with secondhand
rain bottle from Learning Experience 3
1 rock for holding cup in place
supply of water
measuring cup
4 pairs of plastic gloves
Group Recording Sheet
Student Directions Sheet

For the teacher:
1 waterproof box
paper towels
red food coloring
1 insulated cup (8-ounce size)
1 pushpin
1 rock for holding paper cup in place

Advance Preparation

- The waterproof boxes need to be the same size for all groups. Possible sources include polystyrene salad-bar containers, or shoe boxes lined with plastic.

- Assign each group to one of the following models. Each group should use a total of 3 cups of soil types—1 cup of each.

Model A	Model B	Model C	Model D
gravel	pebbles	sand	clay
sand	clay	soil	gravel
soil	soil	clay	soil

- Prepare the dye-marked paper toweling for each group by dropping 15 drops of red food coloring onto half a sheet of paper toweling; prepare an extra for your classroom demonstration.

- Prepare one model reservoir as described on the Student Directions Sheet.

- Have the rain bottles from Learning Experience 3 available.

- Make a copy of the Student Directions Sheet and the Group Recording Sheet for each group and of the Home-School Worksheet for each student.

Assessment

✔ Can students connect their models to the real world?
✔ Are students showing evidence of understanding and applying concepts from previous learning experiences?

Challenge — Keeping the Water from Escaping Teaching Sequence

Session One

Tell students that today they are going to think of themselves as civil engineers specializing in hydrology. A number of communities are having a problem—they have built wonderful incinerators for their trash but are now faced with the problem of getting rid of the ash residues. Each community has called in a team of experts and has given the team the task of constructing a sanitary landfill for the community. Although the materials available for each team are somewhat different, all the teams face the same challenge, which is to construct the landfill in such a way that it does not contaminate nearby water sources. The first task of each team is to design and build a model to test the team's ideas and to demonstrate the model to the community.

Show the class a box with a dye-marked paper towel representing the toxic ash left over from the city incinerator at one end and a paper cup with holes as the reservoir at the opposite end. Tell students that the challenge for the team of engineers is to use its landfill materials around the disposal area and the reservoir in such a way that the leachate from the toxic ash reaches the reservoir as slowly as possible or not at all.

Divide the class into its groups, assign each group its model, and pass out the Student Directions Sheet and the Group Recording Sheet. Give students a few minutes to review the directions.

Invite the groups to pick up their assigned soils, proceed to develop their plan, and record the plan on the Group Recording Sheet.

Remind the groups, as they complete their plans, to check with you before they have the materials manager pick up the rest of the materials they will need.

Getting Started

Students use their knowledge to plan the soil arrangement of a landfill to keep groundwater clean.

> **NOTE**
>
> Hydrology is the scientific study of the properties, distribution, and effects of water on the earth's surface.

Challenge — Keeping the Water from Escaping Teaching Sequence

Exploring and Discovering

Groups build and test their models.

Invite the groups to build their models with the dye-marked paper towel buried at one end of the box. Make sure students are wearing their gloves.

Remind group members to think carefully as they build and to record any changes in their plans.

When the groups have completed their models, ask them to reflect on what they have done and to write a brief statement on why they believe this is the best model. When the groups have written this statement, it is time to test their model. Remind the groups to measure the amount of water they use carefully, to be accurate in their timing, and to record their results.

Have the groups clean up, leaving their models for others to look at.

Session Two

Gather the groups together and ask the reporter from each group to report on the time it took for the dye to reach the reservoir.

Processing for Meaning

Students share and analyze the results of their investigation.

Discuss the results by asking group members to share their thinking. Ask questions like the following:

> How did the dye reach the water in the reservoir? How can you describe the process?
> Did any reservoirs stay clear?
> What do you think were the key factors in slowing down or preventing the dye from reaching the reservoir?
> Do you think that a clear reservoir would stay that way forever? Why or why not?
> What problems exist in the models where the dye reached the reservoir?
> What problems exist in the models where the dye didn't reach the reservoir?
> Which problems do you think may be easier to deal with?

NOTE

The movement of leachate from the landfill depends on amounts of rain and the subsurface geology. Land (sands, gravels, cracked rocks) that allows a rapid flow of water also allows leachate to move great distances, especially when rainfall is high. It is difficult to predict where the contamination will end up.

A carefully designed landfill will contain or at least slow the movement of contamination and

Help students reach the conclusion that, regardless of what is done, the matter dissolved in the water contaminates the ground or the water there or somewhere else. Ask:

Challenge — Keeping the Water from Escaping Teaching Sequence

What is the advantage of containment over letting the contamination seep throughout the earth?

What are the problems for us if the contamination gets too far away?

Tell students that in the next learning experience they will consider the problem of cleaning up contaminated water.

Remind students to take care of their "dumps" and landfills as they have planned (rain, temperature, light) and to record their observations.

limit the distance it travels. It is easier to predict the area of contamination and make sure land use in that area does not promote ill health. Many modern, contained landfills in areas where there are homes and water supplies nearby have mechanisms for pumping out the leachate to prevent overflow into the surrounding area. This contaminated water still has to be put somewhere, but at least the location can be carefully selected and documented.

Extending Ideas

Distribute the Home-School Worksheet, explaining that students are to (a) test soil in various sites to see the speed with which water percolates down through the soil and (b) record their findings on the worksheet. Make sure students have permission and assistance from an older person at home.

Home-School Work

Invite someone from the Environmental Protection Agency or the city sanitation department to speak to the class about landfills.

Have students explore what work hydrologists do, what education they need, who employs them, and how much money they make. If possible, have a hydrologist speak to the class. Make an effort to invite both male and female hydrologists.

Ask students to look for magazine articles concerning good and bad experiences with landfills and to examine some present problems with waste buried in the ground.

Extending the Learning Experience

Models in Technology and Science (MITS)

Publisher:	Pitsco P.O. Box 1708 Pittsburg, KS 66762 (800) 835-0686
Website:	http://www.pitsco.com
Years Published:	1993, 1999
Developer:	Bernie Zubrowski, Children's Museum, Boston, MA
Grade Levels:	5–9
Science Domains:	Physics, chemistry; some modules integrate technology and physical science

Overview

Models in Technology and Science (MITS) gives students the opportunity to carry out extended investigations of basic physical phenomena and technological systems. The curriculum emphasizes direct experiences with materials and development of science concepts. The curriculum modules use a specific phenomenon or technology as the context for introducing the concepts. Scientific content and scientific processes are closely integrated.

> " A lot of curricula seem to start with the science, and then introduce activities to help kids learn the science concepts. This curriculum reverses the plan: it starts with what's intrinsically interesting to kids—toys, food, making things move and work—and then moves into good, rich science."
>
> — Science teacher

The specific physical phenomenon investigated in each module serves as a model for other related phenomena. For instance, in the module *Air and Water Movement,* students explore and study the patterns that food coloring make in a tray of water. The patterns and their creation are analogous to cloud movements and ocean currents. In addition, the curriculum's activities model for students the processes that scientists use to carry out research.

The following principles guide the curriculum's approach to teaching and learning science:

- Extended, in-depth investigations help students master important skills and concepts.
- Students progress from a concrete, everyday acquaintance with phenomena to a more abstract, scientific understanding.
- Scientific problems and questions grow naturally out of the properties of the materials and the students' interests.
- Concepts and processes developed in the investigation of one phenomenon or technology are connected to related phenomena or technologies.
- Mathematics is used to represent and help students make sense of data.

The curriculum also emphasizes using assessment to help guide instruction. The modules suggest ways for teachers to attend to how students work with the materials and to probe students' thinking. In some modules, assessment tasks are an integral part of the learning activities.

Curriculum Focus

The *MITS* modules comprise two strands. Strand One focuses on physical phenomena. Strand Two uses technology topics to introduce physical science concepts and centers on design problems.

Strand One

Inks and Papers (Grade 5 or 6): Students explore the properties of water-based and permanent inks. The module introduces concepts related to basic physical properties of matter such as solubility, physical and chemical change, and reversible and irreversible chemical change. Students use the technique of chromatography in several activities.

Mirrors (Grade 5 or 6): In the first part of this investigation, students play specially designed games to explore the images created by plane mirrors and learn about some of the reflective properties of mirrors. Students then apply their understanding of plane mirrors to studying how images are created with transparent mirrors, and they encounter the concept of transmission. In the third part of the investigation, students explore some properties of curved mirrors.

Shadows (Grade 5 or 6): Students begin this module by making shadows outdoors with sunlight and indoors with a slide projector, discovering that the two light sources are different. The investigation then centers on a specially constructed box that is used to study shadows cast by small objects. Students learn about some of the properties of light beams. In the second part of the investigation, students convert the box into a camera, using it to study how lenses create images. In the course of these experiments, students learn about the refractive properties of lenses and make connections to the function of a camera and the human eye.

Air and Water Movement (Grade 6 or 7): Using simple materials, students investigate and map outdoor and indoor air currents. The module introduces concepts basic to fluid dynamics, including laminar and turbulent flow, vortex formations, convection, and Reynold's number.

Ice Cream Making (Grade 6 or 7): This module challenges students to find the best container and procedure for making ice cream, using common household materials. Students begin by investigating how small ice cubes melt in containers made of different materials and then investigate the cooling rate of hot water when surrounded by different coolants. Students' investigations involve the concepts of conduction, convection, radiation, and phase change. The container and the surrounding medium also represent a model for heat exchange in other situations. The culminating activity of this module is making ice cream.

Waves (Grade 6 or 7): In the first part of this three-part investigation, students generate waves on water and soap film, discovering some of the general properties of waves. In the second part they compare and contrast waves generated in water with those created with materials such as rope, Slinkies, and string. Students also learn about characteristics of waves such as amplitude and frequency. In the third part they experiment with a model wave machine, determining some of the ways that wave energy is transferred.

Salad Dressing Physics (Grade 7 or 8): This investigation begins with a pair of mystery bottles that contain different liquids. As students carry out a series of tests to identify the liquids, they learn the concepts of solubility and density. Students then compare the density of these liquids to the density of four different kinds of solid balls.

Tops and Yo-yos (Grade 7 or 8): Using simple materials such as plastic plates, dowels, and rubber stoppers, students construct different kinds of tops. They launch the tops and isolate the major variables that determine how long each of the tops will spin. As students systematically test the tops, they learn about rotational motion. Students then use the same set of materials to create different kinds of yo-yos. They apply what they have learned from working with tops to make predictions and experiment with the yo-yos.

Strand Two

Structures (Grade 6, 7, or 8): This module challenges students to build a house, a bridge, and a tower out of plastic drinking straws and paper clips. Students test the strength of each of these structures by hanging from it a cup into which nails can be added, and, with help from the teacher, analyze each structure. The models provide the concrete context for introducing the concepts of force, tension, compression, and equilibrium of forces.

Windmills (Grade 7 or 8): This module challenges students to build a working model of a windmill using index cards, a yogurt container, and a few other simple materials. The wind source is a small table fan. Students refine their initial designs to improve performance. This module introduces concepts related to simple machines, rotational momentum, work, and power. In the second part of the investigation, students experiment with measuring power output using different windmill designs.

Water Wheels (Grade 8 or 9): This module challenges students to build a working model of a water wheel using plastic plates, cups, and other simple materials. Water siphons onto their models to make them turn and lift a cup of nails. Students then try to maximize the number of nails lifted. The module develops concepts related to levers, simple machines, torque, and rotational momentum. In the second part of the investigation, students are challenged to find ways to measure the rotational speed of the wheel.

Curriculum Format

Each *MITS* module's extended investigation of a basic physical phenomenon or technological artifact takes between six and eight weeks. Each module follows this general format:

General Goals and Design of the Program: Provides a general statement of the goals of the curriculum materials, describes the instructional approach, and outlines the information available to teachers to guide student investigations.

Introduction: Describes the scientific ideas behind the module's investigations and provides general guidance regarding materials needed for the module, classroom management, possible safety issues, pacing and sequencing, record keeping, class discussion, assessment of student work, and further investigations.

Activities: Outlines the individual student activities and teacher-led investigations that comprise the module; provides a rationale for the module; and offers ideas about overseeing students' work during each activity, leading class discussion, assessing student work, and encouraging further investigation of the phenomenon.

Academic Rigor

The teacher guides for the four most recently published *MITS* modules include a section that indicates how the activities match the content and process standards of the National Research Council's *National Science Education Standards*.

Activities in each module are carefully sequenced to move students from an intuition-based solution to a problem to a solution that is more explicit, articulated, and grounded in experimental evidence. Students' understanding of scientific terms and concepts grows out of their experiences with the concrete phenomena being investigated. Students must test the hypotheses that they generate with the physical materials they are using, rather than gathering evidence from secondary sources such as books or the Internet. For example, in *Air and Water Movement* students study the patterns food coloring makes in moving water, creating shapes of their own design and testing the kinds of flow patterns that result. They conduct studies that show the similarities of air and water movement. At the end of the module, their own investigations serve as the vehicle for introducing the concept of Reynold's number.

The suggested activities for each module follow a logical progression. Each investigation begins with an open-ended activity that generally poses a challenge or problem to students and invites students to explore the materials. The materials and the manner in which the problems are presented structure these explorations. Students learn to isolate variables and manipulate them in a formal, experimental manner. They learn to use observations and collected data to test their hypotheses. Following the investigation of the first problem or phenomenon, the curriculum introduces a second, but closely related, problem or phenomenon. Students must apply what they have learned to this new variation. For example, in *Tops and Yo-yos,* students use their understanding of the factors that affect the spinning time of tops to construct yo-yos and then to determine the factors that contribute to the spinning time of the yo-yos. In *Structures,* they apply their learning about the construction of a model house to making a model bridge.

The structure of the curriculum ensures that students don't arrive at a solution or a final prototype model simply by trial and error. In the technology modules, for example, students systematically test a standard model as part of the design process. A critical phase of each activity is the time for teacher-guided discussion following student explorations. The teacher is encouraged to spend sufficient time to help students process the observations and data that they have gathered during the hands-on portion of the investigation. Teachers then introduce scientific terms and concepts, connecting these directly to the problems that students are solving. These teacher-guided discussions help move students from their initial, intuitive conceptions toward more accurate scientific explanations.

A teacher leader who has observed colleagues using the *MITS* materials offered this comment:

> "Each topic poses an interesting challenge; it's not just getting students to know the facts. But by doing test after test, just like 'real' scientists, they begin to understand a particular concept in considerable depth. For instance, in *Inks and Papers* they learn about chemistry through testing water-based pens with common household liquids and then use the same procedure to test permanent pens to see if they behave in the same manner. This is a way for them to study the concept of solubility and the chemical properties of liquids. They are applying scientific processes and concepts to a real situation."

Connections to Other Disciplines

In some of the modules students draw on mathematics: making graphs, looking for relationships, using proportional reasoning. Each of the technology modules presents a design challenge which students meet by designing, building, and testing models to produce a final prototype. Although their approach differs from the usual approach to formal technology education, these modules can be used to meet technology education requirements.

Assessment

The program emphasizes that the teacher should think of assessment as an ongoing process. Because the activities in most of the modules build upon one another, students continually need to apply their recently gained knowledge and understanding to the next activity. The section of the teacher's guide "Assisting Students During the Activity" identifies particular kinds of student behavior that teachers can look for, including nonverbal cues and spoken comments.

In the section "Interpreting the Results and Observations," the teacher's guide offers questions for the teacher to use to probe student thinking. Some of these questions are generally related to the phenomenon being investigated and some are specific to the activity. The combination allows the teacher to assess what students have learned in the specific activity and what they understand about the overall investigation.

The type of assessment suggested varies with each phenomenon or technical artifact under investigation. For example, at the end of *Inks and Papers,* students receive a sheet with a set of marks from an unknown pen. To identify the type of pen, they have to use the information collected from all the previous activities. In addition, teachers can assess students' records of measurements and other observations, along with the types of comments and drawings they make in their notebooks.

Equity

The *MITS* materials were field tested in urban and suburban schools with students representing a wide range of social and academic experiences. Because of the frequent opportunities for hands-on engagement with the materials, students with different learning styles have many opportunities to become engaged and demonstrate their learning. For instance, observations in *Air and Water Movement* can be described in words, in visual representations, and in movement. The curriculum provides opportunities for direct experience with some of the forces involved in the investigations.

Modules also offer students different ways to communicate their results. Depending on the topic and activity, students may make oral reports during the follow-up discussions or may act out what they have observed in their explorations. In the modules involving model construction, students demonstrate solutions through the action of their models. Students are encouraged to draw and diagram in their notebooks, and these are used as one means of assessment.

The problems and design challenges are sufficiently open-ended that each group of students can adapt the materials to their current level of understanding and skill. While the groups' final products will differ, each group carries out experiments or assembles a model that contributes to the overall knowledge of the class.

Developmental Appropriateness

Field tests and teachers' experience suggest that, because of the aesthetic appeal of many of the phenomena and the challenge of devising their own designs, students are readily motivated to engage in the *MITS* investigations. For example, the patterns of food coloring in trays of water in the module *Air and Water Movement* and the arrangements of straws in *Structures* are visually appealing. One teacher describes the curriculum as follows:

> "Kids learn scientific concepts but have a lot of fun doing it! Some teachers think if students are having too much fun, the curriculum can't be rigorous. I disagree. The curriculum, in fact, meets all the characteristics that research attributes to disciplined inquiry. . . . I hear animated talk about ideas and scientific concepts and observe what we in schools refer to as 'higher-order thinking.'"

The careful sequencing of activities allows students to move from a relatively constrained, concrete understanding to more abstract understanding of basic concepts. In *Salad Dressing Physics*, for example, students can understand the formal definition of density after they have weighed a set of liquids several different ways and studied the relationship between volume and weight.

Teaching Resources and Support

Print Materials

The teacher's guide for each module offers strategies for planning and carrying out the activities. It includes the following sections for each activity:

Rationale: Purpose of the activity and its role in the context of the whole investigation.

Materials List: Materials and equipment needed for the activity.

Preparation Ahead: Specific directions for what needs to be done prior to the activity.

Introducing the Activity: Suggested ways for teachers to help students understand the nature of the investigations.

Assisting Students During the Activity: Strategies for helping students work with the materials to carry out the activity; in some cases the guide identifies observations that can serve as assessments.

Follow-up Discussion: Strategies for helping students report and interpret their observations and data, for introducing concepts and terms, and for relating these concepts and terms to the activities.

Assessment: Specific and general questions to pose, and suggestions for observing students as they work.

Homework: Some modules include ideas for further experiments and explorations for students to do at home.

Teacher Hints and Guidance

Scheduling: Teachers have mixed feelings about the length of time required for each module: on the one hand, they see the value of the in-depth investigation; on the other hand, they feel pressure to cover more concepts than is feasible with this curriculum. One compromise is for the teacher and science coordinator or department chair to select two or three *MITS* modules, leaving the rest of the year for using other materials to teach the remaining concepts in the district's framework or standards. The in-depth modules can be used to address many of the process standards and prepare students for open-ended questions on state or district tests.

Teachers who were using the curriculum for the first time often encountered problems with implementation and, in some cases, did not complete all of the activities in a module. Some who taught the same module again the following year found it easier and less time-consuming to teach. By the third year, these teachers felt comfortable that they had mastered the module and believed student learning had increased substantially.

Classroom Management: The student projects in some modules need to be stored between sessions. For instance, the constructions made in the modules *Structures, Windmills,* and *Water Wheels* cannot be disassembled between classes. Schools have to plan ahead for storing materials throughout the investigation. Some modules, such as *Salad Dressing Physics* and *Ice Cream Making,* are potentially messy. Teachers can recruit students to help in the distribution of materials and in organizing an orderly cleanup.

Preparation: Experienced teachers recommend that teachers construct the models or explore the materials before presenting them to students. This practice gives teachers a sense of what to expect in class and suggests ways to generate questions and carry out assessment.

Technology: School districts can use *MITS* to add a design technology component to their programs in order to meet their state or district standards.

Sample Lessons

The following is an excerpt from *Ice Cream Making and Cake Baking.* Reproduced with permission from Pitsco. Copyright 2001.

ACTIVITY SIX
Cooling Hot Water with Ice and Salt

▼ *Students determine the cooling rate of hot water when an ice-salt-water solution is used as a coolant.*

Rationale

In order for ice cream to freeze, the temperature of the cream must be 32°. In the previous activities, the coolant lowered the temperature of the hot water to 32° but could not freeze it. This is because in order to bring the liquid or cream to freezing, the coolant must be cooler than 32°. Adding salt to the ice-water solution can reduce the coolant's temperature to as low as 20°, allowing the container's liquid to freeze. If students are patient, they can observe ice forming in the container. They will also see that even though heat moves from the container into the solution, the ice-salt-water solution doesn't change temperature. The constant temperature of the solution will reinforce the concept that ice absorbs heat when it changes from solid to liquid.

Time 1–3 periods

Important Reminder If you have time and you wish to do Parts 4 and 5 of the oven experiments, do them before you come to Activity 7. See page 45.

Each Group Needs

▼ 1 container (used in Activities 4 and 5)
▼ 1 8-oz paper container
▼ 16 oz hot water
▼ 4 oz cold water
▼ 4 oz rock salt
▼ 1 1-gal plastic bucket
▼ ice to fill bucket halfway

▼ 2 short thermometers
▼ 1 watch
▼ 1 stirrer
▼ data tables
▼ 1 sheet of graph paper
▼ newspaper (to cover work surface)
▼ *For the Student* 6 (1 per student)

Teacher Needs

▼ 2–3 bags of ice
▼ a cooler (optional)

Planning Ahead

You will need the same amount of ice as for Activity 5.

Leading the Activity

Introducing the Activity Remind students that they will be following the same basic procedures as for the previous activity—only they now will add salt to the ice-water solution in the bucket. Ask students what effect they think this will have on the cooling curve.

Assisting Students During the Investigation Remind students to stir the ice-salt-water solution thoroughly and to take a temperature reading right after stirring. Circulate through the classroom and urge students to be careful that none of the salt or salt solution falls into the hot water container. If this happens, the water will not freeze because the salt will lower the freezing point of the water in the container.

The temperature of the hot water will drop quickly until it reaches 32° and will remain there. If you have enough time left in the period, have students keep watching the water inside the container. Ice will form on the bottom of it. If the water is not stirred and the room temperature is not too hot, ice crystals also will start forming on the surface of the water. The longer the container sits in the ice-salt-water solution, the more the ice that will form.

Students often have difficulty seeing any of the ice. To help them to observe it, have them carefully discard the water inside the container when they clean up. Then suggest that students look closely at the bottom of the container and feel around with their hands for ice. They can also bang on the container to try to free any ice that has formed.

Leading the Discussion

Reporting Results Have students compare the results of this investigation with the results of the previous two. Plot the cooling curve for the hot water in the ice-salt-water environment, as shown in the graph on page 61.

Then plot the cooling curves for the hot water in the metal containers in the three different environments in Activities 4, 5, and 6 as shown on the graph on page 62.

The three cooling curves should be noticeably different. Have students discuss the differences and indicate what implications this has for making ice cream in the metal container.

Interpreting and Processing Results In this activity, the temperature of the water in the container changes quickly at first but eventually reaches a point at which it remains the same: 32°. At this point, heat is still leaving the water. This is the transition point at which the liquid water becomes a solid. As a result, ice forms on the bottom of the can.

In the ice-salt-water solution, the temperature also remains the same because it too is undergoing a phase change. The heat leaving the hot-water container is melting the ice instead of heating the water. So two phase changes are occurring: The water in the container goes from a liquid to a solid and the ice cubes in the bucket go from a solid to a liquid.

Two objects can be at the same temperature but hold different amounts of heat. Consider what would happen if you heated two coffee cans, one full of water and one full of air, so that they reached the same high temperature. The water-filled can would take longer to heat up but would remain warmer longer than the can containing only air. This is because water must absorb much more heat than air to reach the same high temperature.

COMPARING CONTAINERS OF HOT WATER PLACED IN ICE AND SALT AND WATER

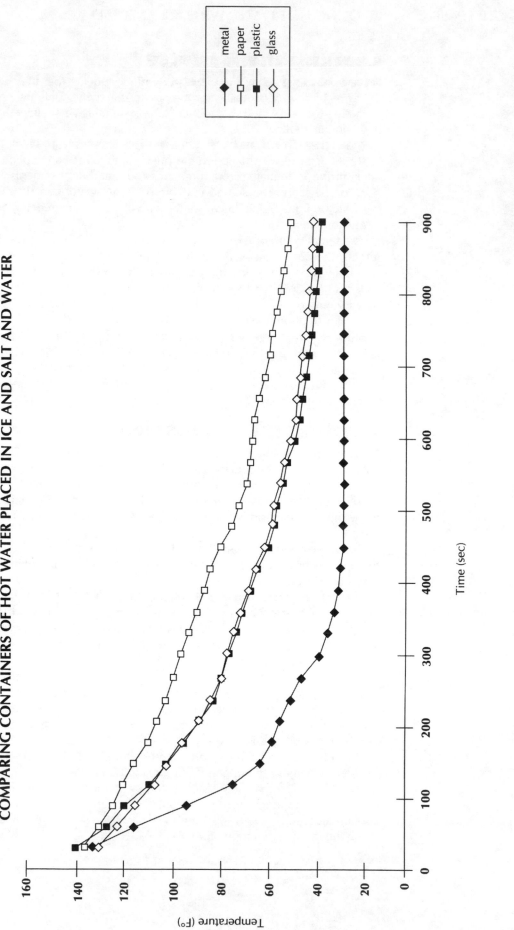

COOLING CURVES OF THE METAL CONTAINER IN THREE ENVIRONMENTS

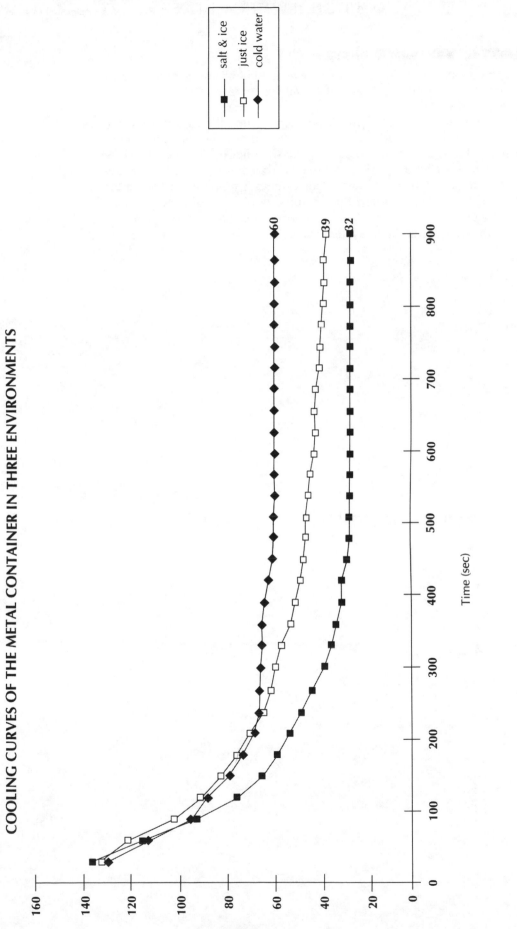

Further Investigation

Students can conduct other investigations involving cooling curves to discover whether or not the amount of salt added to the ice-water solution affects the temperature of the mixture.

If these investigations are done in class, each group should add different quantities of salt to its bucket. Students should follow the same basic procedures as before, using a hot-water container surrounded by a bucket of coolant. Have students prepare the coolant, stir the mixture thoroughly, and check the temperature repeatedly. Once the water starts to freeze, they should record the length of time it took and compare their results with those of other groups. Students will discover that after more than 16 ounces of salt are added to the ice-water solution, the temperature differs little among the different solutions.

New Directions Teaching Units

Publisher:	Michigan Science Education Resources Project Michigan Department of Education P.O. Box 30008 Lansing, MI 48909 (517) 373-0454
Year Published:	1993
Developer:	Michigan Department of Education
Grade Levels:	5–10
Science Domains:	Physical science, life science, earth science, and chemistry

Overview

Five *New Directions Teaching Units* have been developed for the middle grades. These thematic, "hands-on, minds-on" units explore major concepts in earth, life, and physical science, and chemistry related to everyday phenomena. Each unit is designed for use in one of several grades. This curriculum is distinguished by a design based on research about commonly held student misconceptions.

The Michigan Department of Education created these units to help Michigan teachers develop the scientific literacy and conceptual understanding of all students in the middle grades. The department had four goals in developing the *New Directions* units: achieving scientific literacy for all students, valuing depth of understanding over breadth of content coverage, developing an appreciation that learning is useful and relevant outside of school, and supporting interdisciplinary learning. Teachers in states outside of Michigan have also found the units to be effective in their classrooms.

> " I think about *New Directions* as being a sense-making curriculum. Students are really required to make sense out of science, to take the new ideas they are learning and use those ideas, applying them in new contexts. "
> —Science teacher

New Directions defines developing scientific literacy as acquiring an understanding of science that can be put to good use outside of school. Scientific literacy includes the ability to use scientific ideas to understand the world around us, to construct new explanations by asking questions and searching for answers, and to reflect critically on the adequacy of explanations and solutions. The design of the *New Directions* units helps students construct a clear understanding of scientific concepts and principles and become familiar with the scientific approach to experimentation and the application of experiments to real-world problems. Units are designed to elicit students' misconceptions and challenge those misconceptions through direct observation, demonstration, and experimentation. Unit activities lead students through a process of experimentation for which students gradually assume most of the responsibility for design and follow-through. As they experiment, discover, and discuss, students improve their own understanding of how the world works.

Curriculum Focus

The five *New Directions* units designed for the middle grades are as follows:

Hard as Ice (Grade 5 or 6) is about water in its various forms in the hydrosphere, including lakes, rivers, snow, ice, and steam. This unit focuses on water in its solid and liquid states as a context for learning about molecules. Students learn how to describe different forms of water in lakes, rivers, snow fields, and ice floes at a level of detail that gives them clues about the deeper molecular structure of ice and liquid water. They learn how to use the concept of molecules to explain melting and freezing as they see these phenomena in their environment. (This unit was revised in 1998.)

Steamed Up! (Grade 6 or 7) helps students understand how evaporation and condensation work at the molecular and macroscopic levels. Students use measurement and experimentation to develop ideas about evaporation and condensation. They explore the nature of air as a mixture, the nature of water in its liquid and gaseous states, and the causes of change in water's physical state. This unit is a companion to *Hard as Ice,* and the developers strongly suggest that students work through *Hard as Ice* before using *Steamed Up!*

The Lives of Plants (Grade 5 or 6) helps students find answers to the following questions: "Why do plants need light?" "How, where, and why do plants use light to make energy-containing food?" Students develop an understanding of how a plant transforms raw materials and sunlight into food for itself and for people. They study how a plant gets raw materials and transports them to where they are needed. Students explore how a plant absorbs light energy with the help of specialized chlorophyll-containing cells in which water and carbon dioxide combine to make sugar (food) for the plant. Finally, students learn how the plant stores food in order to survive periods without light.

Food, Energy, and Growth (Grade 8, 9, or 10) helps students understand how our bodies use food for energy, growth, and repair. It focuses on the importance of food, considering it at the level of the cell, the system, and the organism. Students see how concepts such as cellular respiration and protein synthesis connect to the food we eat, our need for energy, our changing energy needs during exercise, and gaining and losing weight. The unit draws from several scientific disciplines, including cell biology, human physiology, chemistry, and nutrition.

Chemistry That Applies (Grade 8, 9, or 10) serves as an introduction to chemistry, giving students opportunities to explore various everyday chemical reactions, contrast them to physical changes, and construct explanations for them in terms of molecular changes. Students study the properties of many everyday substances, such as gasoline, baking soda, bleach, metal, bread, wood, and paper, and learn about important, everyday reactions, such as burning, rusting and other oxidation reactions, baking, and the effects of acids.

Curriculum Format

Each teacher's guide (called a *Teacher's Unit*) in *New Directions* is divided into "lesson clusters," and each cluster is built around a story. For example, the *Steamed Up!* unit begins with a story about a young woman named Meredith Gourdine who, during a particularly hot August in 1940, needs to figure out how to keep the block of ice in the family icebox from melting too quickly. Students are challenged to devise an invention or solution to help Meredith solve this problem.

The number of lessons in each cluster varies from unit to unit, as does the number of lessons in each unit. Units contain between two and four lesson clusters.

Each lesson cluster follows a learning cycle: Establish the Problem or Question, Explore Phenomena, Develop Content, Apply and Extend Content, and Pose New Questions. The first few lessons in each cluster allow students to explore the problem, followed by lessons in which the teacher and students work together to construct solutions. The sequence of lessons in each cluster is specifically designed to enhance students' conceptual understanding. At the end of each cluster, students extend and solidify their understandings and skills in slightly different contexts and (except in the final cluster) generate ideas and questions that lead to the following cluster. Each lesson cluster completes one full learning cycle.

Each lesson has two parts: "Introduction" and "Activity." Some lessons conclude with a third part: "What's Next?" The introduction is designed to get students interested in and thinking about the focal idea or concept. Students may be asked to read and discuss a paragraph, view a video, solve a problem, or answer a question based on their previous experiences. During the activity portion of a lesson, students conduct hands-on experiments, make models, engage in extended investigations and projects, and write about their work. The "What's Next?" part of a lesson previews upcoming projects.

Academic Rigor

Each unit targets science concepts and processes that lay the foundation for more sophisticated ideas that students will encounter in high school. For example, the concepts of atoms and molecules are too easily confused by students to introduce them both at the same time. So, in two units, *Hard as Ice* and *Steamed Up!,* students encounter the concept of molecules. Students learn about atoms later, when chemical change is the focus of the unit *Chemistry That Applies.*

Lesson clusters are designed to give students the opportunity to dig deeply into a few concepts. The first lesson cluster in a unit usually begins by bringing out students' prior knowledge about a particular topic or phenomenon. In the ensuing clusters, students pursue activities that help them build an understanding of the key concepts. They can then revise and refine their initial ideas and explanations. The final cluster helps students apply the concepts to real-world contexts.

One teacher described the careful sequencing of a *New Directions* unit:

> "The unit starts out with very basic, simple ideas and, through carefully scaffolded activities, the sophistication level builds. But the unit never introduces an idea or even a term before

students are ready to understand it, until they've had sufficient opportunities to go to that next level."

Teachers believe this curriculum offers students an opportunity to learn significant concepts in depth. As one teacher commented:

> "*New Directions* has some really excellent units that address some ideas that are very, very difficult to teach and to develop an understanding of. . . . The whole notion of molecules and the kinetic theory of matter, that's a difficult, difficult concept to teach, and the curriculum does it very well."

Another teacher described concept development in *New Directions* this way:

> "The units target some really important big ideas, focus on them, and don't try to pull in a lot of other ideas. Students stay really focused on a particular idea that plays out over time with these carefully sequenced activities."

The curriculum also provides students with the opportunity to try out their ideas and explain their reasoning. Students design investigations, interpret the results of their investigations, and reflect on the evidence needed to support their arguments and decisions. Students continually try things out, discuss their ideas, debate solutions to problems, remain both critical and open-minded, listen, and think.

Connections to Other Disciplines

These units draw from as many scientific disciplines as is necessary to delve deeply into a topic. For example, *Food, Energy, and Growth* includes concepts from cell biology, human physiology, chemistry, and nutrition. Chemistry, physics, and environmental science are closely woven in *Chemistry That Applies*, and *The Lives of Plants* employs chemistry and physics concepts to support and explain the plant science.

Some units—*Hard as Ice,* for example—make connections to social studies. Because the program was developed by the Michigan Department of Education, references are made to Michigan geography and history, but the lessons can be adapted to reflect the geography and history of other areas.

Units also provide students with multiple opportunities to apply their communication skills by writing and discussing explanations, descriptions, and predictions. Student pages are provided for some lessons, but students are also encouraged to keep a science notebook or journal to record data, take notes, make drawings, and write their thoughts.

Assessment

Each unit suggests how teachers can use journal entries to assess students' understanding of key ideas and concepts, and particular strategies for assessing journals when students work in cooperative groups. Ideas for assessing the overall quality of the journals are described in each unit. Several units contain additional assessment resources.

Unit Assessments: The Lives of Plants includes a unit assessment. This paper-and-pencil test consists primarily of open-ended and reflective questions, along with a few multiple-choice questions. This assessment can be used as both a pre- and post-test.

Key Questions: In several units, students explore and attempt to answer a key question for each activity. These key questions easily lend themselves for use as assessment questions.

In addition, the Michigan Department of Education has developed *Model Assessment Items,* a resource that contains more than 540 pages of assessment examples written by teachers, including student-tested items.

Equity

The units target classes with a diverse population of students and use approaches that are often successful with students who have special needs. Student activities provide an opportunity for students to work together, using their individual strengths to accomplish a group goal. Many questions are intended for discussion by small groups of students working together to find solutions to problems. Students must write individual answers to questions, so that those who do not contribute or learn well in group discussions have opportunities to articulate their own ideas in writing. The units also suggest alternative methods for students to record their ideas, including drawings, which are recommended for students who are less verbally adept. Talking about their drawings with others may help such students find the words to describe the concepts. As one teacher reported:

> "I think the materials can be used for all students. There are a variety of activities in which they work together in groups and have opportunities to share their ideas in many different formats."

Developmental Appropriateness

Based on prior research on students' pre- and misconceptions, *New Directions* focuses on helping students develop their current conceptions into more scientifically accurate understanding of concepts. The materials inform teachers of what students may be thinking about the relevant concepts, and encourage teachers to let students wrestle with their own possible misconceptions. Students have the chance to alter their conceptions through a sequence of activities that challenge their previous assumptions and understandings.

Teachers find this information particularly useful, as one teacher noted:

> "A section titled 'Pitfalls and Cautions' in each lesson alerts you to what the students are going to be thinking and to watch out for that thinking. It's really neat because you're working on existing ideas, and you're showing the students, through these experiments, how their ideas change. They are steadfast in their beliefs ahead of time. You can't convince them otherwise and you don't try to. . . . You say to yourself, 'Wow, I don't know if I can let them just go on thinking that.' But you have to say nothing. They have to try it and do it. They work collaboratively on different problems and end up proving it to themselves. They've done enough so that they really see what happened, and they believe what they see. They're true, firm believers by that time."

New Directions units connect scientific ideas, skills, and habits of mind with important real-world systems, events, and problems. Students begin by trying to explain real-world phenomena, using what they already know. Next, they explore related concepts and work to develop explanations. Finally, they return to the real-world phenomena to develop more complete explanations.

In these units, students work alone, as a whole class, or, for the majority of time, in cooperative groups. Sometimes all members of a cooperative group do the same work; at other times, each member does something different that contributes to the common endeavor.

Teaching Resources and Support

Print Materials

Each *Teacher's Unit* contains teaching objectives, content background, materials lists, interdisciplinary connections, and project ideas. Also included is information about arranging the classroom, managing materials, dealing with science notebooks and journals, using journals for assessment purposes, and organizing and managing cooperative group learning (for example, establishing groups, setting group rules, helping students learn group roles, monitoring groups).

Every unit contains similar overview materials that include the components listed below. In some units, these materials appear at the beginning of the unit; in others, they are included at the beginning of each lesson.

Background: Explains the science content and commonly held student misconceptions on which the unit or lesson focuses.

Purpose: Provides information about the concept(s) students will explore.

Advanced Preparation: Provides information about what materials or student sheets to prepare.

About This Lesson or *What Students Are Doing:* Describes the activities in the lesson.

Approximate Time: Indicates the number of class sessions the lesson will take.

Key Question (in some lessons): Poses a question that students will attempt to answer while working on the activities.

Each lesson includes a "Procedure" section that serves as a blueprint for the lesson. The procedure is carefully scripted and contains clear directions and step-by-step instructions for organizing and teaching the lesson. Included are questions to ask the students, possible student answers, activity directions, charts, graphs, suggestions for group discussions, and instructions for using the student pages.

Each unit has a reproducible student book. One unit, *The Lives of Plants,* has a companion video. Kits of equipment are available for all units, with the exceptions of *Food, Energy, and Growth* and *Chemistry That Applies.* Most lessons contain transparencies—charts, graphs, data tables, or journal and notebook pages designed for use with the lesson. Some also include "Optional Activities and Projects," with suggestions for activities that will extend the lesson and give students further opportunities to explore particular concepts.

Professional Development

Professional development workshops for any of the units can be arranged by contacting the science education consultant at the Michigan Department of Education, (517) 373-0454.

Teacher Hints and Guidance

Student Thinking: Each unit and lesson alerts teachers to commonly held student misconceptions about the topic discussed. Key questions challenge students' thinking and provide opportunities for them to explore their ideas. Teachers find that being aware of student thinking helps them guide students through the activities and discussions.

Materials Management: Teachers find the list of materials for each section very helpful. The units describe in detail how to set up experiments, with "user friendly" instructions. Materials are primarily substances that teachers can easily acquire, such as juice and window cleaner.

Professional Development: While the information in the *Teacher's Unit* is extremely helpful, teachers who have used the curriculum believe that professional development is important. Professional development can help teachers understand how each unit is designed as a coherent whole, building on students' current understanding and focusing on a few concepts in depth.

Sample Lesson

The following is an excerpt from *Hard as Ice.* Reproduced with permission of Michigan Science Education Resources Project, Michigan Department of Education.

Lesson 8 Which weighs more?

Materials needed:
- ice cubes and liquid water
- styrofoam and clear plastic cups
- plastic wrap
- balances, preferably ones that measure from 1 g to 50 g.
- 1/4 stick of butter, pan for melting butter, hot plate (optional; see step 7)
- photos of ice and water together
- transparencies 12, 13, 14, 15

Advance preparation
1) Allow an ice cube to melt in a clear plastic cup.
2) If students need practice using the balances, weigh several small objects and record their weights on the board, then let students practice with these objects. With the weights recorded on the board, students will know what weight they are trying to get, and will learn to use the balances more quickly. You may want to give them one or two objects to weigh that you know the weight of, but that aren't recorded on the board, to check their skills.
3) You may want to use large charts, drawn on newsprint and hung on the wall, for recording predictions, reasons for predictions, experiment designs, experiment results, and post-experiment explanations. Sample charts are shown in the text.

---

1. Often students say that liquids weigh less than solids, because solids are "solid and hard" or because liquids are more spread out. Some students may talk about molecules in their answers, and some may not. Don't debate the explanations at this point; that will be done later in the unit. This is just a brainstorming opportunity.

2. Students may suggest weighing the frozen ice cube and melted ice cube shown at the beginning of the lesson. This would not be a good experiment, because it uses two different ice cubes, which may have started out with different weights.

Students may want to speed up the process of melting. This is O.K., but don't heat the cup, since it might melt or burn. Direct sunlight or a lamp works well, but students need to cover the cup with plastic wrap so that no water evaporates—see next note. Some students have put their cups, covered with plastic wrap, in shoe boxes lined with black paper, then under a lamp, to speed the heating.

Key Question: How do the weights compare of an ice cube and the puddle of water it melts into? How can you explain this?

What students are doing: Students predict which will weigh more (if either), an ice cube or the puddle of water it melts into. They then design an experiment to test their prediction, and carry it out. They then attempt to explain their results.

Purpose: To continue to explore the molecular design of ice and liquid water, and build a foundation for the theory of conservation of mass — that the mass or weight of an object doesn't change when it melts or freezes, because the total number of molecules stays the same.

Approx. time: 1 class period (close to 60 minutes)

Wall charts may be a good way to record students' predictions, explanations, and designs for this experiment. Samples are shown in the procedure, below.

Procedure _____

1. Show an ice cube in a plastic cup, and the melted ice cube, mentioning that the water is not just water from the faucet, but actually a melted ice cube. **Pose the question:** *How does the weight of an ice cube change, if at all, after it melts?* Let students voice their predictions and

sample wall chart

Will the weight change? *What are your ideas?*	
predictions	beginning explanations
1.	
2.	
3.	
4.	
5.	
6.	
7.	

individual theories and write them down for all to consider (transparency 12 or wall chart.) Don't present a correct scientific explanation yet, just brainstorm.

2. Have students design an experiment to test their predictions. This can be done in teams. This experiment would be very simple, something like weighing an ice cube in a cup, then letting it melt, and weighing it again. Do not use transparency 13 until students have had time to think through a possible experiment in their small groups. If students are still having a difficult time after 5 minutes or so, show transparency 13, which briefly describes a good experiment to test their predictions.

---

3. Let students do their proposed experiments. You may need to teach them how to use the balances or scales, or supervise their use so they do it accurately. Reading the scales is not always that easy for novices— see Advance Preparation. **To get good results, it is extremely important that students do not touch their ice cube or water, or in any way spill any.**

4. While students wait for the ice cubes to melt, have them draw "before" and "after" pictures of an ice cube and the puddle of water it melts into, showing how the molecules are arranged and how they move. Have each student explain why they think their prediction is correct.

Some students will use molecules in their explanations and some will not. You might challenge them to think about what is happening to the molecules when the ice cube melts, and ask if that would have any effect on its weight.

5. When the experiments are complete, **record the results** of each on the board, using three columns to record "weight before melting," "weight after melting," and "weight change." A sample chart is at the right, which can also be used as a wall chart on which students can write their experiment designs as well as their results.

Experiments to find out			
designs	data and results		
	weight before	weight after	weight change
1.			
2.			
3.			
4.			
5.			
6.			

Ask the class, after all data has been recorded on the board, whether they think that the data in front of them indicate that there is or is not a weight change. Let them argue about what the data shows. (In theory, there should be no weight change. If some water evaporates during melting, there may be less weight, although the amount that would evaporate would be small. If some water condenses from the air onto the container, there may be a weight increase.) Try to get the class to agree that the experiments show no weight change.

Weight will decrease as water evaporates from the container, but it will be so little that it is not measurable — unless students use a heat lamp to speed up the melting. Evaporation could be prevented by letting the ice melt in a baggie (although water may condense on it) or by covering the container with plastic wrap (before weighing, of course.) You probably should not suggest the plastic wrap unless some students come up with the idea that water may evaporate; on the other hand, if you know that your students know about evaporation (not all do at this age) you might want to push their thinking about this aspect of the experiment.

Weight will increase if water condenses on the outside of the container. This would be especially true if a baggie or plastic cup is used and the experiment is done on a humid day. This weight would probably be measurable. A styrofoam cup would probably insulate the ice well enough so that very little water would condense on the outside. If water does condense on the container, students may wipe it off with a paper towel before weighing. This may be confusing to them, though, if they think (as many do) that the condensation comes from inside the cup (it really comes from the air. This is discussed in the companion unit *Steamed Up!*)

Proposed scientific explanations	
We believe the weight (did, did not) change:	because...
1.	
2.	
3.	
4.	
5.	
6.	

Some students suggested explanations at the beginning of class, but this is an opportunity for all students to articulate their own thinking in writing.

Does the weight go up, go down, or stay the same?

an ice cube   the puddle of water it melts into

Think about molecules

Say the ice cube has 200,000,000,000 (that's 200 billion) molecules

How many molecules would the puddle have?

What does this tell you about the weight before and after?

Michigan Dept. of Education   Hard As Ice

trans. 15

When ice melts, its molecules

a. weigh less, because they melt into a puddle

b. weigh less, because liquids weigh less than solids

c. stay the same weight, but break apart from each other

d. weigh more, because the puddle they melt into is more dense than the ice cube

7. As with the ice cube, there will be no change of weight, because none of the butter molecules has left the container — they have just started moving faster. The molecules themselves have not changed.

6. Construct an explanation of why there would be no weight change. Have each group construct an explanation. They should look at what they wrote under their before- and after- pictures (from #4 above), although those explanations may be challenged by the finding that there is no weight change.

If no one in the group has used ideas about molecules in their explanations, suggest that they think about what they're learning about molecules, and try to use what they know in these explanations. After a couple minutes of group time, let each group present their explanation to the whole class.

Try to come to consensus within the class. This may not produce the scientific explanation. You may have to help shape the explanation, using transparency 14. The explanation is as follows:

The weight doesn't change when an ice cube melts into a puddle of water, because the number of molecules doesn't change. As the ice melts, all of its molecules simply move faster and break out of the rigid array they were in, but none of the molecules left the container. When ice melts, all the molecules are still there — they don't weigh more or less, they just move faster.

The critical idea for students to come to understand is that the molecules themselves do not weigh more or less after melting. Melting does not make larger or smaller molecules, or heavier or lighter ones—it only speeds them up. Use transparency 15 if you like.

7. What's next? *What else can you think of that melts? Come tomorrow with a list and be ready to explain what's happening when those things melt.*

Science Education for Public Understanding Program (SEPUP) Modules

Publisher:	**Lab-Aids, Inc.** **17 Colt Court** **Ronkonkoma, NY 11779** **(800) 381-8003**
Website:	**http://www.Lab-Aids.com**
Years Published:	**1992, 1996–1998**
Developer:	**Lawrence Hall of Science,** **University of California, Berkeley**
Website:	**http://www.lhs.berkeley.edu/SEPUP**
Grade Levels:	**7–12**
Science Domains:	**Earth science, life science, and physical science**

Overview

Each of the 12 *SEPUP Modules* uses an environmental issue to engage students in science experiences that relate to their own lives. The modules are designed to help students begin to build the knowledge and skills they need to become informed citizens. *SEPUP* encourages students to develop an understanding of how science and technology affect people and the environment. The curriculum uses a problem-solving approach in which students work individually or in groups on a series of conceptually related activities, including experiments, simulations, explorations, and the collection and examination of scientific data.

> " With *SEPUP*, you don't teach the concepts first; students do the investigation first. With learning-disabled students, who have a lot of difficulties with reading information, I noticed that this way of teaching is working better. But it's good for other students as well. Because many times students just memorize concepts without understanding them, and that's not what we want. Whatever concepts students learn during the first activities, they have to continue using throughout the whole curriculum. So if they've just memorized, that won't help them."
>
> — Science teacher

Questions, problems, and background information included in the lessons provide students with guidelines and clues about the facts and additional data that they will need to collect in order to support their conclusions. Supplementary resources and readings reinforce the development of the science concepts related to particular social issues. Most teachers who use *SEPUP Modules*, however, find them most valuable in combination with other curriculum units, reference books, and materials. In many classrooms, a few different modules are used over the course of a year. Teachers and students experienced in using *SEPUP Modules* should be comfortable using some of the newer comprehensive materials by the same developer: *Issues, Evidence and You (IEY)* and *Science and Life Issues (SALI)*. IEY is profiled separately in this chapter; *SALI* is described briefly in Chapter 4.

Curriculum Focus

SEPUP Modules are structured around the following topics and questions:

Chemical Survey & Solutions and Pollution: What is a chemical? Are chemicals necessary? What is a solution? Is dilution the answer to pollution? In the process of investigating these questions, students reflect on their perceptions about chemicals by applying principles of acid–base chemistry to address selected water pollution problems.

Risk Comparison: What are risks to life? Can lifestyle decisions make a difference? As they investigate these questions, students gain experience with probability, risk, risk comparison, and decision making.

Determining Threshold Limits: How do chemists analyze samples to determine what and how much of a certain chemical is present? Students conduct experiments that introduce them to qualitative and quantitative analysis. A toxicity simulation presents opportunities to determine the need for, and limitations of, extrapolating animal data to humans.

Investigating Groundwater: The Fruitvale Story: This hands-on simulation illustrates how to determine the source and extent of a groundwater contamination plume. Students assume the roles of concerned professionals and community members and develop clean-up strategies.

Toxic Waste: A Teaching Simulation: What is toxic waste? Can hazardous and toxic materials be stabilized and rendered relatively harmless? Students explore the use of precipitation, oxidation–reduction, and single replacement reactions in waste reduction and waste treatment processes.

Plastics in Our Lives: What are the advantages and disadvantages of choosing plastics over other materials? As students investigate this question, they learn about physical properties and environmental issues involved in the production, use, recyclability, and degradability of plastics.

Investigating Chemical Processes: Your Island Factory: Students study chemical reactions and their importance in many industries. Then students imagine that they reside on an island and decide how to use island resources to provide employment opportunities and products for the local economy.

Chemicals in Foods: Additives: What chemicals are added to foods? Students explore food preservation, food labels, processing additives, and tests for pesticide residues.

The Waste Hierarchy: Where Is "Away"?: What ultimately happens to the materials categorized as "waste"? Students examine categories of trash and consider methods of disposal based on the concept of a waste hierarchy.

Investigating Hazardous Materials: What happens when we find barrels of hazardous waste in an abandoned field? Students learn methods for physically separating, sampling, and identifying the contents of a barrel of simulated hazardous waste and explore problems of hazardous waste disposal.

Household Chemicals: How much of a household chemical is enough? Will two household chemicals mixed together work better than one? How do household chemicals work? Students study the hazards of household chemicals and discuss appropriate storage and disposal methods.

Understanding Environmental Health Risks: What is an environmental health risk? Students consider personal actions to reduce their exposure to environmental health risks such as biological and chemical contaminants in the water supply and pesticide residues.

Curriculum Format

Every *SEPUP Module* engages students in exploring and considering the tradeoffs between solutions to social problems in modern life and the environmental risks the solutions pose. This process helps students learn how to assess and manage environmental health risks. Each module has between five and ten activities and takes about two to four weeks to teach.

All modules use a standard activity format and the following instructional sequence:

Challenge: Poses a question to grab students' interest and leads to an investigation of the subject.

Readings: Provide additional information and historical perspectives on the issue or concept under study, or background information necessary for data analysis.

Experimental Procedure: Allows students to collect data needed to make decisions.

Modules: Include tables for students to organize their data and procedural models for data analysis and interpretation.

Group Work: Allows students to share and discuss findings and debate evidence used in making decisions.

Questionnaires: Guide students through discussions and deliberations with peers as they present their data, explain their results, and support their conclusions with evidence.

The module activities help students make sense of the information they collect and identify strategies for resolving environmental risks. The activities encourage students' questions rather than providing them with answers. The following comment of one teacher echoes the view of several colleagues:

> "Students really come away understanding that frequently there is not one clear-cut answer. They learn to identify and describe different options. After they are done with the labs, they have collected a lot of important data. At that point, they have to examine the data carefully, and make decisions based on the data."

The *SEPUP* challenges, questionnaires, and readings guide students through the investigations by providing prompts about the data and information they need to back up their decisions. However, teachers may find they need to provide additional information, readings, and content background to strengthen students' understanding of the science concepts relevant to the social issue they are studying.

Academic Rigor

A central goal of *SEPUP* is to promote scientific literacy. The modules address concepts related to the standards for "Science in Personal and Social Perspectives" included in the National Research Council's *National Science Education Standards*. The combined focus on social issues and problem solving contributes to students' awareness of the issues and to their understanding of the basic scientific concepts relevant to assessment of environmental risks. Students learn science processes as well as content. They learn how to conduct a scientific investigation; carry out a qualitative and quantitative assessment of the risks, benefits, and implications involved in particular decisions—including implications from a social perspective; and prepare a substantial argument to support their conclusions.

Connections to Other Disciplines

Instructional strategies used in the materials call for making connections with other disciplines. Throughout the investigations, students have opportunities to use skills and knowledge acquired in language arts, mathematics, and social studies. Because of the need to analyze and interpret data, students can develop new mathematical concepts and skills, and because of the social issues focus of the modules, students also have the opportunity to learn some social studies concepts.

Students exercise language arts skills to read about issues and concepts, record results and observations, and write their own reflections on their findings in their journals. They also consult other bibliographic and media resources, including books, periodicals, journals, newspapers, radio, and television.

Students use mathematics when they analyze the data collected and interpret their results, doing calculations, making projections with mathematical models, creating graphical representations of data, and making comparisons using qualitative and quantitative measures.

Students make social studies connections by considering the social and political factors that might play a role in the decisions they make. They identify various factors that influence these decisions, such as public policy, the presence or absence and use of evidence, and personal actions.

One teacher described the connections the modules make with other subject areas.

> "The activities involve a lot of math. . . . What I noticed is that the students understand why they have to use the math, and how. So, when I am explaining the math concepts, the students are so engaged in what they are doing. The activities have the students use all areas of language: reading, writing, speaking, and listening. They also have to understand maps at some point."

Assessment

Each module approaches assessment in two ways: embedded assessments that are part of the learning activities and end-of-unit tests from a test item bank.

Embedded assessments include strategies to assess students' progress in collecting data; organizing and analyzing data; identifying and using evidence; and using tables, models, and maps to display and interpret data. The modules also include questionnaires that teachers can use to assess students' development of concepts and skills.

Test item bank questions address the science content, processes, and societal issues listed in the conceptual overview of that module. The bank contains multiple-choice, open-ended, and essay items which assess students' recall, comprehension, application, analysis, and synthesis skills.

At the time this guide was written, the *SEPUP* assessments were under revision. However, teachers find the original assessments useful. As one teacher reported:

> "I use some of the test questions. They're really good because they're not memorization questions. . . . I try to tell kids, you don't need to memorize to understand particular concepts. *SEPUP* has questions based on the data and information the kids have collected. The curriculum assumes students can do what they might have to do in real life and apply what they have learned in one situation to a totally different situation."

Equity

SEPUP Modules address different learning styles by having students take responsibility for thinking about alternative ways to pursue the investigation; identifying the most appropriate strategy; designing the investigation; determining the type of data needed; and collecting, analyzing, and interpreting the data. The variety of options available make it possible for students with different learning styles to succeed.

Teachers can modify and adapt the materials to draw on students' diversity of experiences and cultures. The extensive use of group work, discussions, and deliberations offers ways to challenge students with different interests and needs.

Lessons start with questions about social issues that have global relevance. The intent of the program is to provide students with opportunities to experience scientific concepts in particular situations and establish the relationship of these concepts to social issues pertinent to a wide range of geographic, social, and political contexts. Teachers may need to adapt some lessons and supply supplementary resources if the particular contexts used are unfamiliar to their students.

Developmental Appropriateness

The emphasis on concrete experiences combined with opportunities to make inferences and evaluate decisions helps foster the transition from concrete to abstract thinking for learners at the middle-grades level. In order to facilitate this progression, the program bases its approach on a working definition of science as "a way of asking and seeking answers to questions." This definition serves as the foundation for the issue-oriented approach of the program, which, in addition to stimulating students' interest, demonstrates respect for students' views and opinions and allows for both independence and peer interactions.

Teaching Resources and Support

Print Materials

Teacher's Guide: Each module includes a teacher's guide with the following components:

- Conceptual Overview: Displays in a matrix format the major concepts and processes addressed in the module, and cross-references them to the related societal issues.

- Module Overview: Describes the module and its activities, and includes information about the student's role and work.
- Activity: Includes an overview of the activity; pacing information; statement of purpose; materials list for the teacher, the class, and the individual students; and suggestions for advance preparation. An introductory section presents the lesson's concept(s) and provides step-by-step recommendations for the presentation of the concept(s). It also includes recommendations for teaching strategies and suggestions for discussions, describing for the teacher how the activity should unfold in the classroom. At the end of the activity are blackline masters to be duplicated for classroom use.
- Achievement Test Item Bank: Includes factual, short-answer, and essay-type questions. Answers are included.
- Glossary: Explains terms likely to be unfamiliar to students. Brief glossaries and background information sections are also included in the activities.
- Tips for Solution Preparation: Provides directions for preparing additional amounts of the required solutions and obtaining the other materials used in the activities (when the materials in the accompanying kit become depleted).

The Kit: Contains all the laboratory equipment and materials—containers and reagents—as well as printed support materials for a class of 32 students and their teacher.

Student Books: Contain directions for laboratory activities and investigations, and sample data tables.

Professional Development

On-site professional development workshops are available. The publisher recommends professional development for teachers before they implement the curriculum and follow-up as needed. The basic professional development component consists of a two- to three-day hands-on workshop series that covers the philosophy and instructional design of the program and the use of activities. The publisher offers workshops and seminars on a regular basis. In-service presentations vary in length and content, based upon the needs of districts, schools, and teachers. Offerings range from one-hour awareness sessions to multiple-day, in-depth professional development. All workshop leaders are classroom teachers.

For information about professional development offerings, visit <www.Lab-Aids.com>, or call Lab-Aids at (800) 381-8003.

Additional professional development options include the National SEPUP Fellows Program and the National Leadership Institute in Berkeley, California, offered by the developer (Lawrence Hall of Science). These professional development programs, which are held during the summer months, are more focused and specialized, and require an application process. Visit the developer's website for more information.

Teacher Hints and Guidance

Content Knowledge: The modules alone do not provide students with all the information they need to fully master the science content. Teachers need to provide additional materials and resources to help students learn the content.

Teaching Strategies: Because of the way the activities are structured, students must learn how to find and use evidence and formulate their own questions. Teachers, therefore, have to be knowledgeable about relevant science resources and skilled in questioning strategies.

Extensions: Modules present options for extending the learning experiences. Teachers can add activities when needed in order to clarify or strengthen the development of science concepts.

Flexibility: Each module stands alone. This characteristic makes the program flexible for teachers as they decide how to use and combine different pieces of curricula. Teachers can integrate individual modules into other curriculum programs.

Preparation: Kits are available for all modules, but teachers frequently have to refurbish and replace materials and reagents.

Sample Lesson

The following is an excerpt from the teacher's guide for *Toxic Waste*. Copyright 1996 by The Regents of the University of California. All rights reserved.

Metal Replacement

Overview

Students are given a problem to investigate: Do other metals besides aluminum remove copper ions from solution? Students test three different metals in the used copper chloride solution. After deciding which of the metals tested removes copper ions from the solution, they examine cost and safety information to decide which metal would be the best to use. The weighing of various factors in making a use decision is highlighted.

Time

One 40- to 50-minute class period for the student activity and additional period for questions and discussion. Optional activities will require extra time.

Purpose

The students will

1. Discover that other metals remove copper ions from a solution of copper chloride
2. Learn that some of the metals tested remove copper better than others
3. Appreciate that many factors such as cost, safety, and effectiveness must be considered before the final choice of which metal to use can be made

Materials

For the class:
• A large container (beaker or jar) to collect used solutions

For each pair of students:
• SEPUP tray
• Medicine dropper
• Aluminum washer
• Iron washer
• Zinc shot
• Stirring stick or plastic spoon
• Paper towels

For each group of four students:
• 30 ml dropping bottle of used copper chloride solution
• 30 ml dropping bottle of household ammonia

For the teacher:
• 3 small containers to collect used metal washers and zinc shot for recycling
• Blackline master of student sheet **4.1** Waste Reduction by Metal Displacement
• Overhead transparency master, Metal Costs/Waste Water Limitations (see page 84)

Getting ready

Make all materials readily available. Duplicate blackline master 4.1 for each student. Make an overhead transparency of Metal Costs/Wastewater Limitations, put the information on the board, or have a copy available for use as you see fit. To save the metals, provide a cup or suitable receptacle for each one (zinc, aluminum, and iron).

1. Introduction

In Activity Three, the students observed that aluminum foil was able to remove copper ions from a solution of copper chloride. This represents one method of waste reduction: removal of a toxic or valuable component before disposal.

Ask the students if they think that other metals besides aluminum will remove copper ions. Ask them what kind of experiment we would do to find out.

Remind students that the used copper chloride solution represents a solution that contains toxic metal (copper) ions we have to remove before disposal. We know that aluminum foil will remove copper ions and want to find out whether other metals will, too.

Students may ask why this is necessary. After all, since aluminum works fairly well, why try something else? Ask them whether they would change their minds if the aluminum was found to be as toxic, or more toxic than copper, costs too much to use, or is not so easy to find. Remind them that these other factors–cost, availability and safety–might influence the decision. As a matter of fact, it would be very expensive to use aluminum to reclaim copper.

Students might suggest that metals found in a junkyard would be a good place to start. They may suggest aluminum cans and junk iron. We will use these metals in the form of metal washers. We will also use zinc, another commonly occurring but less widely known metal.

2. Doing the experiment

Safety note: Remind students not to handle copper chloride solution or the used washers directly and to wash their hands at the end of the lab. In accordance with your school safety policies, make safety eyewear available for each student.

Review the procedure with the students. Each pair will test both washers and the zinc.

Make the materials available. Encourage students to discuss the questions with their partners as they do the experiment and to write out their answers. As you observe their progress, encourage them to record all observations in the data table.

Provide containers for recycling the washers and zinc shot. The used solutions can be collected in a large jar or beaker for disposal in accordance with your local regulations.

3. Clean up

Metal washers can be saved and recycled. Have students sort them into suitable containers. The next time they are used, provide some fine sandpaper to remove the tarnish. The pieces of zinc may or may not be used again. They may be difficult to clean because of their irregular shape. Students should wash their own trays. Collect rinse water in a large container for evaporation—dispose of it in accordance with your local regulation. This material may be saved for disposal in Activity Seven.

4. Post-lab discussion

Begin a class discussion of the activity by asking the students to share their observations and answers to the questions. Summarize their data on the chalkboard or overhead projector. Sample data is provided on the next page as a reference. Accept students' answers but insist they give evidence. If there is not a consensus on any of the observations or answers, encourage discussion among the groups. Emphasize that differences in observations can be resolved only by further experimentation.

Sample data for solutions and washers

Cup	Metal	Metal Before	Metal After	Used Copper Chloride Solution Before	Used Copper Chloride Solution After
1	Aluminum	dull gray	red-brown coating	deep blue	gray to gray-white
2	Zinc	shiny or metallic	dark red-brown coating	deep blue	clear and colorless
3	Iron	black-gray	black-red coating	deep blue	light yellow-green with red or brown bits
4	Control			deep blue	no change

Sample data table for ammonia added to five drops of solution

Cup	Metal	Observations
4	Aluminum	gray gel-like precipitate forms
5	Zinc	white precipitate forms
6	Iron	brown precipitate forms
7	Control	bluish green to dark blue precipitate forms

5. Answers to the questions

Question 1. Which one of the metals seemed to react the most? What is the evidence? Most will say that the aluminum or zinc seemed to react the most and will cite the vigorous bubbling, rapid deposition of presumably copper metal, and rapid disappearance of the blue color.

Question 2. The blue color of the copper chloride solution disappears as copper is removed. Which metal seemed to do this best? Aluminum or zinc.

Question 3. Which metal has the most copper deposited on it? Aluminum or zinc.

Question 4. Did you notice differences in the way each solution reacts with household ammonia? Be specific. Yes. (See sample data in chart.) The control forms the blue precipitate while the other precipitates do not.

Question 5. Do you have evidence that the metal in the washers removed some copper from the copper chloride solution? There is visual evidence that the blue color is gone, the red-brown coating on the washer or shot, and chemical evidence from the ammonia test.

Question 6. If you were to use one of these metals to remove the copper ions from the used solution, which would you choose? Give reasons for your choice. (Decide whether you want to make available to students all of the information contained on the transparency master titled Metal Costs/Waste Water Limitations, page 84. If so, they can use this information to answer the question. For up-to-date metal costs, check commodities prices, which appear weekly in the financial section of many newspapers.) Answers will vary. Some students might suggest that they want to use aluminum or zinc, since these two generally removed copper best. Others would say that zinc is their choice because it works well and is cheaper than aluminum. Some students will choose iron even if it didn't seem to remove as much copper. This may be because it is cheap and the permitted disposal concentrations are more lenient than for the others.

6. Discussing student choices in Question 6

Question 6 explores a key consideration. The point to make here is that we must often consider many factors when we attempt to treat a hazardous waste. Aluminum, our first choice for copper ion removal based on reactivity, has high value as a recyclable scrap metal. It is eliminated as a possibility even though its disposal concentration is not currently regulated. Iron is not so reactive as the others, but it is attractive because it is cheap. Zinc, though very reactive and slightly more expensive than aluminum, can be toxic to some organisms at levels below 5 ppm. Blue gill, salmon fry, and crustacea are especially susceptible to zinc toxicity. In summary, we may have to compromise in our choice since many factors besides reactivity must be considered.

Ask the students if they can remember an instance when they had to settle for a second or even a third choice. What were the other factors they had to consider as they made a decision? One example may be the selection of electives in their class schedule. Popular electives may be over-enrolled, times may conflict with required courses, and so on.

Another important point to emphasize with students is that, according to most regulations (See Section 3 b., page 39), dilution by adding large amounts of water to a waste stream would not be permitted. In general, we will find that progressive waste management techniques seek to reduce the volume or amount of waste material that is generated. This is done by reducing the waste stream at the source.

Some students may suggest a combination of metals, using one that is cheap (say, iron) for the first stage, in which the bulk of the copper is removed. A more effective metal may then be used in smaller amounts. This approach may have merit, but students should consider that in each case they are replacing each copper ion with another metal ion that may require subsequent removal. Students may begin to appreciate the complexity of the problem.

Science and Technology for Children (STC)

Publisher: Carolina Biological Supply Company
2700 York Road
Burlington, NC 27215
(800) 334-5551

Year Published: 1994

Developer: National Science Resource Center
(NSRC), Washington, DC

Website: http://www.si.edu/nsrc

Grade Levels: K–6

Science Domains: Earth science, life science, physical science, and technology

Overview

Science and Technology for Children (STC) units were developed as a complete K–6 science program. Districts that use the elementary grade units find the grade 6 units a good way to continue a standards-based program in the middle grades. The grade 6 program includes four units, one each for life science, earth science, physical science, and design technology. Some schools use the four modules over the course of the school year; others use one or two units in addition to other grade 6 curriculum materials.

> " The focus of each module is naturally appealing to students. As one example, kids always fool around with magnets and motors. When I see them working on the *Magnets and Motors* module, I can tell that they finally see the connection between magnetism and electricity."
>
> — Science teacher

STC activities involve students in questioning; hands-on investigations; exploration; collection, analysis, and interpretation of data; and discussions in which they draw conclusions and make recommendations. *STC's* instructional approach is based on a four-step learning cycle—focus, explore, reflect, and apply. This approach promotes the development of students' understanding of scientific concepts as well as application of their learning to technological contexts.

At the time this guide was written, NSRC, the developer of *STC,* was developing and piloting a new curriculum program—*Science and Technology Concepts for Middle Schools (STC/MS)*—comprised of eight modules for grades 7 and 8, which has the same general orientation as the *STC* units. (Chapter 4 includes a brief description of this forthcoming curriculum.)

Curriculum Focus

Sixth-grade *STC* units focus on the following topics within each strand:

Experiments with Plants (Life Science Strand): Students formulate questions about plant development, and design and conduct controlled experiments to investigate variables that affect plant growth and development. As students identify, control, and manipulate variables, they learn about the structure and function of plants, plant ecology, germination, and tropism.

Measuring Time (Earth Science Strand): Students explore phases of the moon and learn about the use of natural phenomena to keep time. They investigate and conduct experiments to study the characteristics of a pendulum, learning about astronomy as well as how to measure time. They investigate machines and explore concepts such as energy and motion.

Magnets and Motors (Physical Science Strand): Students explore the properties of magnets and the magnetic properties of electrical currents. They make a compass, investigate the relationship between magnetism and electricity by exploring the characteristics of switches and circuits, and apply their learning as they dismantle and reassemble three different kinds of motors.

The Technology of Paper (Technology Strand): Students explore the properties of paper, make paper by hand, and learn about the relationship between the properties of paper and its use. They test different types of paper for smoothness, tear resistance, opacity, water resistance, and ink receptivity. They also investigate the role of additives, embedding, and embossing in the creation of paper with a variety of properties. Students apply their learning by creating their own product through a four-step technological design process using recycled paper.

Curriculum Format

Each *STC* unit, which generally consists of 16 activities, uses a four-step learning cycle. This learning cycle is designed to develop a sequence of scientific concepts and reasoning skills.

Focus: Students examine what they know about a topic and identify questions they want to explore. After a whole-group brainstorming session, students produce a list of ideas.

Explore: Students explore scientific concepts through hands-on investigations organized as a sequence of activities. They work in groups, recording their observations on record sheets and in science journals.

Reflect: Students discuss the results of investigations, analyze their findings with their team partners, and draw conclusions. They reinforce their learning by recording their conclusions in their journals.

Apply: Students use their new learning in different contexts and apply it to real-world situations both inside and outside of the classroom.

STC has a student activity book with step-by-step instructions to guide students through classroom activities. The student book also serves as a record of student work and can be used to share student accomplishments with parents, teachers, and students themselves. Each lesson in the student book has three sections that organize students' activities and procedures.

Think and Wonder: Describes the purpose of the activities in the lesson for the student and presents concrete questions as advance organizers of the key ideas to be explored in the lesson.

Find Out for Yourself: Introduces terms and ideas related to the main concept and encourages students' reflection, both individually and in groups. Guides students through exploration of new ideas and provides suggestions for organizing information collected after brainstorming and group discussions.

Ideas to Explore: Poses questions to guide students in extending their reflections and explorations outside the classroom.

Academic Rigor

STC Meets the Standards is a tool that helps teachers determine how the curriculum aligns with specific science standards. The document describes each unit's fundamental concepts and principles, and analyzes science content, teaching methods, and assessment.

STC units encourage students to ask questions, test ideas, and draw conclusions on the basis of evidence; discuss their findings; and make links between science and the real world and between science and other areas of the curriculum. The units highlight the key concepts that are the focus of the learning experiences. Throughout the units, classroom investigations engage students in planning and conducting experiments and using resource materials. Working in teams, students formulate questions and carry out controlled experiments designed to provide data to help answer the questions. In doing their experiments, students are guided to identify, control, and manipulate variables. At the end of the unit, students apply their learning and experience to activities that involve a range of tasks that include assembling, dismantling, experimenting with, reassembling, or modifying the object of study.

Throughout the units, students also learn firsthand about the technological design process. They design products, implement their designs, evaluate them, and communicate the processes of designing and building products. They design and conduct controlled tests and support their conclusions with evidence. Classroom investigations enable students to appreciate that the quality of such products depends on appropriate design.

Connections to Other Disciplines

STC units provide opportunities for students to use their writing, speaking, and listening skills as they complete recording sheets, maintain science journals, discuss their work with peers, and write stories about topics that they are studying in science class. Students also have opportunities to develop and apply mathematics skills as they measure, weigh, compare, design data tables, and create graphs and charts.

Lessons in each unit include suggested extensions such as field trips, visits from local experts, or activities that relate science to art and music. These extensions offer opportunities to make connections between curriculum areas. For example, the *Technology of Paper* unit suggests taking a field trip to a local recycling station and inviting environmentalists and paper industry representatives to the classroom, providing the chance to explore social issues involved in paper production and use.

Assessment

The program encourages teachers to incorporate their observations of classroom activities, products of student work, and oral communication in their evaluation of students' progress. The program's assessments offer diverse opportunities for students to demonstrate their growth in scientific reasoning skills and conceptual understanding.

Units include a teacher's recording chart of student progress as well as a student's rating scale. Teachers use the charts to record the progress of individual students, tracking their work and their development of skills. Students use the rating scales to conduct self-assessments. Assessment strategies include:

Pre- and post-unit assessments: At the beginning of each unit students are asked to reflect on their current knowledge and answer questions about the topic and concepts under study. Students are encouraged to brainstorm what they know about carrying out an experiment. In subsequent lessons and in an end-of-the-unit assessment, they revisit these questions. This student information is available for the teacher to use to evaluate student growth.

Embedded assessments: Within the context of each unit, lessons present multiple opportunities for students to demonstrate and apply what they have learned. Teachers can also assess students' final projects in written or oral form. This type of assessment allows teachers to support students as they progress through the activities.

Additional assessments: At the end of every unit, students are challenged to solve a new problem using the available materials. Teachers can also supplement these assessments through the use of student portfolios, field observations, paper-and-pencil assessments, oral presentations, and participation of students in group debates and discussions.

Student self-assessment: Students complete assessments that help them to judge their own progress. Teachers can also use these as assessment tools.

Equity

As students share and consider the different opinions that emerge from group work in *STC* units, they learn to respect and value diversity of perspectives and experience. The occasions *STC* offers students to observe, experiment, interpret results, communicate, and record their observations and ideas in science journals provide opportunities for students to make sense of the phenomena under study based on their own backgrounds, experiences, and preferred styles of learning. Supplementary materials are available that offer additional, related learning experiences geared to students' varied learning styles. Spanish translations of student materials are available.

Developmental Appropriateness

The four-step learning cycle helps students understand scientific concepts, develop scientific reasoning skills, and apply their understanding and skills in an age-appropriate sequence. *STC* emphasizes cooperative learning and independent research coupled with opportunities for discussion and debate. Discussion and debate in class help students to build social and interpersonal skills.

Teaching Resources and Support

Print Materials

Teacher's Guide: The teacher's guide for each unit contains a unit overview, master materials list, and unit goals. For many units, it contains assessment strategies for each goal. It provides specific guidance for teaching strategies, such as how to conduct brainstorming sessions and assess student learning. A bibliography at the end of the guide provides information about science trade books, videotapes, software, and other learning resources relevant to the unit.

For each lesson, the main section of the teacher's guide provides the following:

- Overview and Objectives: Learning objectives and a brief explanation of how the lesson fits into the overall sequence of the unit.
- Background: Information and explanations of science content, plus classroom management tips.

- Preparation: Detailed guidance about how to prepare and distribute materials.
- Procedure: Explicit instructions for facilitating student learning experiences.
- Final Activities: Suggestions for ending the lesson, helping students reflect on their learning, and preparing students for what's to come.
- Extensions: Suggestions for optional additional activities that integrate the lesson with other areas of the curriculum or with students' real-world experiences.
- Reading Selections: Some lessons contain suggested additional readings that extend the lesson content or link it with other science disciplines or topic areas.
- Student Sheets: Master sheets for students to record information and data plus other materials that need to be photocopied.
- Notes and Tips: Additional suggestions about how to prepare materials or handle activities.
- Assessment Suggestions: Matched pre- and post-unit assessments, and strategies for ongoing assessment.

Student Materials: All sixth-grade *STC* units include student activity books that contain lesson outlines, steps to guide students through activities, and reading selections. Spanish translations of student books for all units are available on a CD-ROM, *STC en Español.*

Science Kits: Each unit kit includes most of the materials needed for a class of 30 students working in teams of two or more. The teacher's guide clearly states which materials the teacher must supply, but these are commonly available items, such as glue, scissors, tape, and overhead projector.

STC Discovery Decks: Packages of resource cards for grades 4–6. Each deck contains about 30 large cards outlining activities designed to appeal to a variety of learning styles.

Teacher Training Videos: Videotaped demonstrations accompany each unit portraying a master teacher setting up and using the materials in the science kit and classroom clips of students engaged in the unit activities.

STC Meets the Standards: This booklet provides an analysis of the STC curriculum in light of three criteria outlined by the National Research Council's *National Science Education Standards:* science content, teaching methods, and assessment.

Professional Development

The publisher offers professional development workshops to schools and districts implementing *STC*. For information about professional development, contact Carolina Biological Supply Company at (800) 334-5551.

Teacher Hints and Guidance

Preparation: Teachers who use *STC* units for the first time sometimes find preparation difficult. As they become more familiar with the materials, they become more efficient at set-up. One way to facilitate preparation is to enlist the help of students.

Materials: The supply of materials in the kits accompanying *STC* units is adequate, eliminating the problem teachers often face when they must purchase consumables on their own. Timely refurbishment of consumable kit materials remains a critical element for successful implementation of the program.

Instructional Approach/Professional Development: Teaching the materials for the first time is challenging for teachers because the instructional approach is very different from that of traditional science textbooks. Teachers need to become comfortable with an inquiry approach to teaching and learning and with having students work in groups. One teacher who has used the curriculum described how important it is for teachers to have formal professional development preparation as well as ongoing opportunities to share their experiences.

> "At first, I couldn't understand why I needed professional development to use *STC*. After having used it and taught it, I think it's essential that teachers be trained in it. . . . Each time you use it, you get insights on how to teach it better and those things get discussed during professional development sessions or when we get together and talk about using the kits."

Readings: Student activity books are very useful, but sometimes students who struggle with reading have difficulty with them. Teachers may need to provide additional support for these students.

Sample Lesson

The following is an excerpt from the teacher's edition of *Measuring Time*. Reproduced with permission from National Science Resources Center, from *Measuring Time* (Science and Technology for Children® curriculum). Copyright 1994, National Academy of Sciences.

Section II: Investigating Invented Clocks

LESSON 7 | # Using Water to Measure Time

Overview and Objectives

In this first lesson of **Section II: Investigating Time with Invented Clocks,** students investigate one way to use water to measure time. They construct a sinking water clock capable of timing an interval of 15 seconds, and they begin identifying the variables involved in determining how rapidly or slowly the clock sinks. In Lessons 8 and 9, students will plan and conduct an investigation of how changing one of the variables affects the time it takes a funnel to sink. This cycle of exploration and investigation will be repeated in Lessons 10, 11, and 12, when students plan and conduct experiments with pendulums.

- Students construct sinking water clocks.

- Students identify the variables that have an effect on the time it takes their water clocks to sink.

- Students read about water clocks used by early cultures.

Background

This lesson marks the beginning of a new section of the unit. In this section, instead of observing the natural cycles of the sun and the moon, students begin to manipulate variables to change the rate at which observable events, such as sinking objects and swinging pendulums, take place. This shift in focus corresponds with the historical shift in timekeeping methods that occurred when people first looked for improvements to the methods that relied on the sun and moon. Through ongoing observations of the moon's phases and appropriate reading selections, students will be given a context for comparing timekeeping methods.

For your information, background about the history of water clocks has been included below. The **Reading Selection** on pg. 71 of the Teacher's Guide and pg. 30 of the Student Activity Book includes additional information.

Water clocks have been in use in one form or another for more than three thousand years. They were developed to meet a real need: how to tell time on cloudy days and at night. First used in Egypt and Babylonia, water clocks were brought across the Mediterranean by the Greeks. The Greeks called water clocks **klepsydra,** which means "thief of water."

The use of water clocks shifted people's thinking about time. Sun clocks were good for telling the time of day, but water clocks could be used easily to measure the length of shorter intervals of time. For example, in ancient Greece, citizens were allotted a certain amount of time—measured by sinking water clocks—to address the Senate or a jury. In China and in the Middle East, people created very elaborate water clocks. The most elaborate used gears and simple machines.

Materials

For each student
1   science notebook
1   piece of aluminum foil, 10 cm (4″) square

For every two students
1   plastic flex tank, 4 liters (1 gal), with water
3   brass washers, 9 mm (⅜″) diameter

For the class
1   clock with a sweep second hand
1   class list, "What We Know about Measuring Time" (from Lesson 1), and a marker of a different color from previous entries
3   buckets with handles, each approx. 4 liters (1 gal)
    Several sponges
    Several sheets of newsprint and marker(s)

Preparation

1. Cut one 10-cm (4″) square piece of aluminum foil for each student.

2. Fill each plastic tank about three-fourths full with water. You may want to ask students to help with this task. If your classroom is not equipped with a sink, buckets with handles are one way to transport and pour water efficiently.

3. Display a clock with a sweep second hand in the classroom.

Procedure

1. Remind students to continue recording their observations of the moon for the next several weeks. The record of moon observations will be important evidence of the pattern of the moon's phases.

2. Ask students to describe some of the problems they encountered using the sun and moon to keep track of time. Here are some of the things they are likely to come up with:

   ■ It is impossible to tell time when it is dark or cloudy.

   ■ Sun clocks aren't portable.

   ■ It is hard to be precise.

3. Show students the "What We Know about Measuring Time" list from Lesson 1. Ask students whether the list includes ways to keep track of time without depending only on the sun or moon. Encourage them to brainstorm new ideas to add to the list.

4. Explain to students that because people had problems keeping time with the sun and moon, they began to make different types of clocks. One type—sinking water clocks—used objects sinking in water to keep track of the passage of time.

5. Ask students to discuss with their partners their ideas about how to use water to keep track of time. Have them sketch a few possible designs in their notebooks and write explanations for their sketches.

6. Now ask students to use a piece of aluminum foil and brass washers to construct a sinking water clock. Challenge them to try to find a way to make a clock that will sink in 15 seconds. Have students use the clock on the wall to compare how long it takes their water clocks to sink. Encourage a variety of designs.

Figure 7-1

Constructing a
sinking water clock

7. Distribute the materials to students. Ask them to take turns testing their sinking clocks. Encourage them to talk with each other about what they are trying to accomplish.

8. After students have completed their work with water clocks, ask them to return the materials to the storage area and dry off their work area.

9. Have students describe and illustrate in their notebooks how they made their sinking water clocks. What worked? What didn't work?

Final Activities

1. Discuss with students the various strategies they used to construct their water clocks. Have students share one of their designs. Ask questions such as the following to focus the discussion. List students' responses on a sheet of newsprint.

   ■ What are some things you did to make the clock sink more quickly? More slowly?

■ How do you know that your sinking clock is consistent—that it sinks at the same rate each time?

■ How would you change your clock if you did this activity again?

Note: Save this class list to use in Lesson 8.

2. Explain that the things students changed to make the clock sink faster or slower are called **variables**, because they are able to be "varied." Tell students that in the next two lessons they will plan and conduct an experiment with sinking water clocks. The experiment will provide evidence of what happens when one variable is changed. Students can use this evidence to design different kinds of sinking water clocks.

3. Ask students to read "Water Clocks," on pg. 30 of the Student Activity Book (pg. 71 of the Teacher's Guide). Ask them to focus on the following questions as they read.

■ What are some advantages and disadvantages of water clocks compared with sun clocks?

■ What are some types of water clocks that have been invented other than those that sink?

Extensions

1. Encourage students to design and build timers that use water to keep track of the passage of time. Ask them to explain and demonstrate their timers for the rest of the class.

2. Ask students to create advertisements to sell their sinking water clocks. Have them include at least three good reasons why someone should buy them.

Assessment

This lesson is the first of a sequence of three lessons involving the investigation of sinking water clocks and the planning and carrying out of water clock experiments.

The specific process skills involved in these three lessons are listed below.

■ Planning an experiment

■ Identifying and controlling variables

■ Collecting and interpreting data

■ Presenting results in graph form

Because development of these skills requires practice, students apply them again with pendulums in Lessons 10, 11, and 12.

At the end of Lesson 9, you will have information with which to assess students' ability to plan and conduct an experiment. For example, the plan and graph students construct in Lessons 8 and 9 will provide information about questions such as the following.

■ Is the plan reasonable? Can the students do it?

■ Do students select one and only one variable to investigate? Have students controlled all but one variable in carrying out their experiments?

■ Do the experiments carry out the plan?

■ Are the graphs that students construct labeled?

By comparing your assessment of students' skills at the end of Lesson 9 with your assessment at the end of Lesson 12, you may be able to document changes in students' skill development.

CHAPTER 4

Annotated Resources

In addition to the materials profiled in Chapter 3, there are a variety of other science curriculum materials that districts committed to standards-based reform may want to consider. In particular, at the time this guide was written, several comprehensive and year-long middle-grades curriculum programs were under development. Several of these are extensions of curriculum programs profiled or are being developed by the same groups that created profiled programs; others are new.

The first part of this chapter ("Curriculum Materials") briefly describes these forthcoming programs, as well as a number of other materials, including series of modular units which can be used to supplement other curricula or combined into yearlong programs. Also described are a number of technology-based programs. We have not reviewed these materials in depth, nor did we identify educators to interview who have had experience in using them—although the practitioners who spoke with us mentioned several of them. We urge you to learn more about these materials and examine them carefully in light of the criteria described in this guide and your own state and local standards and frameworks.

The second part of this chapter ("Additional Resources") describes a number of resources that can help districts identify, evaluate, select, adopt, and implement standards-based science curricula. These resources include published science standards and guides, curriculum evaluations and criteria, NSF-funded curriculum dissemination and implementation centers, U.S. Department of Education-funded regional consortia, professional organizations, and other sources of professional development.

At the time this guide was prepared, a number of curriculum materials were under development, and school districts should keep an eye out for their completion. These curricula—both comprehensive and supplementary—are based on research and reflect the national science standards. They have been recommended

Curriculum Materials

Forthcoming Curriculum Materials

by teachers in reform-minded districts, and are expected to meet the same kinds of criteria as the materials profiled in Chapter 3.

Constructing Ideas in Physical Science (CIPS)

Publisher:	To be determined (TBD)
Year Published:	Estimated completion date, 2003
Developers:	San Diego State University, University of Minnesota, Western Michigan University
Contact:	fgoldber@sciences.sdsu.edu
Grade Levels:	6–9
Science Domain:	Physical science

CIPS, an inquiry-based, yearlong physical science course, engages middle-grades students in constructing an understanding of important physical science concepts. The program will make use of extensive hands-on experiences, complemented by innovative computer software. CIPS includes six units: *Course Overview, Motion and Force, Light and Color, Electricity and Magnetism, The Nature of Matter,* and *Chemical Interactions.* A science fiction storyline weaves through the modules, and ideas about systems interactions, energy transformations, and energy conservation are developed and applied in a variety of contexts.

FOSS (Full Option Science System) for Middle School

Publisher:	Delta Education
Year Published:	2000
Developer:	Lawrence Hall of Science, University of California, Berkeley
Website:	http://www.lhs.berkeley.edu/FOSS/
Grade Levels:	6–8
Science Domains:	Earth, space, life, and physical science

FOSS for Middle School is a general science curriculum for middle-grades students. The curriculum is organized into topical units, called courses, within three strands: *Earth and Space Science, Life Science,* and *Physical Science and Technology.* Each course is an in-depth unit requiring nine to twelve weeks of instruction. The units have approximately ten investigations, each with three to seven parts.

Each unit contains a detailed teacher's guide (overview, materials preparation, goals and objectives, at-a-glance investigation chart, science background, lesson plans, transparency masters, teacher answer sheets, assessments with masters and scoring guides, CD-ROM user's guide, and references); a kit of student laboratory equipment; a resources book (100 pages containing images, data, and readings for each student); an investigations book (43 student sheets and organizers for the investigations); and a CD-ROM (for use as a whole class demonstration tool as well as an individual or small group instructional tool).

GLACIER: Global Connections

Publisher:	TBD
Year Published:	TBD
Developers:	Education Development Center, Inc., Rice University
Website:	http://www.glacier.rice.edu
Grade Levels:	6–9
Science Domains:	Earth, ocean, and space science

Glacier, a thematic curriculum consisting of four modules, is designed to supplement an existing science curriculum. *Glacier* allows students to explore the geology, glacial geology, geomorphology, geography, oceanography, meteorology, astronomy, and environmental science of Antarctica while honing critical-thinking skills. Students use actual data collected in Antarctica to conduct their experiments and access scientists, explorers, and other students via the World Wide Web. In *Glacier,* students conduct multidisciplinary, open-ended activities in cooperative groups.

Modules have eight to twelve student investigations, each requiring one to three days of classroom time. An entire module takes from three to six weeks to complete. The theme of each module is a real-world, scientific problem. Modules include a teacher's guide, reproducible masters, and a website that contains the Antarctica data and images. The materials also include teaching suggestions and background information to assist the teacher with each of the investigations.

PUSD Middle School Curriculum

Publisher:	TBD
Year Published:	TBD
Developers:	Pasadena Unified School District, Caltech Precollege Science Initiative (CAPSI)
Website:	http://www.capsi.caltech.edu/
Grade Levels:	7–10
Science Domains:	Life, earth, and physical science

At the time this guide was written, four units of the *PUSD Middle School Curriculum* had been completed—two for seventh grade (*Microbiology* and *Health Biology*) and two for eighth grade (*Moving Through the Universe and Matter* and *Chemical Change*). Other units are planned for grades 9 and 10. In addition to the written units, this program includes a CD-ROM that contains the units in electronic format, samples of student work for the teacher, homework assignments, pre-tests, and assessments for students. A website will also support *PUSD Middle School Curriculum* by providing additional materials and corrections and updates to the already existing units. It will also reference relevant websites and other documents that can support both students and teachers. Teachers using one or more units of this program will be networked via e-mail and encouraged to share information and suggestions about the units they are teaching.

Investigating Earth Systems

Publisher:	It's About Time
Website:	http://www.its-about-time.com
Year Published:	Fall 2000 (expected date of publication)
Developer:	American Geological Institute
Grade Levels:	5–8
Science Domain:	Earth science

Investigating Earth Systems includes nine activity-based modules designed to address the earth science components of the *National Science Education Standards.* It focuses on student questions and investigations, and incorporates collaborative learning strategies. Modules for grades 5 and 6 include *Investigating Soil, Investigating Oceans,* and *Investigating Materials and Minerals.* Modules for grades 6 and 7 include *Investigating Water as a Resource, Investigating Climate and Weather,* and *Investigating Rocks and Landforms.* The three modules for grades 7 and 8 are *Investigating Dynamic Earth, Investigating Energy Resources,* and *Investigating Life Through Time.*

Investigating Earth Systems makes connections across disciplines. It provides substantial teacher support. Student journals allow students to record progress and track their understanding of ideas, and serve as a component of performance assessments. Teachers also use journals to note how particular investigations worked and to keep track of management strategies and organizational resources. Additional components of this program include a video for each module, a CD-ROM, and an interactive website.

SEPUP Science and Life Issues (SALI)

Publisher:	Lab-Aids, Inc.
Year Published:	TBD
Developer:	Lawrence Hall of Science, University of California, Berkeley
Website:	http://www.lhs.berkeley.edu/SEPUP/sali.html
Grade Levels:	6–8
Science Domain:	Life science

SALI is a life science course for use in grade 6, 7, or 8. It can serve as a yearlong program, or it can be combined with *Issues, Evidence and You* (profiled in Chapter 3) to make an integrated two-year program. Modules of *Issues, Evidence and You* and *SALI* are also available individually. *SALI* is divided into three thematic segments: *My Body and Me, Living Partnerships,* and *Using Tools and Ideas.* These segments are designed to facilitate conceptual understanding and to provide opportunities for students to link their learning on various topics. The course also emphasizes scientific thinking, personal and societal decision making, science and technology as professions, and science as a predictive activity.

Science and Technology Concepts (STC) for Middle Schools

Publisher:	Carolina Biological Supply Company
Years Published:	Fall 2000 (first four modules); 2002 (remaining modules)
Developer:	National Science Resources Center
Website:	http://www.si.edu/nsrc/stcms/overview.htm
Grade Levels:	7–8
Science Domains:	Life, earth, and physical science, and technological design

When completed, *STC* will comprise eight units for grades 7 and 8, including teacher and student guides, resource books, and professional development modules for teachers. The instructional units will be balanced among life science, earth science, physical science, and technological design. The components are designed to be offered as two one-year courses (each with one unit from each of the scientific strands) or as four single-semester courses. The eight units in this program include *Catastrophic Events; Energy, Machines and Motion; Human Body Systems; Properties of Matter; The Earth in Space; Light; Organisms;* and *Electric Circuits and Control Systems.* The first four modules, along with the materials and apparatus kits for each module, are available in the fall of 2000. The remaining four modules and materials will be available in 2002.

Other Published Curriculum Materials

The following materials are similar to those profiled in Chapter 3. They include self-contained units that can stand alone and units that can be combined into a full-year course or "mixed and matched" to supplement other modular units or texts. They vary in their structure, however, from one or more coherent units that focus on particular subject matter (e.g., *Cambridge Physics Outlet* and *Matter and Molecules*), to more wide-ranging sequences of units (e.g., *GEMS, IMaST*), to collections of activities that do not develop concepts over time (e.g., *Microcosmos, Thinking Science*).

Astronomy Resources for Intercurricular Elementary Science (ARIES)

Publisher:	Charlesbridge Publishing
Website:	http://www.charlesbridge.com/school/
Year Published:	1998 (first three units)
Developer:	Harvard Smithsonian Center for Astrophysics
Grade Levels:	3–8
Science Domains:	Earth, space, and physical science

ARIES is an astronomy-based physical science program for students in grades 3 through 8. *ARIES* consists of eight modules, five of which were still in development at the time this guide was written. The modules are *Exploring Time, Exploring Light and Color, Exploring the Earth in Motion,*

Exploring Waves, Exploring Navigation, Exploring Space, Exploring Energy, and *Exploring Motion and Forces.* The modules can be used in any sequence to fit the needs of the local science curriculum and each one requires about 16 weeks of instructional time.

The program engages students in a series of structured explorations and offers procedures for using readily available materials to build models and equipment for the investigations. The two main components are a teacher's manual and a student science journal. The teacher's manual organizes instruction for each unit with detailed lesson plans, assessments, and connections to other content areas. The student journal provides a structure for students to record observations, make hypotheses, and draw conclusions. An optional apparatus kit is also available.

Cambridge Physics Outlet (CPO)

Publisher:	Cambridge Physics Outlet
Year Published:	1996
Developer:	Tom Hsu
Website:	http://www.cpo.com
Grade Levels:	4–12
Science Domain:	Physical science

CPO is an integrated mathematics and science curriculum comprised of 11 modules. Each module is a two-part package: (1) a teacher's guide which includes information necessary to use the activities in the classroom, and (2) photocopy masters for a set of student activity guides, a cut-and-paste quiz builder, and scoring rubrics for assessment. Most of the CPO activities have three skill levels to accommodate students at three grade ranges: 4–8, 7–11, and 11–12+. The three levels of learning activities are: Level A which builds students' familiarity with the concepts and skills being introduced, Level B which builds from Level A and helps students tie together related concepts, and Level C which examines the concepts in Level B in greater depth and for deeper understanding. Teachers and the program's developer consider Level A appropriate for students in grades 5 to 9. Some of the titles in Level A are *Car and Ramp, Sound and Waves, Electric Circuits, Periodic Puzzle, Roller Coaster,* and *Gears and Levers.*

Cradleboard Teaching Project

Publisher:	Nihewan Foundation
Year Published:	1997
Developer:	Buffy Sainte-Marie
Website:	http://www.cradleboard.org
Grade Levels:	K–12
Science Domain:	Physical science

The *Cradleboard Teaching Project* provides three kinds of curriculum materials: core curriculum materials from a Native American perspective, tribe-specific materials developed with participating Native American communities, and technology-based interactive materials. At the middle-grades level, the project offers curriculum units in science and four other subject areas. Each of the units is supplemented with appropriate maps, videos, charts, lesson plans, and activities. In most classes that use *Cradleboard,* students study one or two Native American core curriculum units per year.

Another component is an interactive CD-ROM, *Science Through Native American Eyes,* designed for use at grade 6, which uses video, speech, animation, text, and music to present principles of friction and sound, and the benefits and constraints of building materials used in various Native American lodges. The CD-ROM also engages students in tests of their content understanding, thinking skills, reading, writing, and computer keyboarding skills.

Great Explorations in Math and Science (GEMS)

Publisher:	**Lawrence Hall of Science, University of California, Berkeley**
Year Published:	**1989**
Developer:	**Lawrence Hall of Science**
Website:	**http://www/lhs.berkeley.edu/**
Grade Levels:	**PreK–10**
Science Domains:	**Life, earth, and physical science**

GEMS consists of approximately 60 units, 40 of which are appropriate for middle-grades students. Titles include *Chemical Reactions; Terrarium Habitats; Earth, Moon and Stars;* and *Bubble-ology.* The units cover a range of mathematics and science topics and can serve as a supplement to existing curricula or be grouped together to create a curriculum sequence. Each unit varies in length and may be taught over a range of two to ten weeks. Although many *GEMS* units are designed, written, and tested for specific grade levels, many guides contain suggestions for ways to modify or adapt the activities for younger or older students.

While there is no student book, the teacher's guide includes step-by-step instructions for each activity, background information on the topic, lists of resources for teachers and students, assessment suggestions, and literature connections. In addition, the handbook *Once Upon a GEMS Guide* provides an extensive listing of literature selections that connect to the *GEMS* units. A parents' guide suggests ways that the units can be used at home, in the community, or by classroom volunteers. The handbook *Insights and Outcomes: Assessments for Great Explorations in Math and Science* provides ready-made assessments to accompany the units.

Human Biology

Publisher:	Glencoe/McGraw-Hill
Website:	http://www.everydaylearning.com
Year Published:	1999
Developer:	Program in Human Biology at Stanford University
Grade Levels:	6–9
Science Domain:	Life science

Human Biology is a modular life science curriculum program with ten units that can supplement or extend any life science or health curriculum. The units are grouped into three categories: Human Systems (*Digestion and Nutrition, Lives of Cells, Circulation, Nervous System, Genetics,* and *Breathing*), Adolescent Topics (*Your Changing Body, Reproduction,* and *Sexuality*), and The Environment (*Ecology*). The units require about three weeks to complete and can be used in any combination or in any order. They are also designed to make connections to other curriculum areas, including mathematics, social studies, health, language arts, and physical education.

The program includes softbound student books that contain readings, activities, data, and questions to promote student investigation and learning of science content. Teacher's guides provide an overview of the unit, an activity guide, and suggestions for teaching each section. A program guide explains features of the teacher's and student guides and offers suggestions for modifying the program for a variety of middle-grades settings and tips on implementing the *Human Biology* curriculum.

Integrated Mathematics, Science, and Technology (IMaST)

Publisher:	Glencoe/McGraw-Hill
Years Published:	1996–1998
Developer:	Center for Mathematics, Science and Technology Education, Illinois State University
Website:	http://www.ilstu.edu/depts/cemast
Grade Levels:	7–8
Science Domains:	Life, earth, and physical science

IMaST is a two-year, integrated mathematics, science, and technology curriculum that includes ten modules intended to provide a full curriculum for each of the three disciplines. It is designed to be taught by a team of three or more teachers for approximately 120 minutes per day for a full year. The modules are *Wellness, Food Production, Waste Management, Energy Transformations, Manufacturing, Forecasting, Animal Habitats, Human Settlements, Systems,* and *Communication Pathways.*

IMaST promotes experience-based, hands-on learning for students. In addition to the three integrated subjects, *IMaST* also connects to other disciplines such as social studies and language arts. The program provides opportunities for students to apply the concepts and skills taught to new situations. Assessments focus on how well students can apply knowledge and skills to new situations. *IMaST* includes a student text, a booklet of journal sheets, a teacher resource binder, activity assessments, and a rubric outlining evaluation criteria.

Matter and Molecules

Publisher:	The Institute for Research on Teaching, College of Education, Michigan State University
Year Published:	1988
Developer:	Michigan State University
Website:	http://ed-web3.educ.msu.edu/Publications
Grade Levels:	6–8
Science Domain:	Physical science

Matter and Molecules is a single unit designed to teach middle-grades students about kinetic molecular theory. It has four main themes: understanding the nature and properties of matter, identifying and describing physical changes in matter, developing molecular explanations for observable properties and phenomena, and describing and explaining the world around us. The unit is arranged in lesson clusters, with the number of lessons in each cluster varying from three to five. Not all lessons have the same format; however, each takes about 45 minutes to complete. Thirty-five lessons make up the unit, and teachers should allow at least seven weeks to teach the entire unit.

The program includes a *Science Book* (student text), which explains the important ideas about matter and molecules. It also includes a set of teaching strategies and student activities to facilitate student comprehension of the text. An *Activity Book* contains questions for students to answer about each activity and demonstration. Separately packaged questions and tests help students consolidate their understanding of an entire lesson cluster. A set of overhead transparencies is designed to help teachers facilitate class discussions about the key ideas in the unit. Charts and posters help students remember and organize key ideas. The videotape *Making Dew,* from the *Voyage of the Mimi* television series, is also used to help students envision molecular motion.

The Microcosmos Curriculum Guide to Exploring Microbial Space

Publisher:	Kendall/Hunt Publishing Company
Phone:	(800) KH-BOOKS
Year Published:	1992
Developer:	Boston University
Grade Levels:	7–9
Science Domains:	Life and earth science

Microcosmos is a collection of explorations intended to make students familiar with microorganisms and their importance in life and earth science. The program is inexpensive and offers hands-on experiences that do not require elaborate equipment or materials. It focuses on developing process and critical-thinking skills and can be integrated into an existing science curriculum.

The program includes a three-ring binder that allows for periodic updates, background, and enrichment pieces to be added to the original materials. Teachers can move activities around, add notes, build or re-create the book to fit their needs. There is no set sequence to the activities, although the authors do suggest one. Teachers determine the sequence based on their students' needs. In addition to the explorations, a section of the binder lists books and articles that provide background information and supplemental reading about the concepts presented.

Thinking Science

Publisher:	**Research for Better Schools (RBS) Publications**
Website:	**http://www.rbs.org**
Year Published:	**1992**
Developer:	**Center for Educational Studies, King's College, London**
Grade Levels:	**7–12**
Science Domains:	**Life and physical science**

Thinking Science is a collection of 30 classroom activities designed to provide students with opportunities to develop and practice higher-order thinking skills. Intended to supplement and enrich a science curriculum for grades 7 to 12, it helps students to develop concepts and integrate ideas. Each activity involves an experiment, begins with an introduction describing the activity's objectives, and includes an apparatus summary, a procedure summary outlining steps and ideas of the lesson, and a full procedure description. Each activity requires one or two class periods to complete. Many of the activities can be taught as a mini-series in a sequence of two or three. Although the activities are not labeled "biology," "chemistry," or "physics," they may be grouped by concept.

The materials include both student and teacher manuals. Student manuals include worksheets for recording data and observations; work cards that provide instructions, information, and problems; and activities that include example cards containing illustrations of concepts for discussion. Teacher manuals describe various instructional strategies and ways for teachers to assess students' learning. Some of the concepts addressed by the 30 activities are: variables and relationships, proportionality, formal models, compound variables, and equilibrium.

A World in Motion II: The Design Experience

Publisher:	**Society of Automotive Engineers**
Year Published:	**1998**
Developers:	**Education Development Center, Inc., Society of Automotive Engineers**
Website:	**http://www.sae.org/students/awim.htm**
Grade Levels:	**7–8**
Science Domains:	**Design engineering and physical science**

A World in Motion II is a multidisciplinary curriculum centered on two engineering design projects. Challenge 2, for seventh grade, centers around designing a moving toy for a fictional toy company. Challenge 3, for eighth grade, focuses on designing a flying toy for a fictional publishing company. These design challenges provide a storyline that closely integrates the science learning activities, which form the core of the experience, with mathematics, technology education, social studies, and language arts. Over the course of eight weeks, students work together in engineering design teams, as a team of teachers leads them through a six-phase design process: set goals, build knowledge, design, build and test, finalize the model, and present. Key concepts include force, motion, gears, and gear trains in Challenge 2, and lift, drag, and equilibrium in Challenge 3.

The programs consist of a teacher's guide and a set of construction materials. The teacher's guide provides an overview and detailed lesson plans for all the disciplines involved. The guide also contains student sheets for recording data and suggestions for planning and preparing for the various steps in the engineering design process. The guide and the kit materials are available free of charge to teachers who have a community sponsor.

Although other materials described in this chapter include optional technology components, those listed in this section require use of the technology. These materials can be used to supplement other curricula.

Technology-Based Materials

Biodiversity Counts

Publisher:	American Museum of Natural History
Year Published:	1998
Developer:	American Museum of Natural History
Website:	http://www.amnh.org/
Grade Levels:	6–9
Science Domain:	Life science

Biodiversity Counts is an inquiry-based outdoor education project that integrates hands-on science with telecommunications technology. In this program, students and teachers inventory the plant and arthropod life in their local environment and observe the relationships among them. In conducting field research, students make scientific observations, collect evidence and record data, keep field journals, identify and classify evidence, analyze data, publish work for peer review, and make public exhibitions of their work. Students learn how museum scientists conduct their investigations and apply that knowledge to their own field-work. In the classroom, students learn technological skills by using e-mail and the World Wide Web to share their data with other participants, both regionally and nationally.

A website hosted by the American Museum of Natural History is the hub of the project. "Data Central," one area of the website, has students use electronic field journals to identify and quantify the species that they find. Resources include links to other useful websites such as plant identification guides and museum staff biographies. *National Student Journal* is an electronic, peer- and teacher-reviewed journal in which students publish their work. "School Sites" provides information about participating schools across the country.

Global Lab: An Integrated Science Program

Publisher:	Kendall/Hunt Publishing Company
Year Published:	2000
Developer:	TERC
Website:	http://globallab.terc.edu/
Grade Levels:	8–10
Science Domains:	Earth, life, and physical science

Global Lab is an interdisciplinary science course for students in grades 8 to 10. It is a full-year, introductory course with an environmental theme. Students select a site in which to investigate the terrestrial, aquatic, and aerial aspects of the environment. They collect and then submit their data over the Internet. They also post data to a website for other classes around the world to retrieve. This program involves extensive use of web-based collaborations, online publishing, and e-mail.

Global Lab includes six units that introduce four scientific themes: interaction of matter and energy, biogeochemical cycles, biomes and biodiversity, and the earth as a system. By the end of the *Global Lab* year, students will have designed and directed extended investigations related to the four scientific themes. The *Global Lab* materials include a teacher's notebook, student team research guides, a toolkit, tools for telecollaboration and data exchange, and background and reference materials.

Global Learning and Observations to Benefit the Environment (GLOBE) Program

Publisher:	National Oceanographic and Atmospheric Administration (NOAA)
Year Published:	1997
Developer:	Globe Development Group
Website:	http://www.globe.gov
Grade Levels:	K–12
Science Domain:	Environmental science

GLOBE is a hands-on environmental science and education program that links students, teachers, and scientists from around the world in learning about the environment. Students from over 80 countries collect environmental data and transmit them to a central processing facility via the Internet. Students can then access data collected from other *GLOBE* sites in three ways, downloading data as raw numbers, graphical representations, or geographic visualizations. Students collect data on the atmosphere, hydrology, soil, land cover/biology, and seasons. They use a unit on Global Positioning Systems (GPS) to establish locations of their study sites. In addition, students learn to carry out scientifically rigorous observations of the earth and learn to use measurements and data as part of their study of environmental science. Participating scientists also use students' *GLOBE* data for environmental research.

The program provides a teacher's guide that includes student activities, suggestions for implementation, and instructions (protocols) for conducting the various required measurements. In order to implement the program, teachers are required to attend professional development sessions. The *GLOBE* program provides five days of free professional development at various facilities across the country.

Integrated Science

Publisher:	**Center for Communication and Educational Technology (CCET)**
Years Published:	**1996–1997**
Developer:	**CCET, University of Alabama**
Website:	**http://www.ccet.ua.edu**
Grade Levels:	**6–8**
Science Domains:	**Life, physical, earth, and space science**

Integrated Science is a multiyear program that can be used in conjunction with an existing science program or as a stand-alone. It focuses on thematic concepts integrating perspectives from biology, chemistry, physics, and earth and space science. The program moves from concrete aspects of the integrated concepts in grade 6 to more abstract concepts in grades 7 and 8. The program includes four blocks of study for each grade level. Each block requires about six weeks of classroom time.

Integrated Science provides a number of resources for teachers and students, including regular telecasts, teacher's manuals, student books, science kits, professional development for teachers, and follow-up online communication. Three times per week, an on-air instructor, accompanied by visiting scientists and other guests, introduces major science topics and themes via the telecasts. Teacher's manuals are available for each block of study and include daily lesson plans, hands-on activities, block objectives, and assessments. In addition, science kits contain materials for the hands-on activities and student books provide additional background material and homework assignments. Teachers are supported through summer workshops that help them to master and implement new science content and teaching methods.

Journey North

Publisher:	**Annenberg/CPB Projects**
Year Published:	**2000**
Developers:	**Elizabeth Howard, Julie Brophy, Joel Halvorson, Laura Erickson, Beth Allen, Ed Piou, Wei-Hsin Fu**
Website:	**http://www.learner.org/jnorth**
Grade Levels:	**K–12**
Science Domain:	**Environmental science**

Journey North is an online project in which students track the coming of spring by investigating aspects of their local environment, including the migration patterns of butterflies, birds, and mammals; the budding of plants; and changing daylight. Students track a dozen migratory species and share their field observations with other classrooms across the country and the world. Students also explore such questions as how wind and weather affect species as they migrate, what routes they take, and what risks they face along the way. In addition, students learn about conservation efforts to protect various wintering grounds along the migration path. Students are linked with scientists who serve as resources by sharing their expertise directly with the classroom.

Middle School Gateways

Publisher: Riverdeep Interactive Learning
Year Published: 1999
Developer: Riverdeep Interactive Learning
Website: http://www.riverdeep.net/html/simlibrary_frame.html
Grade Levels: 6–8
Science Domains: Life and physical science

Part of the *Logal Simlibrary Science and Math Program, Middle School Gateways* offers online simulation activities and downloadable teacher lesson plans and handouts for 15 different topics. Some of the titles include *Chemical Reactions, Waves, Understanding Photosynthesis,* and *Human Circulatory System.* A paid subscription to Riverdeep Interactive Learning includes full access to Simlibrary science activities. Students learn through interactive multimedia presentations, science simulations, tool-based activities, and membership in an online community. Teachers are provided with lesson plans, access to community resources (e.g., museums and other informal education providers), various teaching tools, a support center, a calendar of community events, and a monthly newsletter. Once they have subscribed, teachers may also access correlations of the activities to curriculum standards and leading textbooks.

Minorities in Science

Publisher: CSY, Inc.
Year Published: 1996–1997
Developer: CSY, Inc.
Website: http://www.csy.com
Grade Levels: 4–9
Science Domains: Life, physical, and earth science

Minorities in Science is a multimedia instructional program that is designed to extend an existing science curriculum. It provides students with a view of scientists that they may not ordinarily see. The program presents six contemporary minority and women scientists: Dr. Eloy Rodriguez, plant biochemist and toxicologist; Dr. Denise Stephenson-Hawk, atmospheric scientist; Dr. Anthony M. Johnson, physicist; Dr. Lisa D. White, micropaleontologist; Dr. William M. Jackson, astrochemist; and Dr. Alissa J. Arp, ecological physiologist. For each of the six scientists, the program provides a biography, a conversation, and an interactive science simulation. The scientists introduce themselves, tell how they chose their careers, and describe their areas of expertise. In the conversations, scientists answer personal and professional questions students would likely ask. The scientists extend their conversations with students via e-mail on the program's website. In the simulations, the scientists lead students in instructional experiments in their fields. The website also provides data sheets for students to use in organizing data from these experiments.

Additional resources include an *International Faces of Science® (IFS)* CD-ROM database and bilingual videodiscs. The database contains profiles of over 500 women and minority scientists in the United States and Canada, and the videodiscs feature dual audio tracks—one in English and the other in Spanish. The *IFS* database is available on the Internet and may be accessed through the program's website. The program also offers teacher training.

National Geographic Kids Network

Publisher:	National Geographic Society (NGS)
Years Published:	1989, 1997–1999
Developer:	TERC
Websites:	http://www.terc.edu/byterc/ngs.html
Grade Levels:	3–9
Science Domains:	Earth, life, and physical science

National Geographic Kids Network is an interdisciplinary curriculum consisting of web-based units that provide teachers with a great amount of flexibility. Students investigate topics that are of global significance, such as water supply, soil, and the atmosphere. The curriculum includes middle-grades units that are designed to last approximately 25 class sessions, or about eight weeks each: *What Is Our Soil Good For? Is Our Water at Risk? How Loud Is Too Loud? Are We Getting Enough Oxygen?* Older versions of the units required students to share data live through a modem or high-speed Internet connection. The most recent version allows students to post data on a website for retrieval by other classes at a later date.

The program includes a teacher's guide, posters, transparencies, student readings and activity sheets, assessment tools, and reference materials. It also includes *NGS Works,* a software program used with all of the units, providing tools for word processing, graph making, map making, and telecommunications. In the most recent version, all of the student materials are also available online with links to other web resources. The program further supports communication between NGS teachers and students via an electronic bulletin board.

Science 2000+

Publisher:	Kendall/Hunt Publishing Co.
Year Published:	1995
Developer:	Decision Development Corporation
Website:	http://www.kendallhunt.com
Grade Levels:	5–9
Science Domains:	Earth, life, and physical science

Science 2000+ is a multiyear, multimedia science curriculum that takes an integrated, thematic approach to the earth, life, and physical sciences. The curriculum is framed around six themes identified by Project 2061 of AAAS in *Science for All Americans*: energy, evolution, patterns of change, scale and structure, stability, and systems and interactions. The entire program comprises thirteen units, one for grade 5 and four each for grades 6 through 8; some units can also be used in grade 9. At each grade level the yearlong course includes a series of units connected by central themes and a storyline—a narrative that sets a real-world context for the science content. Each unit poses problems related to genuine scientific and social issues. Students address the problems by drawing information from CD-ROM-based resources (text, images, video, and simulations), supplemented by laser disks, web-based resources, and materials kits. Each unit covers between nine and thirteen weeks of instructional time.

The major components of the program include a teacher's guide, implementation guide, and student book. The implementation guide (common to all units) describes the goals and recommended instructional approaches, and reviews hardware requirements and procedures for installing the software. The teacher's guide for each unit includes summaries of lesson clusters, lesson plans, assessment sheets, and answer keys. The student activity book includes an investigation for each lesson in the unit, along with a vocabulary key. Additional resources to support both teachers and students include alphabetized databases (including databases of images, video, maps, and simulations), Internet links, and bibliographies of print materials. The program also provides online notebooks in which students can enter and format text, images, and other media, as well as a personalized home page for each student from which he or she can navigate to familiar sites and resources within the *Science 2000+* program.

Science Sleuths

Publisher:	**Videodiscovery**
Year Published:	**1992**
Developer:	**Videodiscovery**
Website:	**https://www.videodiscovery.com**
Grade Levels:	**6–9**
Science Domains:	**Life, earth, and physical science**

Science Sleuths is a two-volume set of CD-ROMs containing a series of mysteries that combine earth, life, and physical science concepts with problem-solving techniques. The mysteries are real-life puzzles that involve various scientific aspects of the environment. Students can use the resources provided, research the clues, and conduct experiments to solve the mysteries. The program makes connections to technology and real-world issues, and encourages students to pursue science careers. Some of the skills developed include problem solving, measurement, and use of simple and complex scientific tools.

The program includes a teacher's manual, an interactive CD-ROM for students, and an assessment software tool. The student resources include video interviews, graphs and tables, maps and charts, an encyclopedia, and interactive on-screen tools. In Volume One students investigate the mysteries of *The Blob* and *The Exploding Lawnmower.* Volume Two introduces *The Biogenic Picnic* and *The Traffic Accident.* Each mystery has six levels of solutions from apprentice to master. Students may solve the easiest level within a class period, while the higher levels may take up to two or three class periods. Case sheets and end-of-program tests, along with the assessment software, make it possible for teachers to assess students' performance and understanding of the concepts.

University of Michigan Digital Library (UMDL) Project

Publisher:	University of Michigan
Year Published:	1996
Developer:	University of Michigan
Website:	http://www.umich.edu/~aaps
Grade Levels:	6–12
Science Domains:	Earth and space science

The *UMDL Project* is an online inquiry project that focuses on earth and space science and can be used to supplement other curriculum programs. The library includes a collection of online resources: text, simulations, chat spaces, videos, interactive maps, and online mentors. The teaching and learning materials are available online and cover seven areas: *Scavenger Hunt, Astronomy, Ecology, Geology, Weather, Waves and Vibrations,* and *Women in Science.* Each project has six sections: introduction, activity, questions, reference, teacher's guide, and table of contents. The introduction provides a scenario and gives students an initial driving question with links to other documents relevant to the question.

The Web-based Integrated Science Environment (WISE)

Publisher:	Graduate School of Education, University of California, Berkeley
Years Published:	1997–2000
Developer:	Graduate School of Education, University of California, Berkeley
Website:	http://wise.berkeley.edu/WISE
Grade Levels:	6–12
Science Domains:	Life, physical, and earth science

WISE is a sequence of classroom activities, each spanning approximately two to ten days of class time. These activities, which vary widely, include surveying web-based materials, conducting hands-on investigations, participating in online discussions, and critiquing other classmates' work. *WISE* projects are organized around three basic templates: critique, controversy, and design. During "critique," students are presented with web-based materials and are asked to think critically about their source and content validity, as well as their relevance to the project topic. "Controversy" presents students with two sides of a scientific question and asks them to form their own argument using the web-based evidence. In the third template, students are presented with a design problem and are guided through the design process in a sequence of *WISE* activities.

The *WISE* project library is created and developed by a set of authoring partnerships. The partnerships consist of teachers, scientists, and educational researchers who work together online to define project goals, design lesson plans, and compile materials.

Additional Resources

Standards and Guides

Britton, Edward, Mary Ann Huntley, Gloria Jacobs, and Amy Weinberg, *Connecting Mathematics and Science to Workplace Contexts: A Guide to Curriculum Materials* (Thousand Oaks, CA: Corwin Press, Inc., 1998)

Connecting Mathematics and Science to Workplace Contexts: A Guide to Curriculum Materials reviews 23 curricula that incorporate workplace experiences in mathematics and science education. Curriculum samples illustrate opportunities for learning science in work settings, from hematology laboratories to soda bottling companies. The guide may help educators, curriculum developers, and supervisors identify key characteristics of successful curricula and create their own curriculum materials.

Available from:
Corwin Press, Inc., A Sage Publications Company
2455 Teller Road
Thousand Oaks, CA 91320-2218
Phone: (805) 499-9774
E-mail: info@sagepub.com

Council of Chief State School Officers (CCSSO)

CCSSO maintains a website with a link to each state's department of education where you can find the state standards for science as well as links to local district information. In collaboration with four other state-based organizations, CCSSO has also developed the State Education Improvement Partnership (SEIP), which offers a variety of activities and services to states. Among these are training in benchmarking of standards and evaluative feedback regarding states' efforts to implement standards. Information about SEIP can be found on the CCSSO website.

For information, contact
Council of Chief State School Officers
One Massachusetts Avenue NW, Suite 700
Washington, DC 20001-1431
Phone: (202) 408-5505
Website: http://www.ccsso.org

National Research Council, *National Science Education Standards* **(Washington, DC: National Academy Press, 1996)**

The *National Science Education Standards* offers a vision of what it means to be scientifically literate. The document reflects the contributions of thousands of teachers, scientists, science educators, and other experts from across the country and outlines what students should know and be able to do in science at different grade levels. It describes teaching practices that help students to become scientifically literate, and outlines criteria for assessing and analyzing student achievement and learning opportunities. Furthermore, the document describes the nature and design of an effective school and district science program and the resources needed for students to learn successfully.

Available from:
National Academy Press
2101 Constitution Avenue, NW
Lockbox 285
Washington, DC 20055
Phone: (888) 624-8373 or (202) 334-3313
Website: http://www.nap.edu

National Research Council, Maxine Singer and Jan Tuomi (Eds.), *Selecting Instructional Materials: A Guide for K–12 Science* **(Washington, DC: National Academy Press, 1999)**

Selecting Instructional Materials presents a procedure to help educational decision makers evaluate and choose materials for science classrooms. This book outlines the evaluation process for school district facilitators and provides review instruments for each step. It reviews current selection processes for science materials across the country—some in states where the board of education determines the materials and others where local decision makers choose the materials. *Selecting Instructional Materials* explores how purchasing decisions are influenced by parent attitudes, political considerations, and marketing skills. It is intended for use by state and local decision makers, program administrators, and teachers.

Available from:
National Academy Press
2101 Constitution Avenue, NW
Lockbox 285
Washington, DC 20055
Phone: (888) 624-8373 or (202) 334-3313
Website: http://www.nap.edu

National Science Resources Center, *Resources for Teaching Middle School Science* (Washington, DC: National Academy Press, 1998)

Resources for Teaching Middle School Science is the second in the NSRC's series of resource guides for K–12 educators. It follows the 1996 publication of *Resources for Teaching Elementary School Science* and describes more than 400 curricula that reflect the *National Science Education Standards*. The materials are grouped by scientific domain—physical science, life science, environmental science, earth and space science, and multidisciplinary and applied science—and include core materials, supplementary units, activity books, educational software, and multimedia programs. Reference materials include resource directories and guides to science trade books, books about teaching science, and periodicals for teachers and students. The latter part of the guide features an extensive compilation of resources (including museums and other science-rich places to visit) organized by region and state, professional associations and government organizations that support science education, and publishers and suppliers of curricula and science materials. One of the appendices also includes the NSRC criteria for reviewing middle-grades curriculum materials.

Available from:
National Academy Press
2101 Constitution Avenue, NW
Lockbox 285
Washington, DC 20055
Phone: (888) 624-8373 or (202) 334-3313
Website: http://www.nap.edu

New Standards™ Student Performance Standards (Washington, DC: National Center on Education and the Economy and University of Pittsburgh, 1997)

The *New Standards* are designed to make national standards in the content areas operational by not only describing what students should know and be able to do but also including numerous examples of student work illustrating what meeting the standards looks like. Each example of student work is accompanied by an explanation of how the example illustrates the relevant standard. The *New Standards* volume for the middle grades includes standards in English language arts, mathematics, science, and applied learning. In each subject area, the *New Standards* performance standards build on the content standards developed by the national professional organizations. The developers of the *New Standards* have also developed a performance assessment system linked to the standards and adopted by a number of states and districts.

Available from:
National Center on Education and the Economy
P.O. Box 10391
Rochester, NY 14610
(888) 882-9538
http://www.ncee.org

Project 2061, American Association for the Advancement of Science, *Benchmarks for Science Literacy* (New York: Oxford University Press, 1993)

Benchmarks for Science Literacy is a companion to Project 2061's previously released *Science for All Americans*. While *Science for All Americans* recommends what students should know and be able to do in science, mathematics, and technology by the time they graduate from high school, *Benchmarks* outlines how they should progress and what they should be able to do at critical junctures in their K–12 education—the ends of grades 2, 5, 8, and 12. *Benchmarks* reflects input from elementary, middle, and high school teachers, administrators, scientists, mathematicians, engineers, historians, and experts on learning and curriculum design. It serves as a tool to help educators design a curriculum that reflects the standards of scientific literacy and makes sense in their particular contexts.

Project 2061, American Association for the Advancement of Science, *Resources for Science Literacy: Professional Development* (New York: Oxford University Press, 1997)

Project 2061's first CD-ROM tool offers a wide array of materials designed to provide educators with a deeper understanding of how to help their students achieve science literacy. The CD-ROM contains six components that can be used by higher education faculty in planning pre-service education, by school districts in designing in-service staff development programs, and by teachers for self-guided study of the learning goals in *Science for All Americans* and *Benchmarks*. Organized around the goals presented in *Science for All Americans*, it offers a carefully selected collection of bibliographies, research findings, comparisons of *Benchmarks* to national standards documents in other subject areas, college course plans, and a diverse set of workshop designs. Annual updates will be available via disk or online.

Information about this and other Project 2061 tools is available from:
Project 2061, American Association for the Advancement of Science
1333 H Street, NW
P.O. Box 34446
Washington, DC 20005
Phone: (202) 326-7002
Website: http://www.project2061.org/tools/

Curriculum Evaluations and Criteria

Resources for Science Literacy: Curriculum Materials Evaluation

Project 2061, in collaboration with hundreds of K–12 teachers, curriculum specialists, teacher educators, scientists, and materials developers, has developed a process for evaluating middle-grades science curriculum materials. Field tests suggest that Project 2061's evaluation procedure will not only serve schools' materials adoption purposes, but will also help teachers revise existing materials and guide developers in the creation of new materials. *Resources for Science Literacy: Curriculum Materials Evaluation,* which is available as a CD-ROM, includes a detailed description of Project 2061's materials evaluation procedure and its uses. It provides a rationale and an overview of the research supporting this analytical approach. Also included is information about selected evaluated materials—bibliographic information, summaries of activities, descriptions of intended audiences and goals, evaluation reports, and samples from the instructional materials themselves. Print versions of these materials will also be available.

Information about this and other Project 2061 tools is available from:
Project 2061
American Association for the Advancement of Science
1333 H Street, NW
P.O. Box 34446
Washington, DC 20005
Phone: (202) 326-7002
Website: http://www/project2061.org/tools/

NSF Study of Comprehensive Science Instructional Materials
In 1996, the NSF, through its Division of Elementary, Secondary, and Informal Education, undertook a study of comprehensive instructional materials in science for the middle grades. NSF wanted to determine the characteristics of comprehensive instructional materials for middle-grades science developed with NSF funds, as well as determine how well those materials succeeded in providing comprehensive programs consistent with national standards. The study results were published in 1997, and include criteria used for carrying out the review.

Available from:
National Science Foundation
Division of Elementary, Secondary, and Informal Education
Room 885
4201 Wilson Boulevard
Arlington, VA 22230
Phone: (703) 306-1234
Website: http://www.nsf.gov

NSRC Evaluation Criteria for Middle School Science Curriculum Materials
These criteria concentrate on six main topics: pedagogical appropriateness of materials, science content, presentation, organization, format, and equity. This evaluation document appears in Appendix B of the NSRC's *Resources for Teaching Middle School Science* (listed above under "Standards and Guides").

Mathematics and Science Education Expert Panel

In 1997, the U.S. Department of Education's Office of Educational Research and Improvement (OERI) convened a Mathematics and Science Education Expert Panel to develop a high-quality, research-based process for selecting curricula, and to use that selection process to identify exemplary and promising programs. The goal was to help practitioners make better and more informed curriculum decisions. The panel is composed of 15 experts in mathematics or science from around the country. It includes university educators, representatives of professional associations and regional laboratories, and practitioners. The results of the science review are expected to be available in time for the 2000–2001 school year. Descriptions of each program will include a general overview, program costs, description of program quality, evidence of effectiveness and success, related professional development, and ordering and contact information.

Available from:
Mathematics and Science Education Expert Panel
Office of Educational Research and Improvement
U.S. Department of Education
555 New Jersey Avenue, NW
Washington, DC 20208-5000
Phone: (202) 219-2087
Website: http://www.ed.gov/offices/OERI/

Over the past decade, the NSF has funded a number of curriculum development projects with the goal of improving the selection of science education materials available to teachers and students. More recently, NSF has funded four dissemination and implementation centers to share information with and provide assistance to school districts across the country interested in choosing among and implementing these various science curricula.

NSF Curriculum Dissemination and Implementation Centers

EDC K–12 Science Curriculum Dissemination Center

This center is part of a nationwide effort to introduce school districts to NSF-supported, exemplary K–12 science instructional materials, and help them critically assess and use the materials to address their state standards and local science curriculum frameworks. The center helps teams select and adopt standards-based materials and plan for challenges they are likely to encounter in implementing them. The center's ten regional hubs are Colorado, Indiana, Inland Northwest, Kentucky, Mississippi, Montana, Northern Michigan, Northern Plains, Oregon, and

TriState (FL, GA, AL). Through these hubs, the center offers seminars, on-site consultation and technical assistance, planning tools, and a wide variety of resources.

For more information, contact
Center for Science Education
Education Development Center, Inc.
55 Chapel Street
Newton, MA 02458-1060
Phone: (617) 618-2562
Website: http://www.edc.org

LASER (Leadership and Assistance for Science Education Reform)

LASER is a long-term, nationwide initiative launched by the National Science Resources Center (NSRC). It is designed to help school districts explore, adopt, and implement effective, inquiry-based, K–8 science education programs and to bring about science education reform in their communities. The initiative involves partnerships established by the NSRC with three groups: regional LASER sites, publishers, and corporations. The NSRC provides ongoing technical assistance to LASER districts as they move toward realizing their vision of science education reform. Educators from eight regional sites are partners with the NSRC in this undertaking. Other partners in this initiative are publishers of NSF-supported science curriculum materials and several major corporations and foundations. LASER sites are located in Alabama; the tri-state region of New Jersey, eastern Pennsylvania, and southern Connecticut; Oklahoma; Rhode Island; South Carolina; southern California; Washington; and western Pennsylvania.

For more information, contact
National Science Resources Center
955 L'Enfant Plaza, SW, Suite 8400
Washington, DC 20560-0952
Phone: (202) 287-2063
Website: http://www.si.edu/nsrc/laser.htm

BSCS High School Science Curriculum Implementation Center

This center assists high school teachers, schools, and districts in learning about, selecting among, and implementing standards-based curriculum programs developed with NSF funding. Center work is organized around three topics: evaluating and selecting curriculum materials, designing professional development and support for teachers implementing new materials, and special issues in high school science reform. The center is writing guides about each topic, sponsoring three-day seminars on each topic to begin in Spring 2001, and establishing an Academy for Curriculum Leadership, which will provide two-year intensive assistance to selected school and district teams. In addition to its emphasis on curriculum reform, the center is developing and piloting institutes for teachers teaching out-of-field in both earth science and physics.

For more information, contact
BSCS High School Science Curriculum Implementation Center
5415 Mark Dabling Boulevard
Colorado Springs, CO 80918-3842
Phone: (719) 531-5550
E-mail: info@bscs.org

Center for the Enhancement of Science and Mathematics Education (CESAME)

CESAME uses the experience it has gained from its Statewide Implementation Program to inform its IMPACT Project, a regional effort to accelerate the implementation of standards-based instructional materials throughout New England. This effort builds on existing regional structures to provide the information, resources, and support for districts to implement science and mathematics education reform.

A number of regional IMPACT Centers at locations throughout New England assist districts in the selection and implementation of standards-based curricula. An implementation advisor at each center works with districts to plan and support the implementation process. The regional IMPACT Centers network with each other and with IMPACT collaborators. CESAME has also identified and supported over 100 CESAME-certified "Curriculum Trainers" to provide professional development to teachers for specific standards-based curricula. These trainers also evaluate new programs and materials for recommendation to districts.

For more information, contact
CESAME
Northeastern University
716 Columbus Avenue, Suite 378
Boston, MA 02120
Phone: (617) 373-8380
Website: http://projects.terc.edu/impact

Regional Consortia

Eisenhower Regional Mathematics and Science Education Consortia

The *Eisenhower Regional Mathematics and Science Education Consortia* are part of the national network supported by the Eisenhower National Clearinghouse to improve mathematics and science education. Funded by the U.S. Department of Education, the consortia were created to help disseminate effective materials and instructional methods.

For information, contact
Eisenhower Regional Mathematics and Science Education Consortia
Barbara Humes, Coordinator
555 New Jersey Avenue, NW
Washington, DC 20208-5645
Phone: (202) 219-1376
Website: http://www.enc.org/about/consort/index.htm

The ten regional consortia for mathematics and science are as follows:

Northeast and Islands Region
Eisenhower Regional Alliance for Mathematics and Science Education
Region: CT, ME, MA, NH, NY, RI, VT, PR, and the VI
Mark Kaufman, Director
TERC
2067 Massachusetts Avenue
Cambridge, MA 02140
Phone: (617) 547-0430
Website: http://ra.terc.edu/

Mid-Atlantic Region
Mid-Atlantic Eisenhower Consortium for Mathematics and Science Education
Research for Better Schools
Region: DE, MD, NJ, PA, and DC
Keith Kershner, Director
444 North Third Street
Philadelphia, PA 19123
Phone: (215) 574-9300 x279
Website: http://www.rbs.org

Southeastern Region
Eisenhower Consortium for Mathematics and Science Education at SERVE
Region: AL, FL, GA, MS, NC, and SC
Francena Cummings, Director
Southeastern Regional Vision for Education (SERVE)
1203 Governor's Square Boulevard, Suite 400
Tallahassee, FL 32301
Phone: (850) 671-6033
Website: http://www.serve.org/Eisenhower/

Appalachian Region

Eisenhower Regional Math/Science Consortium at AEL
Region: KY, TN, VA, and WV
Roger Bynum, Director
AEL, Inc.
1700 North Moore Street
Suite 1275
Arlington, VA 22209
Phone: (800) 624-9120
Website: http://www.ael.org/eisen/

North Central Region

Midwest Consortium for Mathematics and Science Education (MSC)
Region: IA, IL, IN, MI, MN, OH, and WI
Gilbert Valdez, Director
North Central Regional Educational Laboratory (NCREL)
1120 Diehl Road, Suite 200
Naperville, IL 60563
Phone: (800) 356-2735
Website: http://www.ncrel.org/msc/msc.htm

Mid-Continent Region

Eisenhower High Plains Consortium for Mathematics and Science
Region: CO, KS, MO, NE, ND, SD, and WY
John Sutton, Director
Mid-continent Research for Education and Learning (McREL)
High Plains Consortium
2550 South Parker Road, Suite 500
Aurora, CO 80014
Phone: (800) 949-6387
Website: http://www.mcrel.org/hpc/

Northwest Region

Northwest Consortium for Mathematics and Science Teaching (Northwest CMAST)
Region: AK, ID, MT, OR, and WA
Kit Peixotto, Director
Mathematics and Science Education Center
101 SW Main Street, Suite 500
Portland, OR 97204
Phone: (503) 275-9500
Website: http://www.nwrel.org/msec/nwerc

Far West Region

WestEd Eisenhower Regional Consortium for Science and Mathematics (WERC)
Region: AZ, CA, NV, and UT
Art Sussman and Steve Schneider, Directors
730 Harrison Street
San Francisco, CA 94107
Phone: (415) 615-3029
Website: http://www.wested.org/werc/

Southwest Region

Southwest Consortium for the Improvement of Mathematics and Science Teaching (SCIMAST)
Region: AR, LA, NM, OK, and TX
Stephen Marble, Director
Southwest Educational Development Laboratory (SEDL)
211 East Seventh Street
Austin, TX 78701
Phone: (512) 476-6861
Website: http://www.sedl.org/pitl/scimast/

Pacific Region

Pacific Mathematics and Science Regional Consortium
Region: HI, American Samoa, Commonwealth of the Northern Marianas Islands, Federated States of Micronesia, Guam, Republic of the Marshall Islands, and the Republic of Palau
Paul Dumas, Director
Pacific Resources for Education and Learning (PREL)
Ali'i Place
1099 Alakea Street, 25th floor
Honolulu, HI 96813
Phone: (800) 441-1300
Website: http://www.prel.org

Professional Organizations

National Middle School Association (NMSA)

4151 Executive Parkway, Suite 300
Westerville, OH 43081
Phone: (800) 528-6672
Website: http://www.nmsa.org
Established in 1973, the National Middle School Association (NMSA) serves as a voice for professionals, parents, and others interested in the educational and developmental needs of young adolescents (10–15 years of age). NMSA has over 20,000 members in more than 50 countries, including teachers, principals, parents, college faculty, central office administrators, educational consultants, and community leaders. In addition, NMSA has state, provincial, and international affiliates that

work to provide middle-grades support. NMSA also has working committees and task forces that focus on specific areas: curriculum, professional preparation, publications, research, rural and small schools, and urban issues.

National Science Teachers Association (NSTA)

1840 Wilson Boulevard
Arlington, VA 22201-3000
Phone: (703) 243-7100
Website: http://www.nsta.org
The National Science Teachers Association (NSTA), founded in 1944, is the largest organization in the world committed to promoting excellence and innovation in science teaching and learning for all. NSTA's current membership of more than 53,000 includes science teachers, science supervisors, administrators, scientists, business and industry representatives, and others involved in science education. To address subjects of critical interest to science educators, the association publishes five journals, a newspaper, many books, and numerous other publications. NSTA conducts national and regional conventions that attract more than 30,000 attendees annually and provides many programs and services for science educators, including awards, professional development workshops, and educational tours. NSTA offers professional certification for science teachers in eight teaching level and discipline area categories.

National Staff Development Council (NSDC)

P.O. Box 240
Oxford, OH 45056
Phone: (513) 523-6029
Website: http://www.nsdc.org/
The National Staff Development Council (NSDC), founded in 1969, is a non-profit association committed to ensuring success for all students through staff development and school improvement. The council believes that high-quality staff development programs are key to improving learning in schools. It offers a number of publications and also sponsors projects, consultation services, leadership councils, and training for staff developers. The website offers resources and links that middle-grades educators will find helpful for planning professional development.

Annenberg/CPB

Annenberg/CPB, a partnership between the Annenberg Foundation and the Corporation for Public Broadcasting (CPB), uses media and telecommunications to advance excellent teaching in American schools. Annenberg/CPB funds educational video series and teacher professional development workshops for the Annenberg/CPB channel. The channel is distributed free by satellite to schools and other educational and community organizations nationwide. The channel provides non-commercial satellite broadcasts (via PBS) of renowned educational series for use in

Professional Development Resources

teacher training and as video supplements to classroom curricula. It also offers professional development workshops in which educators can participate individually or as part of school in-service programs. Participants can see educational standards in action around the country and earn in-service and graduate credits. The channel's website offers supplementary materials, including classroom handouts, online activities for teachers and students, and links to relevant sites, as well as video previews, basic program schedules, and workshop registration. It also enables teachers to communicate with each other during and after the workshops.

For more information, contact
Annenberg/CPB
401 9th Street, NW
Washington, DC 20004
Phone: (202) 879-9600; (800) LEARNER (to request a catalog)
Website: http://www.learner.org/

Eisenhower National Clearinghouse for Mathematics and Science Education (ENC)

Website: http://www.enc.org
The website for the Eisenhower National Clearinghouse for Mathematics and Science Education is a significant resource for online information, resources, free publications, current news in mathematics and science education, and links to other resources in science education. A section called "Under the Action" highlights 13 outstanding mathematics and science Internet sites, which are called the "ENC Digital Dozen." The site also presents an "Innovator of the Month," describing educators who are "re-inventing learning with their students."

Center for Highly Interactive Computing in Education at the University of Michigan (hi-ce)

Website: http://www.hi-ce.org
Hi-ce develops technology-based materials that engage teachers and students in meaningful and motivating learning experiences. Some of its programs include *Middle Years Digital Library* (tools that help search for useful science information on the web); *Knowledge Networks on the Web* (shows teachers classroom activities as they were enacted by other schools and allows them to communicate with other teachers using the curriculum); and *Science Laboratory* (collection of software tools for data gathering, graphing, and modeling). The center also develops models for professional development, assessment, instructional strategies, and home–school–community integration.

MiddleWeb: Exploring Middle School Reform

Website: http://www.middleweb.com
MiddleWeb describes itself as a website devoted to "exploring the challenges of middle school reform." Sponsored by the Edna McConnell Clark Foundation, *MiddleWeb* offers extensive resources and information of

interest to any educator or parent of middle-grades students. It includes teacher and principal diaries, teacher interviews, and news items (updated weekly) which link to articles in *Education Week* and newspapers around the country. An index allows the visitor to view journal articles in categories such as Assessment and Evaluation, Curriculum and Instruction, Standards-Based School Reform, Teacher Professional Development, and Student and School Life. There is a search option to find information within the site and links to other educational sites. A wealth of information on middle schools and school reform is accessible at this site. As of the fall of 2000, *MiddleWeb* is also launching a listserve for middle-grades teachers who are "restless to improve." List members include exemplary teachers in districts across the U.S., and the list features regular guests, including experts in curriculum, professional growth, and standards-based teaching, who converse with list members. The *Guiding Curriculum Decisions* series can be downloaded from this site.

PBS TeacherSource Web Campus for PreK–12 Educators
Website: http://pbs.org/teachersource
PBS TeacherSource features a growing inventory of more than 1,300 free lesson plans, teacher guides, and online student activities. It offers access to curriculum, professional development, and community resources provided by PBS stations across the country. *TeacherSource* correlates each of its classroom activities to national and state curriculum standards, aggregates the services PBS and its member stations provide to educators, and helps teachers learn effective ways to incorporate video and the Internet in the classroom. *TeacherSource* groups its resources into five subject areas: Arts and Literature, Mathematics, Science and Technology, Social Studies, and Health and Fitness, and offers subject, grade level, and keyword searches. Educators visiting the site can customize it to reach any PBS station's TV schedule and then view the slate of programs with off-air taping rights of one year or more. Teachers and school librarians can also learn about a station's education events and professional development workshops as well as community news and outreach activities.

Attaining Excellence: A TIMSS Resource Kit
The Third International Mathematics and Science Study (TIMSS) collected data in more than 40 countries about student achievement in third, fourth, seventh, and eighth grades, and the final year of high school. Students were tested in mathematics and science, and information about the teaching and learning of mathematics and science was collected from students, teachers, and principals. Researchers also collected information about teachers' academic preparation, instructional practices, and views on current issues in mathematics and science education, and about school characteristics and resources. The resource kit has four modules which can be used in professional development and community outreach. These include reports on the TIMSS findings; videotapes of classroom teaching in the United States, Japan, and

Germany; guides for discussion leaders; presentation overheads for speakers; and checklists, leaflets, and fliers.

Available from:
Superintendent of Documents
P.O. Box 371954
Pittsburgh, PA 15250-7954
Phone: (202) 512-1800

For more information about TIMSS, contact
TIMSS International Study Center
Center for the Study of Testing, Evaluation, and Educational Policy
Lynch School of Education
Campion Hall 332
Boston College
Chestnut Hill, MA 02467
Phone: (617) 552-1600
Website: http://timss.bc.edu/

Killion, Joellen, *What Works in the Middle: Results-Based Staff Development* (Oxford, OH: National Staff Development Council, 1999)

This guide provides information and resources to aid in the selection, design, and evaluation of staff development programs in mathematics, science, language arts, social studies, and interdisciplinary studies. The premise of the guide is that the strong link between teacher learning and student achievement argues for professional development that will help teachers deepen their content area expertise and develop the instructional approaches that allow them to teach content effectively. The book is designed to provide guidance for implementing successful professional development in middle schools. It reviews 26 professional development programs that have demonstrated effects on student learning; five of these are programs with science as a focus.

Available from:
National Staff Development Council
P.O. Box 240
Oxford, OH 45056
Phone: (513) 523-6029
Website: http://www.nsdc.org

Wheelock, Anne, *Safe to be Smart: Building a Culture for Standards-Based Reform in the Middle Grades* (Columbus, OH: National Middle School Association, 1998)

Wheelock argues that in order to achieve high standards schools must change the way they operate as well as the content of their curricula. Schools committed to standards-based reforms create cultures that support the beliefs that (1) every student can think well and understand deeply (i.e., "become smart"), and (2) the school and its teachers are responsible for enabling students to learn for understanding. Wheelock draws from many schools and classrooms to illustrate the kinds of practices that follow from these beliefs. These practices include making expectations clear and explicit to students; a focus on student work, supported by good teaching and challenging curriculum; building relationships with students that foster motivation, effort, and investment in schoolwork; and development of professional communities of teachers that focus on achieving high expectations for all students.

Available from:
National Middle School Association
2600 Corporate Exchange Drive
Suite 370
Columbus, OH 43231
(800) 528-6672
http://www.nmsa.org